Praise for

Hedge Fund Risk Fundamentals

Solving the Risk Management and Transparency Challenge

by Richard Horwitz

"An abundance of helpful information ... written with commendable clarity"

Financial Analysts Journal

"An excellent overview of the risks that hedge fund managers take"

GARP (Global Association of Risk Professionals) *Risk Review*

"This book offers an excellent review of the complex topic of hedge fund risk management. Furthermore, **it provides an innovative and pragmatic solution to the key transparency issue.**"

PIERRE JETTÉ, MBA, CFA
Vice President, International Equities, CDP Capital

"Not overly technical, **this book is not only a must-read for neophytes and the newly indoctrinated to risk on derivatives but also a great refocuser for risk professionals!** It covers the spectrum of experience in rish management on derivatives."

ROBERT M. AARON
CEO, DPM Mellon
Chairman of the Board, Managed Funds Association

"**A wonderfully written book on a topic that has vexed investors and professionals alike—balancing the need to know against the desire to provide information.** In a thorough and comprehensive manner, Richard Horwitz takes the reader on an explanatory journey of the risks associated with hedge fund investing. His insight and experience give him the perspective needed to articulate the challenges faced by this industry, as well as offering a sound solution that I believe couldn't come soon enough."

ANDREW A. KANDIEW
Managing Director, Risk Management
Commonfund

"**In a world where risk theory is available to all, but practical insights are hard-won, closely guarded secrets, Richard Horwitz has produced a work of exceptional practical value.** This book deals head-on with the challenges of hedge fund investing by providing intelligent, well-informed, and uniquely accessible advice. Most usefully, he provides a benchmark for hedge fund investors to evaluate their own investment processes."

ANDREW B. WEISMAN
Merrill Lynch & Co., Inc.

"*Hedge Fund Risk Fundamentals* is an insider's guide to understanding the complexity of these new investing styles. In clear, plain language, Horwitz guides both beginning and seasoned investor. **This is required reading for anyone who wishes to understand the fine points of hedge fund risk measurement.**"

STEVE MCMENAMIN
Executive Director, Greenwich Roundtable

"**Richard Horwitz has put together a comprehensive, eye-opening account on risk management that should be read by investors and managers alike.** As the hedge fund industry becomes more mainstream, more institutional and more complex, the concepts become key. He takes complex concepts and makes them easy to understand and illustrates his points with tables and examples. He makes a strong case for standardizing risk fundamentals and presents a possible solution."

LOIS PELTZ
President and CEO, Infovest21

"Richard Horwitz provides a refreshingly fresh and engaging perspective on hedge funds, risk-management, and investing principles. Practitioners all too often forget the basic principles of quantitative risk management, and thus obscure rather than illuminate the trade-off between risk and reward. **This book eloquently bridges the divide between the 'theory' and the 'practice' of investing in hedge funds.**"

ADIL ABDULALI
Director of Risk Management, Protégé Partners

Hedge Fund Risk Fundamentals

Hedge Fund Risk Fundamentals

Solving the Risk Management and Transparency Challenge

Richard Horwitz

Viva Books

New Delhi | Mumbai | Chennai | Kolkata | Bangalore | Hyderabad | Kochi | Guwahati

First Indian Edition 2009

VIVA BOOKS PRIVATE LIMITED

- 4737/23 Ansari Road, Daryaganj, New Delhi 110 002
  E-mail: vivadelhi@vivagroupindia.net, Tel. 42242200
- 76, Service Industries, Shirvane, Sector 1, Nerul, Navi Mumbai 400 706
  E-mail: vivamumbai@vivagroupindia.net, Tel. 27721273, 27721274
- Jamals Fazal Chambers, 26 Greams Road, Chennai 600 006
  E-mail: vivachennai@vivagroupindia.net, Tel. 28290304, 28294241
- B-103, Jindal Towers, 21/1A/3 Darga Road, Kolkata 700 017
  E-mail: vivakolkata@vivagroupindia.net, Tel. 22836381, 22816713
- 7, Sovereign Park Apartments, 56-58, K. R. Road, Basavanagudi, Bangalore 560 004
  E-mail: vivabangalore@vivagroupindia.net, Tel. 26607409, 26607410
- 101-102 Mughal Marc Apartments, 3-4-637 to 641, Narayanguda, Hyderabad 500 029
  E-mail: vivahyderabad@vivagroupindia.net, Tel. 27564481, 27564482
- First Floor, Beevi Towers, SRM Road, Kaloor, Kochi 682 018, Kerala
  E-mail: vivakochi@vivagroupindia.net, Tel: 0484-2403055, 2403056
- H. No. 12, P. B. Road, Rehabari, Near Arya Hospital, Guwahati 781 008
  E-mail: vivaguwahati@vivagroupindia.net, Tel: 0361-2735624

www.vivagroupindia.com

Published by arrangement with

Bloomberg Press
731 Lexington Avenue
New York, NY 10022

ISBN-10: 81-309-1124-8
ISBN-13: 978-81-309-1124-3

Published by Vinod Vasishtha for Viva Books Private Limited, 4737/23, Ansari Road, Daryaganj, New Delhi - 110 002.

Printed and bound by Raj Press, R-3, Inderpuri, New Delhi - 110 012.

To Gillian and Jesse

Contents

Part Four

Risk from the Investor's Viewpoint

Acknowledgments

I would like to acknowledge Kenmar for its forward-looking support. Kenmar and I share a vision of standardized risk management for the hedge fund world that can be institutionalized as an "industry utility." Kenmar has been willing to invest in this vision to transform it into a reality. Kenmar has also demonstrated a strong commitment to long-term results, compared to the short-term focus typical of corporate America. In particular, I would like to thank Kenneth Shewer and Marc and Esther Goodman of Kenmar, who have demonstrated an unparalleled commitment to solving the transparency challenge.

I would also like to thank Adil Abdulali, Francis Owusu, and Jon Lukomnik for reviewing the material. Only true risk experts could have provided the feedback that these professionals were able to contribute. I would like to thank Daniel Lim for his ongoing support, and Carol and Sandy Ross for their strategic and legal counsel. In particular, I thank Paul McDermott, who has committed the past two years of his life to sharing and implementing my vision. Paul has demonstrated a superior ability to combine diverse technologies to develop a rich and user-friendly system. I will always value our many arguments. I would also like to thank all of my other colleagues at Kenmar who have supported this effort in their particular areas of expertise.

Finally, I want to thank Jeff Schmidt for creating the opportunity to write this book. As a totally right-brained person (having written less than 100 pages during five years at MIT), I had never thought about writing a book. However, I do feel passionate about solving the risk management and transparency challenge, making me a risk evangelist. To my great surprise, this book flowed out of me. Thank you, Jeff, for opening the spigot.

Foreword

Different investors and investor groups have different objectives and requirements, but all deserve the best return that risk can buy. Return is simple enough to measure, but at the same time dangerously luring if not seen in the context of risk. Risk, by contrast, is multifaceted and elusive.

Because portfolio risk is often hidden behind apparently quantifiable and orderly intermarket and interstrategy relationships (or nonrelationships), its true dimensions are easy to understate during nonstressed market periods. Underestimation of risk can lead to superb performance followed by sudden substantial losses. Overestimation of risk leads to inefficient utilization of available capital. Consequently, a highly methodical and multidimensional approach toward balancing the naturally interrelated investment companions "return" and "risk" is essential to successful investing.

Risk as a concept is not new, but only in recent times have people started to manage financial risk in a structured fashion. Managing risk necessarily implies identifying and understanding it in its various shapes. This task is as easy to describe as it is hard to accomplish. And it can be near impossible in complex situations such as when dealing with a multitude of seemingly different and diversifying strategies that are nevertheless at their core centered on a concentrated set of risk-drivers.

Investors in hedge funds, whether large or small, face the risk management and transparency challenge on a daily basis. While many allocators are well schooled in the theoretical approaches to assembling diverse funds into optimized portfolios that should generate the desired risk-return profiles, it is readily apparent that such optimization is backward looking. The assumption of repetition of historical results in terms of strategy or market interdependence tends to fail exactly when it counts most. Nevertheless, in order for quantitative analysis to be truly complementary to qualitative, experience-based research and judgment, the best must be made of whatever data is available.

Unfortunately, the data provided by hedge funds and industry observers does not easily support meaningful application. A large part of the problem is caused by the inconsistency of data provided by industry exponents. Each has its own measures and formats, and the data is often questionable, to say the least. The diversity of hedge fund styles, and the fact that each style has its own unique language, exacerbates the problem. Unfortunately, "diversity" and "unique language" can turn into "high correlation" and "remarkably similar behavior" during periods of stress. It is a major quest to create a sound environment enabling comparison and reliable analysis across funds and with a portfolio view contingent on circumstance.

A prudent risk management framework must be based on identification of the key risk factors inherent in each single investment, and the interdependencies among these factors. Because the hedge fund industry is characterized by flexible and often complex or blended investment strategies on the one hand, and a reluctance of managers to provide in-depth transparency on the other, managing multi-strategy alternative portfolios and their risks can at times be —who would admit it—a pseudo-scientific task. Or, as cynics might call it, an involuntary form of art.

Risk transparency has become a much-discussed topic in the hedge fund industry, especially among institutional investors. Despite the fact that the transparency challenge is too important for the industry to ignore, there has been very little progress in solving the problem. The debate is fueled by diverging interests: investors' demand for transparency on one side, and managers' reluctance to divulge sensitive information on the other. The compromise between these two interests is subject to ongoing negotiations.

While this and related issues will continue to be hotly discussed for years to come, the solution proposed by Richard Horwitz is definitely a step in the right direction. His proposition revolves around a framework of standardized reporting that does not compromise proprietary data. By consistently applying such a reporting framework, the investor is able to compare and aggregate the underlying investments. If used appropriately and consistently, more reliable information will be gained than would result from large quantities of detailed but uncontrollably heterogeneous data. This type of solution, combined with the format offered, provides powerful tools to compare data across several dimensions (time frame and markets being the most obvious).

When I first met Richard about two years ago, I was impressed by his enthusiasm for discovering different ways of viewing risk. He had already started developing his own models, often based on existing and well-documented approaches, but always formulated in a very personal fashion. In the meantime, he has come a long way. While I am sure that his proposed solutions will further evolve over time, I believe the approach described in this book meets many current investor requirements without compromising hedge fund manager sensitivities. As such, the book is clearly aligned with this maturing industry's endeavors to improve risk transparency.

RAMON KOSS
Former Head of Alternative Investments and Mutual Funds
Credit Suisse Group

Preface

It is strange how many great ideas and relationships happen by being in the right place at the right time. This book is a result of such timing and luck. Last summer, a colleague at Bloomberg, Kathleen Peterson, came to me looking for a current hot topic for the Bloomberg Press financial book series. At the time, I had been having discussions with Richard Horwitz at Kenmar about a new way of providing hedge fund risk reporting through the Bloomberg Professional service. It was a natural to suggest Richard's "solution" for tracking hedge fund risk as a topic for a book. This is especially true in light of the considerable press coverage surrounding developments emanating out of Washington, D.C. related to hedge fund regulation and transparency. Since Richard together with his colleagues at Kenmar had written several articles on this matter, it seemed logical to pool these ideas, organize and expand the scope, and create this book for publication.

Hedge Fund Risk Fundamentals: Solving the Transparency and Risk Management Challenge came together quickly thanks to the tireless efforts of our author Richard and also Kathleen, his editor. Risk management and ultimately transparency constitute an exceedingly timely and critical topic in a period when better information about hedge funds, mutual funds, and general security practices on Wall Street has become a top priority.

One thing is for sure. Hedge funds are a very important alternative to which investors want access. Furthermore, investors should have a meaningful and standardized way to choose among hedge fund managers and risk profiles. We hope this book establishes a case for just this type of standardized reporting. It is important to note that the Risk Fundamentals® system has been designed to support both traditional and alternative investments, broadening its appeal to the industry. The fact that all asset classes can be holistically analyzed within a single framework is extremely valuable.

There are estimated to be more than 8,000 hedge funds operating today, with these funds representing a multitude of styles available to investors. We certainly aren't suffering from an undersized investment universe, and so making considered decisions on hedge fund managers is difficult and time consuming by any measure. At the same time, recognizing that hedge funds have highly focused strategies, gaining insight into their risks is essential, yet can be difficult considering that many managers have "position paranoia"—fund managers believe that providing position transparency to investors can adversely impact performance of the fund. Thus, a new type of transparency is needed.

Washington has been wrestling for the past five years with the issues surrounding how to better assess and disseminate the risk profile of hedge fund managers, but such efforts have seen only modest sponsorship. Risk reporting today is fragmented and in a format that does not easily allow investors to gauge risk in a consistent fashion.

Therefore the demand for enhanced disclosure by hedge funds will not abate, and a way must be found whereby a fund manager can give true risk profiles without jeopardizing fund performance. This book offers a fresh and compelling argument for a standardized way to judge hedge fund strategies across a comparable set of risk factors. The Risk Fundamentals concept provides hedge funds with a flexible risk management tool, and it provides investors with a standard format with which to compare individual hedge funds or aggregate risk of a portfolio of hedge funds.

Hedge Fund Risk Fundamentals is written using basic terminology and is an essential read for all those interested in new ways to assess risk in alternative investments.

JEFFREY SCHMIDT
Derivative Products Specialist
Bloomberg L.P.

Introduction

The most complex formula you will see in this book is one of simple arithmetic. Although you have been taught that 1 + 1 = 2, Chapter 2 explains how, when it comes to risk management, 1 + 1 really equals 1.41. The level of mathematical sophistication in this book does not exceed the basics taught in high school, although they are applied in a slightly different way.

The typical risk management book is filled with complex formulas and Greek symbols. You will find neither in this volume. Instead you will find very commonsense concepts presented in plain English. Just as many professionals (such as lawyers, doctors, and even record producers as portrayed on the TV show *American Idol*) tend to mystify their craft using esoteric language, so do financial engineers and risk managers. However, just as laymen can understand the

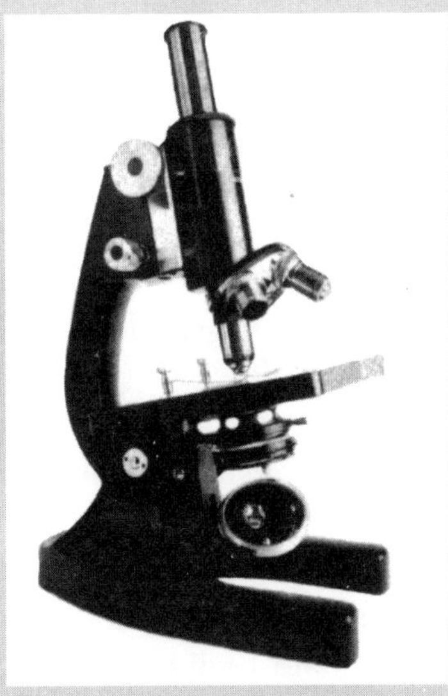

HOW A FUND VIEWS RISK

HOW AN INVESTOR VIEWS RISK

FIGURE I.1 Hedge Fund Strategies

	DIRECTIONAL	RELATIVE VALUE/ ARBITRAGE	EVENT
Fixed Income	Fixed-Income Directional Emerging Market Debt	Fixed-Income Arbitrage	Distressed
Equities	Long/Short Equities Emerging Market Equities Short-Bias Equities	Equity Market Neutral Statistical Arbitrage	Merger Arbitrage
Futures	Managed Futures		
Multi-Asset	Macro	Convertible Arbitrage Multi-Arbitrage	Event-Driven

concepts related to these other professions when communicated intelligently, so can the lay investor or the hedge fund manager who does not have a Ph.D. in mathematics understand risk.

This book explores and explains risk from two viewpoints, that of the fund manager and that of the investor. Although there are significant similarities, there are also significant differences: The fund manager looks at a single fund through a microscope, and the investor searches a universe of funds through a telescope. In this context, *fund* is used broadly to include hedge funds, mutual funds, and managers of separate accounts. Similarly, *investor* is used broadly to include private money, pension funds, endowments, and other institutional investors.

Although there are a number of other works in print that focus on hedge fund risk, this book is unique. The other books address risk by individual hedge fund strategy. This perpetuates the "silo" orientation of hedge funds. Hedge funds typically focus on a single strategy (although an extremely small fraction of funds have bundled these into multistrategy offerings). **Figure I.1** shows an array of common strategies.

The problem with focusing on risk by strategy is that investors want to diversify across strategies and do not know how to aggregate the risk across these silos. This book, and The Risk Fundamentals® Solution described in Chapter 18, deal with risk on a holistic basis that transcends specific strategies. Such an integrated approach is required to permit an investor to construct a "risk-efficient" portfolio of underlying investments, including both traditional and alternative investments.

The book is intended to function, in effect, as four books in one:

- A concise treatise on the theory of risk management
- A how-to guide on the practice of risk management
- A workbook with real-life examples complete with discussions of how to interpret and evaluate results
- A prescriptive handbook on how the hedge fund industry can solve the transparency challenge.

What Are Risk Fundamentals?

Webster's Dictionary defines "fundamental" as:

1 One of the minimum constituents without which a thing or system would not be what it is;
2 Of or relating to essential structure, function, or facts; or
3 Of central importance.

The term *risk fundamentals,* as used here, is a triple entendre, referring to:

- Fundamental risk principles
- Fundamental risk measures
- The Risk Fundamentals® Solution

Fundamental Risk Principles

Here are the fundamental risk principles that this book presents, chapter by chapter:

Chapter 1: ***Volatility*** results from uncertainty of returns. The greater the volatility, the greater the risk. In general, the greater the risk, the greater the potential returns.

Chapter 2: ***Diversification*** reduces risk without necessarily reducing returns.

Chapter 3: ***Leverage*** enhances returns while commensurately increasing risk.

Chapter 4: ***Illiquidity*** is a risk for which hedge funds can be compensated. However, illiquid instruments/portfolios, especially when combined with leverage, can have significant "blow-up" risk.

Chapter 5: Both funds and investors should ***measure risk*** in all market conditions. *Historical simulation* helps you analyze the behavior of a portfolio in normal market environments. *Stress testing* allows you to analyze the behavior of a portfolio in crisis market environments.

Chapter 6: Both funds and investors should ***understand the source of risk.*** A risk factor framework is an *additive* framework to explain and communicate risk, which is inherently nonadditive (which is why 1 + 1 doesn't equal 2).

Chapter 7: Risk is amorphous and difficult to communicate. ***Visualizing and articulating*** risk is as important as analyzing it.

Chapter 8: Hedge funds should develop a ***risk culture*** that nurtures the taking of attractively compensated risk.

Chapter 9: Risks other than those related to market performance are never compensated. ***Non-market risks*** should be minimized or avoided.

Chapter 10: Hedge funds should target idiosyncratic risk exposures through security selection ("stock picking" in the equity world). Hedge funds should actively manage their exposures to market and secondary risks in ***constructing a fund.***

Chapter 11: ***Attributing performance*** by applying the same risk factor framework upon which portfolio constructions are based provides an understanding of how a fund has made money.

Chapter 12: ***Risk budgeting*** is a holistic approach embraced by many large institutional investors. It integrates risk management with other investment processes.

Chapter 13: ***NAV/return reporting*** is currently inefficient, incomplete, imprecise, and misleading.

Chapter 14: Investors have created portfolios of funds by "stacking" funds with good trailing returns. Instead, investors should proactively ***construct a risk-efficient portfolio of hedge funds.***

Chapter 15: Investors should perform comprehensive ***risk due diligence*** as part of the initial manager selection process and should continue to update it as part of their routine monitoring process.

Chapter 16: ***Transparency*** permits investors to fundamentally understand the risks they are taking.

Chapter 17: As proven in many other industries, universal, cost-efficient risk transparency within the hedge fund industry will require an ***industry standard solution.***

Fundamental Risk Measures

In the financial world, business fundamentals are the essential measures that characterize the behavior of a company. For example, company financial fundamentals are the key balance sheet, profit & loss (P&L), and cash flow measures that characterize the financial well being of the company and explain the market behavior of its securities. These are the key statistics that are used in fundamental research.

Similarly, risk fundamentals are the key measures that characterize the risk and return behavior of an investment. To understand the potential value of risk fundamentals to a hedge fund analyst, consider the value of company fundamentals to an equity analyst. Which would an equity analyst performing fundamental research prefer?

- Hard copies of every invoice in their raw form (thirteen tons of paper delivered in a tractor trailer); or
- Net revenues by line of business for the past twenty quarters from the 10Qs (sixty summary statistics presented in a spreadsheet)?

The answer is obvious. The reason that companies report fundamental financial information is to efficiently communicate the essential performance characteristics of the business. Furthermore, financial fundamentals do this without compromising proprietary data. For example, if the company had opted to deliver the truckload of hard copies, this information would have inadvertently revealed the pricing provided to each and every customer. As this became public, customers who were receiving less favorable prices would be up in arms. So providing every detail would not have successfully communicated the essential information, and it would damage the company by disclosing sensitive data.

Now consider the fundamentals you would want to see when comparing the risks of hedge fund investments. Which would better explain the risk associated with an investment?

- A haphazard and inconsistent presentation of the details of each and every position in the portfolio; or
- A structured presentation of standardized summary risk statistics?

The answer is equally as obvious. As with the company financial information, less is more. A select set of summary, standardized statistics is more valuable than comprehensive, detailed, unstructured data. It is significantly more valuable to provide synthesized risk fundamentals than to inundate the investor with raw data that do not fundamentally explain the risks of the investment. Furthermore, fundamental risk data do not compromise proprietary details.

The Risk Fundamentals® Solution

Risk Fundamentals provides risk management and transparency without requiring managers to disclose their specific holdings. As Chapter 16 discusses, the hedge fund industry, investors, and regulators have been actively debating risk transparency for more than five years (since the Long-Term Capital Management crisis in the fall of 1998), but little concrete progress has resulted. As argued in Chapter 17, achieving quality transparency within the hedge fund industry will require the adoption of an industry standard reporting framework.

Risk Fundamentals is a standardized framework to report summary risk measures that are comparable and can be aggregated across all funds. It has been designed and is being provided by Kenmar, a global investment management and fund of hedge funds firm. Kenmar is committed to helping solve the industry's transparency problem, and we intend to provide a basic service available through prime brokers and fund administrators. Not surprisingly, Risk Fundamentals is based on the fundamental risk principles presented in this book, and it applies the fundamental risk measures defined herein.

The vast majority of this book is intended to be a primer on risk management in hedge funds. It is general information that is broadly applicable. However, Chapter 18 presents specific examples of how risk can be managed using Risk Fundamentals. It is intended to illustrate how all of the previously discussed concepts and measures can be implemented. Chapter 18 presents concrete examples of the system's functionality and addresses how to interpret the results. Drilling down to this level of detail demonstrates how to apply the concepts discussed in previous chapters at a very practical level.

Background of the System

During Kenmar's twenty-year history, it has enjoyed access to real-time data (holdings and valuation) in a consistent reporting framework from its underlying futures managers (commodity trading advisers have historically been willing to supply position disclosure). These detailed data available from managed futures funds had permitted Kenmar to implement a variety of sophisticated analytical systems. Yet the poor quality of information that existed in the hedge fund world frustrated Kenmar. Although a sizeable minority of Kenmar's underlying hedge fund managers provided some risk reporting, the total lack of consistent structure across managers made comparing or aggregating the information virtually impossible. Recognizing that dogmatically requiring position disclosure would limit one's investment universe by eliminating many of the industry's best managers, Kenmar opted against making position disclosure a prerequisite.

The solution that Kenmar developed is Bloomberg-centric (built around the "open" Bloomberg Professional terminal) and can be distributed to the fund managers in which Kenmar invests. This architecture permits managers to retain control of their position data while providing a risk profile based on risk fundamentals. Unlike the "centralized" and "closed" nature of most established risk management systems, this solution is both "distributed" and "open." This is enabled by the use of standard and ubiquitous technology and market data (that of Microsoft and the Bloomberg Professional service) coupled with a standardized, transparent, and broadly available set of risk data and analytics.

The initial reviews of Risk Fundamentals among hedge fund industry professionals were outstanding, with repeated suggestions that Kenmar make the system commercially available. Kenmar rapidly recognized, however, that the way to make the greatest contribution to the hedge fund industry was for such a system to become broadly available as an "industry utility." Kenmar's risk factors, discussed below, are designed so as to directly connect hedge fund risks and returns to underlying market data. Risk Fundamentals we believe holds the potential to become an industry standard, just as distributed and open personal computers replaced centralized and closed mainframe computers.

Overview of How the System Works

The distributed system operates at each fund, calculates a comprehensive set of risk fundamentals, and transmits a risk fundamental–based profile without disclosing any position-specific data. This summary profile is automatically sent electronically to a central database and forwarded to permissioned investors. Although the underlying analytics of the system are very powerful, a significant amount of the benefit of the system comes from simply presenting the summary information of each of the underlying managers in a common framework so that it can be compared and aggregated by investors.

The risk fundamentals include sensitivities to a set of hedge fund–oriented risk factors. The risk factor framework permits risk to be treated holistically across all asset classes (including providing VaR statistics) while still supporting the established risk frameworks specific to each asset class. Besides receiving a complete picture of the risks of each underlying fund, investors can consolidate the risk profiles of each underlying fund to analyze the risks of their portfolio of funds.

Risk Fundamentals generates the Risk Fundamentals statistics, a comprehensive set of fundamental risk statistics for every fund using the system. In addition to the typical risk and return statistics that can be calculated based on historical monthly return data, Risk Fundamentals is designed to marry real-time NAV/return data with detailed fund risk statistics, all calculated applying a standard methodology. The application of a standard template permits investors to compare and aggregate risk across hedge funds.

I

Part One

The Components of Risk

CHAPTER 1

Volatility

Volatility is the primary component of risk. Volatility exists when outcomes are uncertain. For example, assume you repeatedly flip a coin and this is the payout from each flip:

- You earn $1 if the coin lands on heads (50 percent probability).
- You earn $3 if the coin lands on tails (50 percent probability).

Your expected return for each flip will be $2, the average of $1 and $3. The average absolute deviation from the expected return—that is, the volatility—will be $1. That's because if the coin lands on heads you will earn $1 less than the expected return, and if it lands on tails you will earn $1 more than the expected return.

Now let's analyze a second payout scenario:

- You do not earn anything if the coin lands on heads (50 percent probability).
- You earn $4 if the coin lands on tails (50 percent probability).

Your expected return for each flip will still be $2, the average of zero and $4. The average absolute deviation will now be $2. (The absolute deviation from the mean of $2 of both outcomes will be $2, so the average absolute deviation will be $2.) The two scenarios have the same return and different volatilities.

In general, the greater the level of risk taken, the greater the level of return expected. If the above examples were restated as alternative investments, no investor would choose to take the second investment, which would have equivalent returns but greater volatility. However, there is a floor to returns called the "risk-free rate." That is, a risk-free investment (such as the 90-day Treasury bill) will earn a baseline return to reward the investor for committing capital. (In our simple example, there was no commitment of capital, just a payout.) Therefore, the typical relationship between return and volatility is as shown in **Figure 1.1**.

Investments that fall on this line are considered to be "efficient." The "efficient market theory" argues that markets are efficient over time and that returns are commensurate with the level of risk. This implies that over the long term returns should fall on the efficient line as shown in Figure 1.1.

FIGURE 1.1 **Relationship between Risk and Return**

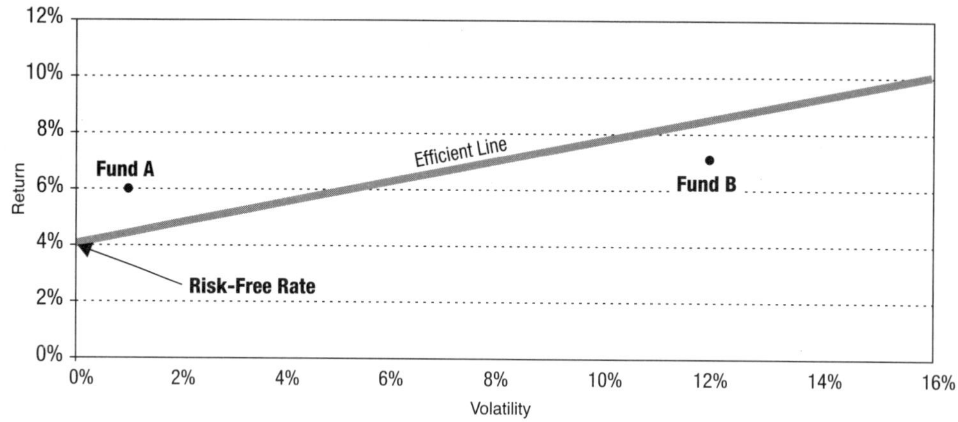

Because investments with higher volatility should command higher returns, you cannot evaluate a return without simultaneously considering the risk associated with that return. For example, the two hypothetical funds in Figure 1.1 had the following payout:

- Fund A had a volatility of 1 percent and a return of 6 percent (above the efficient line).
- Fund B had a volatility of 12 percent and a return of 7 percent (below the efficient line).

From a perspective of risk efficiency, Fund A would be the preferred choice, despite the fact that it generated a lower absolute return. This demonstrates the need to measure performance on a "risk-adjusted" basis, not an "absolute" basis. More than forty years ago, William Sharpe, a Nobel laureate and pioneer in financial theory, developed the Sharpe ratio, which provides a measure that appropriately adjusts returns for the level of volatility. The Sharpe ratio is the mainstay of hedge fund risk statistics:

$$\text{Sharpe Ratio} = \frac{\text{Return} - \text{Risk-Free Rate}}{\text{Volatility}}$$

Assuming a 4 percent risk-free rate, the Sharpe ratio of Fund A, therefore, is 2 (the difference of 6 percent and 4 percent, or 2 percent divided by 1 percent), and the Sharpe ratio for Fund B is 0.25 (the difference of 7 percent and 4 percent, or 3 percent divided by 12 percent). The higher the Sharpe ratio, the better the risk-adjusted returns.

Despite the fact that Sharpe has recently questioned the validity of his formula, given the practical problems with hedge fund return data (discussed in Chapter 5), this formula for comparing the risk-adjusted returns is widely applied throughout the hedge fund world.

The Capital Asset Pricing Model (CAPM) takes the efficient market theory one step further, concluding that the only risk that is compensated (or that produces return) is "market" risk. This is based on the assumption that the markets are 100 percent efficient and that risks other than market risks (such as exposures to styles or sectors) can be diversified away. If risks other than directional market risk can be shed through diversification, the theory concludes, there is no reason that investors should be compensated for taking these other risks.

However, the direct implication of this theory is that hedge funds cannot earn a positive return. Hedge funds, after all, explicitly target, rather than shed, risks other than directional market risk to generate "alpha"—that is, returns in excess of those generated by taking directional market risks only. The superior returns of hedge funds over the last decade is empirical evidence refuting the CAPM theory.

Furthermore, although the favorable composite returns of hedge funds are direct evidence that the underlying markets are not efficient, the returns across hedge funds are similarly evidence that the ability of hedge funds to earn a return is not efficient. The performance of individual hedge funds has varied dramatically, as **Figure 1.2** shows.

FIGURE 1.2 **Hedge Fund Performance (1997–2003)**

	ANNUAL RETURN	STANDARD DEVIATION	LARGEST DRAWDOWN	SHARPE RATIO	CORRELATION TO S&P	BETA TO S&P
Minimum	–20%	0.5%	0%	–2.1	–0.84	-1.5
Maximum	38%	89%	–94%	3.8	0.99	1.8

Based on 568 hedge funds in Hedge Fund Research universe with histories back to January 1997

FIGURE 1.3 **Hedge Fund Return versus Volatility**

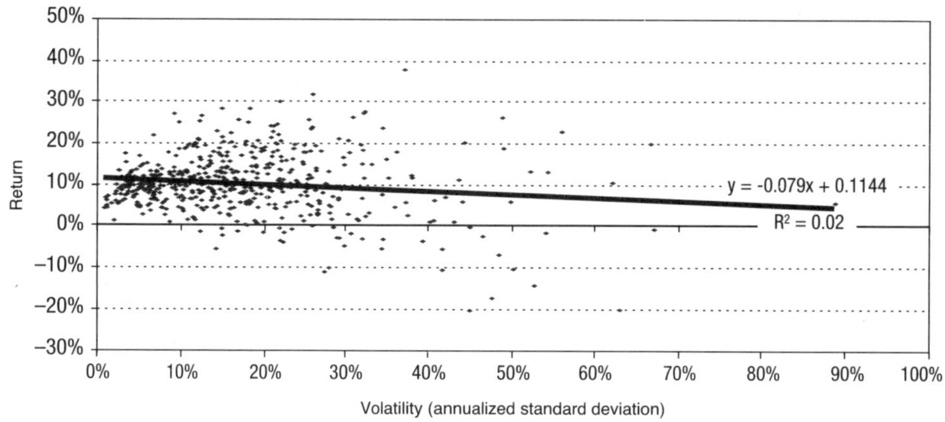

In theory, a hedge fund's level of return should be directly related to its risk (intercepting at the risk-free rate). However, if you statistically analyze the relationship between the risk (measured as the annualized standard deviation of return) and return (measured as the compound annual return) of funds, you find, as in **Figure 1.3**, that the actual relationship is negatively sloping (versus the theoretical positive sloping relationship shown in Figure 1.1).

Although the negative relationship is not statistically significant ($R^2 = 0.02$), it clearly implies that the relationship between hedge fund risk and return is not efficient.

Risks in Hedge Funds versus Traditional Investments

In 1530, Copernicus concluded that the planets circled the sun in a well-defined, systematic behavior, consequently the name "solar system." It took 150 more years for Isaac Newton to explain gravity, the force that caused this systematic behavior.

In the financial world there are equivalent natural forces that similarly cause systematic behavior. The fundamental equity and interest rate market movements represent forces that drive correlated behavior across stocks and bonds, respectively. This correlated behavior is captured in benchmarks, such as the S&P 500 Index. Furthermore, in the traditional investment world, managers are typically judged based on how similarly to these benchmarks they perform, generally measured as tracking error. Therefore, the behavior of individual long-only funds is consequently drawn to the behavior of their specific benchmark. For example, a small-cap value manager is typically measured against a small-cap value benchmark, such as the Russell 3000 value index, and will have a strong incentive to behave similarly to that benchmark, while attempting to beat it. However, in the absolute return world of alternative investments, no similar gravitational force exists, and, consequently, the behavior of individual hedge funds cannot be meaningfully explained by the behavior of indices.

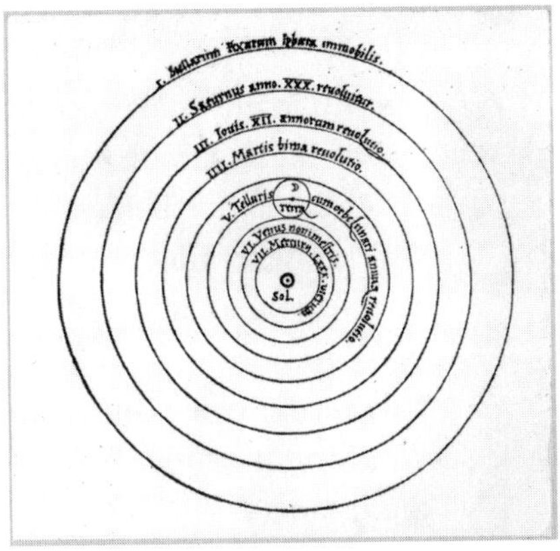

THE COPERNICAN SYSTEM

In traditional investments, the vast majority of risk is explained through linear relationships to the relevant benchmarks. Because hedge funds, measured on absolute returns, generally target risks other than core market exposures, the performance behavior of hedge funds is highly complex. This is exacerbated by the fact that there is no force pulling returns to the norm of an index.

Alternative Investments ≠ Traditional Investments

The fact that the risks of traditional investments are both linear and additive permits you to analyze them using relatively simple approaches. The behavior of hedge funds is significantly more complex because of the following:

Idiosyncratic risk. The primary risk in a long-only, traditional fund is directional market risk. In contrast, hedge funds target "idiosyncratic" risk. "Idiosyncratic" is defined by Webster as "an individualizing characteristic or quality" or "individual hypersensitivity." For example, most long-only U.S. equity managers focus on a universe of 500 or 700 large-capitalization equities, with their greatest focus on the top 100 stocks because of cap-weighted benchmarks. Most hedge fund managers focus on a universe of more than 2,500 U.S. equities, with relatively equal focus on all market-cap ranges because their target is absolute return.

Relative value or spread relationships. Hedge funds often target relative value or spread relationships. They are able to target these specific relationships because of their ability to "go short" (sell a security they do not hold). Looking at

Copernicus's view of the world, each planet goes around the sun in nice, uniform ellipses. This well-defined behavior is equivalent to the directional behavior of the equity market. Now consider the movement of Mars relative to Earth. These two planets have differently shaped ellipses that are not concentric and orbit the sun at different speeds. If you were to view the movement of Mars relative to Earth, the behavior would seem extremely irregular.

The relative behavior of spread trades in hedge funds is similarly irregular and idiosyncratic. For those of you who were not tracking the relative relationship in our solar system, Mars came within 56 million miles of Earth in August 2003, the closest it had been in 60,000 years (a 10-plus standard deviation event). Furthermore, astronomers tell us this will not occur again until August 28, 2287. Wouldn't it be nice if such relative relationships could be as precisely forecast in the financial world?

Optionality. Unlike traditional fund managers, hedge funds can buy or sell options. Unlike the linear behavior of stocks and bonds, options introduce "convexity" (nonlinear behavior) into the portfolio. As Chapter 3 discusses, optionality can introduce significant risk into the portfolio.

Let's briefly discuss the return behavior of an option, using a basic call option as an example. Suppose an investor held a call option on IBM, which was trading at $75 per share. Assume the option was at a strike price of $80. The holder of the option has the right but not the obligation to receive the underlying stock at

FIGURE 1.4 **Example of IBM Call Option**

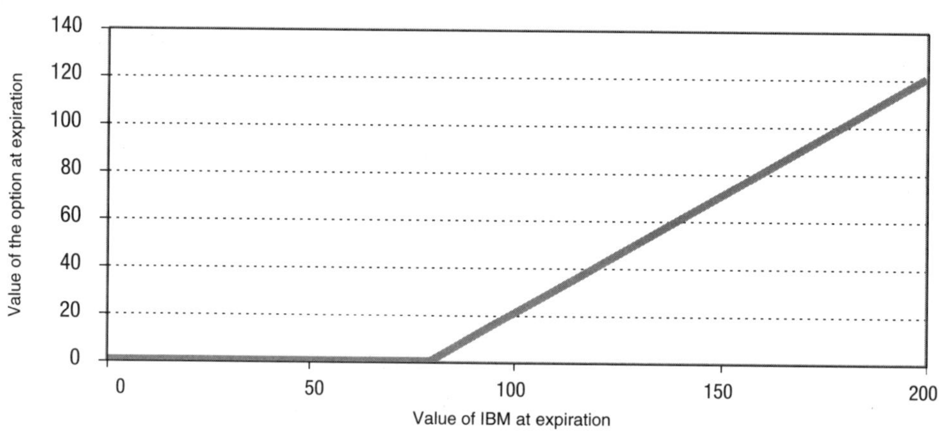

the specified strike price at a specified expiration time. Therefore, if at the time of expiration IBM trades at less than $80 the call is "out of the money," and the option would be worthless. However, if IBM is trading for greater than $80 at expiration the option has value. If at the time the option expires IBM is trading at $85, the option would be worth $5, the premium over the $80 strike price. If IBM is trading at $100, the option would be worth $20 (again, the premium of $100 over the $80 strike price). Therefore, the option will have a "payout function" (the relationship between what the option is worth and the value of the underlying stock at expiration) as shown in **Figure 1.4**.

As you can see, the relationship is kinked, or "convex." Furthermore, the value of such a call option would be relatively small because the option is out of the money when IBM is trading at $75, so the risk exposure per dollar of capital is potentially extremely large. However, the value can increase rapidly (and dramatically as a percent of the price paid for the option) as it comes into the money. If you are long the option, this nonlinear behavior represents only upside. However, if you are short the option, this convexity can result in significant losses.

Beyond directly holding options, portfolios can hold positions with "embedded" options, cash instruments that are bundled with a related option. For example, convertible bonds are corporate bonds bundled with equity options. (Although traditional managers will invest in convertible bonds, they do not explicitly target the optionality as do hedge funds.)

Leverage. Hedge funds can use significant financial leverage by borrowing or using notionally funded instruments. (In contrast, mutual funds can use extremely limited leverage.) Although this does not introduce a new source of risk, it amplifies all the other risks. Chapter 3 discusses leverage in detail.

Asymmetric trading. Traditional investments are typically buy-and-hold strategies. The average holding period is generally a year or more. In contrast, many hedge funds execute trading-oriented strategies. The average holding period is typically one month, although it can be as short as a day. Hedge funds frequently follow asymmetric trading strategies. These strategies can often have option-like behavior (convexity) without actually holding option positions.

Asymmetric trading strategies introduce convexity, or option-like behavior, because the trading rules for holdings that are profitable are different from those that are not. In general, hedge funds hold profitable positions longer than unprofitable positions that are stopped out (closed out having hit a previously established limit). Such asymmetric trading strategies (discussed in Chapter 10) effectively create synthetic options, that is, funds that behave as if they contained

FIGURE 1.5 **Returns of Managed Futures during S&P 500 Declines (1980–2003)**

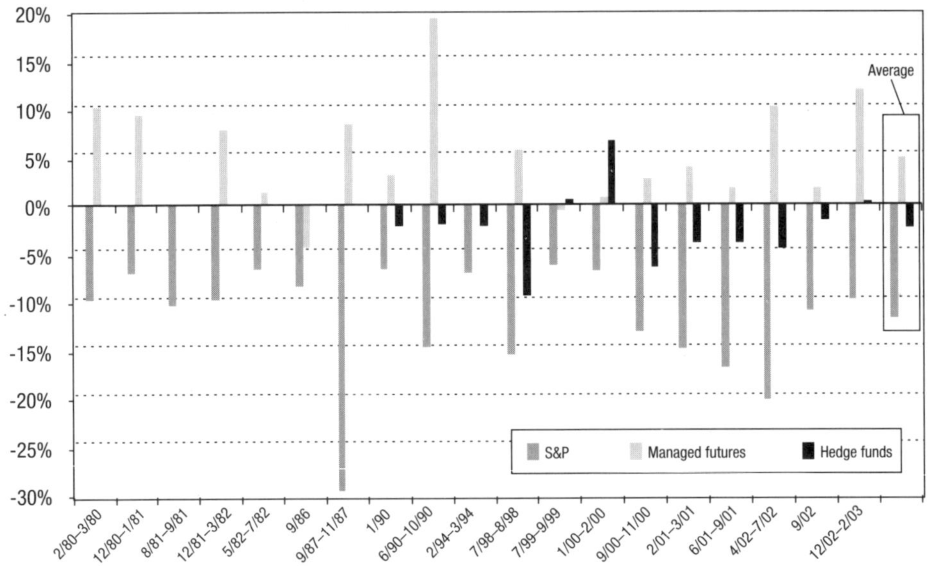

options. As with options, when market-implied volatility increases, such a strategy tends to generate significant gains. Therefore, these strategies are equivalent to being "long volatility."

For example, trend-following commodity trading advisers (CTAs) employ quantitative trading systems that automatically respond to trends. These managers who trade in managed futures demonstrate "long-volatility" behavior. That is, they tend to generate favorable returns when equity volatility increase. Because equity volatility tend to increase when the underlying equity market falls, managed futures generally have positive returns when the returns of the equity markets tumble. **Figure 1.5** shows that managed futures posted positive returns in fifteen of the eighteen periods of consecutive monthly declines of the S&P 500 that occurred since 1980.

Furthermore, unlike short sellers who also generate positive returns when the S&P declines (short sellers demonstrate linear behavior in the opposite direction of that of the market), the returns of CTAs demonstrate convexity, also posting positive returns during periods that the S&P increased (see **Figure 1.6**).

FIGURE 1.6 **Returns of Managed Futures and Short Sellers in Extreme Markets***

	% OF THESE PERIODS WITH GAINS FOR: MANAGED FUTURES	SHORT SELLERS**
Periods of S&P losses >6%	90%	90%
Periods of S&P gains >6%	89%	0%

* Consecutive monthly losses or gains in the S&P 500 between January 1990 and July 2002 (period for which both indices existed)
** HFR Short Selling Index

Event risk. Hedge funds take risks in event-driven strategies such as merger arbitrage, capital structure arbitrage, and distressed debt. Event-driven strategies are characterized by extreme price moves around key events. For example, in merger arbitrage the deal either ultimately goes through, or it is cancelled. In distressed debt the company typically reorganizes and continues to operate, or it is liquidated. In capital structure arbitrage some event affecting the relative value of different components of the capital structure occurs.

Illiquidity. Mutual funds can be "marked to market," or valued, based on fair market value, on a daily basis. This demands that they invest in primarily liquid securities. In contrast, hedge funds can invest in illiquid instruments. Markets that are less liquid are generally significantly less efficient, and this creates an opportunity to create alpha. Some of the less liquid traded securities include mortgage-backed derivatives, asset-backed securities, distressed debt, and microcap stocks. In addition, hedge funds can have holdings in securities that trade on an extremely limited basis, such as private equity and bank loans.

With illiquidity comes risk. There is a correlated behavior across illiquid instruments. When financial crises occur there is typically a general flight to quality, and illiquid instruments underperform. Hedge funds, which are typically long the less liquid instruments and short the more liquid instruments, can have correlated losses (across most asset classes). This is compounded by the portfolio-specific problem that when a loss is sustained, if the capital is invested in illiquid instruments the investor cannot monetize the illiquid instruments to raise cash to fund margin requirements (discussed in Chapter 4). These adverse general market- and portfolio-specific conditions tend to occur simultaneously, as in the fall of 1998 when many hedge fund blow-ups occurred (the Russian debt default, followed by LTCM, followed by dislocations in the mortgage backed markets). Finally, in an effort to respond to market pressure for shorter redemption policies, there is an increasing mismatch between the redemption policies of the fund and the liquidity of the underlying portfolio. This imbalance can be and has been resolved at the expense of the investor.

Many of these hyperactive hedge fund strategies are based on being "liquidity suppliers" to less nimble traditional investors. For example, statistical arbitrage hedge funds respond to increases or decreases in relative demand for stocks (detected by short-term relative price moves), by selling or buying shares, respectively. This strategy results in the fund behaving as if it were "short volatility" (the equivalent of being short a put option). Such funds enjoy positive returns with low volatility (from positive carry) for a period of time until they blow-up, often forfeiting these returns and then some.

Finally, note that a single hedge fund can be exposed to many of these risks simultaneously. For example, a convertible arbitrage fund can use relative value strategies across bonds, extract the embedded option of the convertible bond, dynamically re-hedge the equity exposure, and, especially in the case of "busted converts" (distressed convertible bonds), have significant exposure to event risk and illiquidity.

The Distribution of Hedge Fund Returns

The example of volatility described at the beginning of this chapter used a very simple random process, the flip of a coin. This is an extremely simple stochastic (i.e., probabilistic) process, as the outcome is binary, either heads or tails. Most stochastic processes have significantly more complex distributions. Many natural processes behave consistently with the Gaussian distribution (named after the German mathematician Carl Friedrich Gauss). **Figure 1.7** illustrates this distribution. Although mathematicians call it the Gaussian distribution, it is more commonly known as the "normal" distribution. Furthermore, because of its shape, it is frequently called the "bell curve."

For a variety of reasons, it is generally assumed that traditional financial processes will display this behavior. As Chapter 5 discusses, making this assumption permits a variety of simplifying "closed form" analytical models to be applied. However, for all the reasons just discussed about the differences between alternative and traditional investments, assuming that hedge fund returns will be normally distributed is overly simplistic and misleading. In fact, the significant

FIGURE 1.7 Normal or "Bell-Curve" Distribution

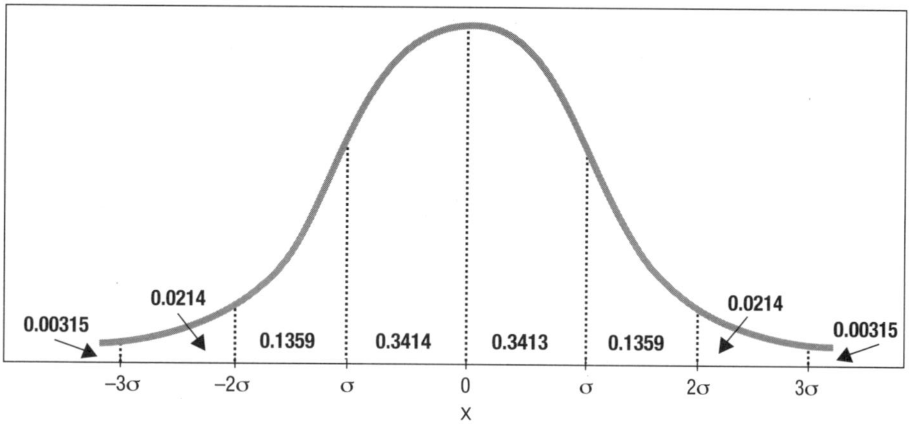

FIGURE 1.8 Fat Tails—Distribution of Returns of the HFR Convertible Arbitrage Index

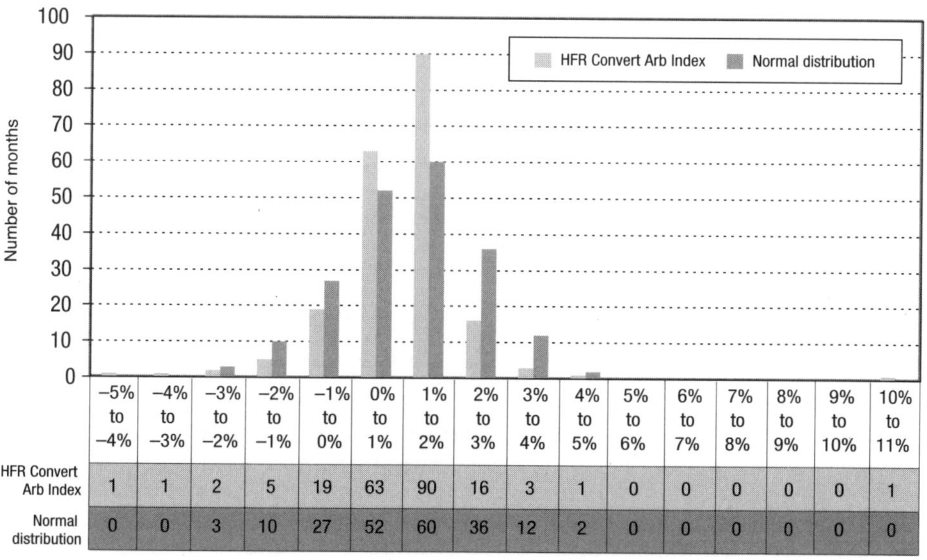

	−5% to −4%	−4% to −3%	−3% to −2%	−2% to −1%	−1% to 0%	0% to 1%	1% to 2%	2% to 3%	3% to 4%	4% to 5%	5% to 6%	6% to 7%	7% to 8%	8% to 9%	9% to 10%	10% to 11%
HFR Convert Arb Index	1	1	2	5	19	63	90	16	3	1	0	0	0	0	0	1
Normal distribution	0	0	3	10	27	52	60	36	12	2	0	0	0	0	0	0

FIGURE 1.9 Asymmetric Returns—Distribution of Returns of the HFR Event-Driven Index

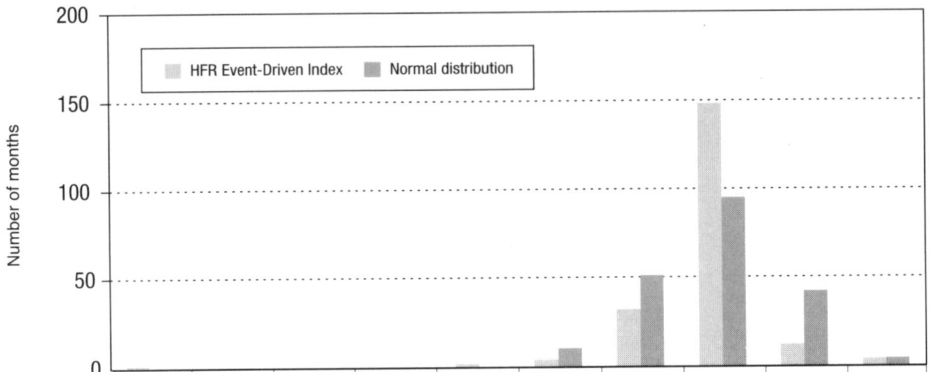

	−28% to −24%	−24% to −20%	−20% to −16%	−16% to −12%	−12% to −8%	−4% to 8%	−4% to 0%	0% to 4%	4% to 8%	8% to 12%
HFR Event-Driven Index	1	0	0	0	1	4	32	148	12	4
Normal	0	0	0	0	0	10	51	95	42	4

difference between the actual return behavior of hedge funds and the normal distribution is the source of much of the alpha hedge funds generate. To ignore the associated risk would be a gross oversimplification.

Hedge fund returns typically deviate from the normal distribution in two ways. First, they tend to display "fat tails," with the distribution of returns being more peaked than the bell curve and the tails extending further. **Figure 1.8** shows the distribution of monthly returns of the Hedge Fund Research (HFR) Convertible Arbitrage Index. Convertible arbitrage is a strategy in which the hedge fund isolates the equity option embedded in a convertible bond. The convexity of the option creates the fat tails. Mathematicians call this "kurtosis."

The second way that hedge fund returns tend to deviate from the normal distribution is that they are typically not symmetrical. Mathematicians call this "skew." The bell curve of the normal distribution is symmetrically shaped around the mean. Hedge fund returns more often than not display asymmetric behavior, or a skewed bell curve.

Figure 1.9 shows the distribution of monthly returns of the HFR Event-Driven Index. This distribution displays both fat-tail and asymmetric behavior. The primary reason is that the outcomes of events are typically binary, so the consequent distribution of returns does not conform to the normal distribution. Events generally include betting on a merger closing or a bankrupt company restructuring. The skew is negative in that these types of events generally resolve as anticipated, resulting in a large number of relatively small positive return periods. However, in the less frequent occurrences when the market is surprised, the downward move is generally significantly larger.

In sum, the result is that hedge fund returns can deviate significantly from the bell curve of the normal distribution. It is because of these fat-tail and asymmetrical behaviors that the hedge fund industry has developed a series of risk measures:

- Drawdown
- Semi-deviation
- Gain and loss standard deviation
- Downside deviation
- Sortino ratio

These measures isolate the upside and downside volatility and explicitly measure the performance in different market environments. Volatility is not a bad thing if it results in more upside than downside.

Value at Risk (VaR)

Recognizing that returns in complex financial instruments are often not normally distributed, Value at Risk, or VaR, is a way to describe risk without assuming a specific underlying distribution of returns. VaR expresses the largest loss a portfolio will probabilistically sustain at a specified "confidence level." For example, a 95 percent VaR is the loss that a portfolio should expect to experience in 95 out of 100 periods (alternatively stated, the investor should anticipate losing more than this value only in 5 percent of the periods). For example, the actual returns of the 100 months through September 2003 of the HFR Composite Index sorted in decreasing sequence are displayed in **Figure 1.10**. The 95 percent confidence VaR would be when there are only five returns of less than or equal to this level, or –2.8 percent (the shaded return). This implies that investors in hedge funds could have anticipated losing no more than 2.8 percent in only five months during this approximate eight-year, or 100 month, period.

Therefore, VaR at a specific confidence level defines one point in the entire distribution of returns. When returns can be legitimately expressed as a normal distribution, the full distribution of returns is defined by two parameters: the mean and

FIGURE 1.10 **Actual Returns of the HFR Index Sorted in Descending Sequence**

100 MONTHS THROUGH SEPTEMBER 2003				
7.7%	2.9%	1.7%	0.5%	–0.8%
6.2%	2.8%	1.6%	0.5%	–0.8%
5.1%	2.7%	1.5%	0.5%	–0.9%
4.5%	2.6%	1.3%	0.3%	–1.2%
4.4%	2.5%	1.3%	0.3%	–1.3%
4.0%	2.3%	1.2%	0.3%	–1.5%
3.9%	2.2%	1.2%	0.2%	–1.5%
3.8%	2.2%	1.2%	0.2%	–1.6%
3.7%	2.1%	1.2%	0.1%	–1.6%
3.7%	2.1%	1.1%	0.0%	–1.8%
3.7%	2.1%	1.0%	0.0%	–1.9%
3.6%	2.1%	1.0%	0.0%	–2.0%
3.6%	2.1%	1.0%	–0.1%	–2.1%
3.4%	2.1%	0.9%	–0.1%	–2.1%
3.3%	2.0%	0.9%	–0.2%	–2.2%
3.2%	2.0%	0.7%	–0.4%	–2.8%
3.2%	2.0%	0.7%	–0.6%	–2.9%
3.1%	1.9%	0.7%	–0.7%	–2.9%
3.1%	1.9%	0.6%	–0.7%	–3.5%
3.0%	1.8%	0.6%	–0.7%	–8.7%

the standard deviation. In contrast, there are an unlimited number of VaR values at varying confidence levels. Furthermore, when comparing two investments, the VaR of one can be higher at some confidence level, say the 90 percent VaR, and the VaR of the other could be larger at another confidence level, say the 99 percent VaR. Unfortunately, this is not a failure in VaR but rather a reality of distributions that are not well behaved. It is something that an investor in hedge funds must deal with.

In the preceding example, the VaR of hedge fund returns is calculated based on the actual monthly returns. In most portfolios, the construction of the portfolio changes over time, and the VaR is calculated by simulating how the current construction of the portfolio might have behaved over time. Chapter 5 discusses in detail alternative approaches to doing this. The VaR is then calculated based on these simulated returns.

CHAPTER 2

Diversification

Diversification is behind the equation 1 + 1 = 1.41. Let's start with a simple example. Suppose you make the investment described in the example in Chapter 1 that pays out $1 with a 50 percent probability and $3 with a 50 percent probability. The expected payout will be $2 [(50% × $1) + (50% × $3)]. The standard deviation (the most common measure of volatility) of the payout is defined as the square root of the expected squared deviation from the mean. (Chapter 1 uses the average absolute return rather than the standard deviation, for simplicity.) Under either outcome, the squared deviation from the mean of $2 is $1, so the expected squared deviation is $1, and the square root of this is also $1.

Now suppose you invest $1 in each of two funds (A and B), each of which has the same payout characteristics ($1 with 50 percent probability and $3 with 50 percent probability), and whose results have no relationship between them (that is, their results are independent). There are four possible outcomes, each having a 25 percent probability, as shown in **Figure 2.1**.

The expected payout is the average of the combined payout, or $4. The actual and squared deviations are shown in the columns titled "deviation from mean" and "squared deviation," respectively. The average squared deviation is $2 (the average of the squared deviation column). The standard deviation is the

FIGURE 2.1 **Example of Possible Outcomes**

PROBABILITY	FUND A	FUND B	COMBINED	DEVIATION FROM MEAN	SQUARED DEVIATION
25%	$1	$1	$2	($2)	$4
25%	$1	$3	$4	$0	$0
25%	$3	$1	$4	$0	$0
25%	$3	$3	$6	$2	$4
		Average	**$4**	**$0**	**$2**

square root of the average squared deviation, or $1.41. Consequently, when you combine two independent funds with a standard deviation of $1, the combined fund has a standard deviation of $1.41. Therefore:

$$1 + 1 = 1.41$$

QED

QED stands for "quod erat demonstrandum," a Latin phrase meaning "that which was to be proven," which mathematicians frequently put at the end of a formal proof to proclaim their success.

For those readers who have taken some probability or statistics (others please skip this paragraph), this equation is the direct result of the fact that the variance of the sum of two independent random numbers (i.e., the covariance is zero) is the sum of the variances of those numbers. Because the variance increases additively, the standard deviation, which is the square root of the variance, increases by the square root. In the above example, 1.41 is the square root of 2. The fact that volatility of a combination of independent random events increases as the square root of the number of events increases is the reason it is generally assumed that the volatility of a period behaves as the square root of the length of the period. For example, converting the standard deviation of monthly returns to the annualized standard deviation is accomplished by multiplying the returns by the square root of 12.

The Power of Diversification

Having worked through this exercise, we are now ready to discuss the concept of diversification. The example above shows two investment strategies. If you invested $2 in Fund A, you would generate an average payout of $4 with a standard deviation of $2 (exactly double the results of investing $1 described above). Alternatively, if you split your $2 investment, putting $1 into Fund A and $1 into Fund B, you would generate an average payout of $2 and a standard deviation of $1.41. Contrary to the old adage, you do get something for nothing. The second alternative generates a significantly more attractive risk-adjusted return—the same expected return with 30 percent less risk (standard deviation of $1.41 versus a standard deviation of $2). This is an example of the power of diversification. Diversification can reduce the risk when combining investments without sacrificing returns, thereby generating superior risk-adjusted returns.

Here's another example: Suppose you were offered an opportunity to roll a die and receive ten times your total wealth if you roll a six, but lose all your wealth if you roll any other number. Even though the ten-to-one payoff is attractive as an expected return, most people would not accept the offer and expose themselves to a five-in-six probability of going broke. Now, suppose the rules were modified so that you would lose only 10 percent of your wealth if the die comes up other than six, but will double your wealth if the die comes up a six (again a ten-to-one payoff). Most people will accept this because it has a favorable expected return and the downside exposure can be tolerated. The fact that you would be willing to gamble (investing in the markets is exactly that) 10 percent of your wealth but not 100 percent of your wealth is an example of diversification.

Hedge funds call that portion of returns that comes from diversification "alpha." Alpha is the residual returns in excess of (unfortunately, they can also be negative) the returns that are explained by the behavior of the underlying markets. Chapter 1 discusses CAPM, which argues that generating alpha is not feasible. However, as Chapter 1 also points out, hedge funds have been very successful in generating alpha. Returns generated simply from directional exposure to the markets are easy to capture and therefore deserve minimum compensation. This is because all investors with such exposures passively enjoy the market returns. However, alpha is a zero-sum game. To earn returns by generating alpha, an investor must take them away from another investor. For every investor who earns positive alpha there must be another investor earning negative alpha. Therefore, alpha deserves to be well compensated, in the form of high hedge fund performance fees.

Diversification is measured by "correlation," a metric that can range from –1.0 to 1.0. When two return series are perfectly correlated, they move in lockstep with each other, and the correlation is 1. When two return series move exactly opposite each other the correlation is –1. When two return series are independent of each other (implying there is no relationship between them so that if the first return is above the average return in a specific period, the probability of the second series being simultaneously above the average is 50 percent/50 percent), the correlation is 0. Therefore, a portfolio whose funds have correlations of approximately 0 is highly diversified; one with high correlations (approaching 1) is highly concentrated; and in a portfolio whose funds have extreme negative correlations (approaching –1), the funds are hedging each other out, resulting in minimal net risk exposure (funded with significant fees to managers with offsetting exposures).

FIGURE 2.2 **Correlation of S&P 500 and MSCI World ex USA (Trailing 52 Weeks)**

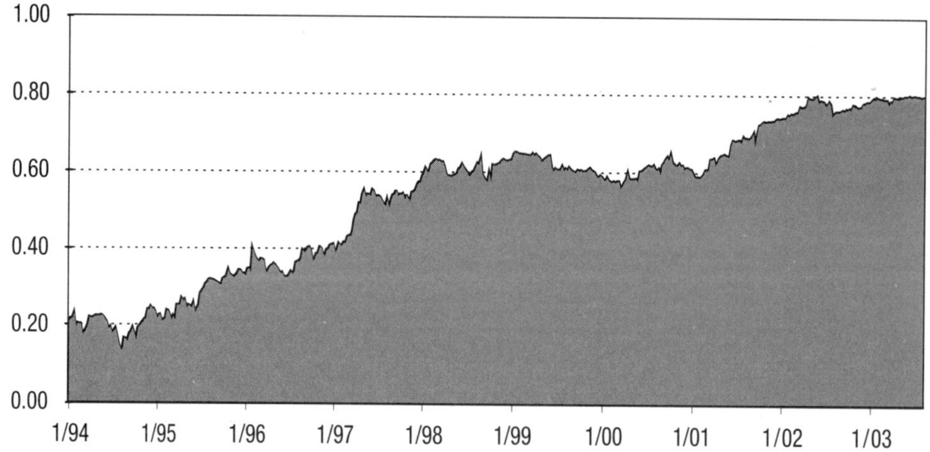

Now that we understand the benefits of diversification, let's explore how to take advantage of it. An investor in hedge funds should take advantage of two opportunities to diversify:

1 She should diversify between her portfolio of hedge funds and her traditional investments.

2 She should diversify among the funds in her portfolio of hedge funds.

Most investors already have significant exposure to the core equity and fixed-income (interest rate and credit) markets through their traditional investments. Investors should be actively seeking diversification from these exposures, because globalization has made the markets increasingly more correlated, as **Figure 2.2** shows.

Consequently, diversification is becoming more difficult to achieve and increasingly more valuable. Furthermore, investors can gain directional exposure to market risks for relatively small fees. For example, the fees associated with exchange-traded funds (such as SPDRs) are approximately 10 basis points. By contrast, hedge funds that offer exposure to the underlying equity and fixed-income markets are offering nondiversifying (concentrating) exposures at twenty to thirty times these fees.

Despite marketing themselves as generating absolute returns, hedge funds

FIGURE 2.3 **Average Correlation of Individual Hedge Fund with the Equity Market**

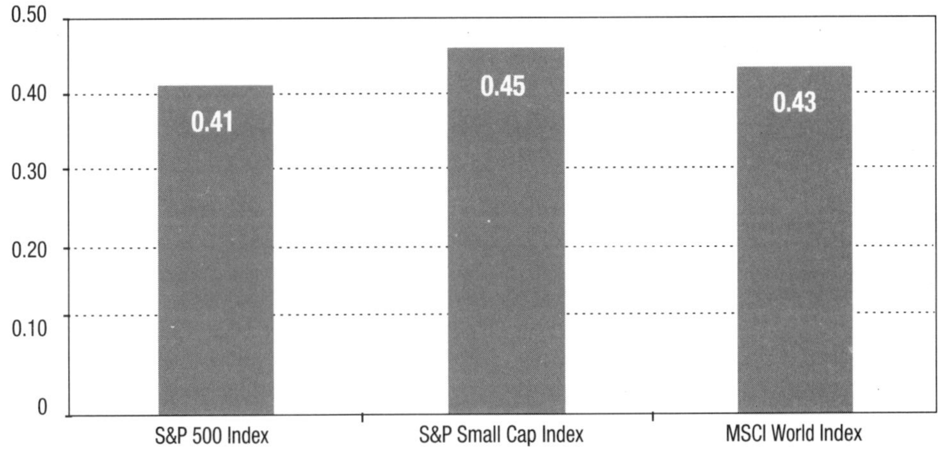

often demonstrate strong equity market biases. Recent history (2001 and 2002) in declining equity markets has refuted many hedge funds' (particularly equity hedge funds) long-stated claim that they can "make money in all market conditions." **Figure 2.3** shows that hedge funds, on average, demonstrate a significant correlation with, and bias to, the equity markets.

As Chapter 6 discusses, market risks are systematic risk exposures that cannot be diversified away in a long-only portfolio. Consequently, many investors already have significant exposure to many market risks through their long-only portfolio. There are six primary market risks:

- ***Equity***—The risk related to the directional movement of the equity market.
- ***Interest rate***—The risk related to the directional movement of interest rates.
- ***Credit***—The risk related to the directional movement of credit spreads.
- ***Commodity***—The risk related to the directional movement of physical commodities.
- ***Currency***—The risk related to the directional movement of the dollar relative to other currencies.
- ***Real estate***—The risk related to the directional movement of direct investment in real estate.

Figure 2.4 shows the correlations among the six primary market risks.

FIGURE 2.4 Correlation of Primary Market Risks

	EQUITY	INTEREST RATES	CREDIT	CURRENCY	COMMODITIES	REAL ESTATE
Equity	1.00					
Interest Rates	–0.08	1.00				
Credit	0.17	–0.11	1.00			
Currency	0.08	–0.18	0.00	1.00		
Commodities	0.03	0.14	–0.01	–0.20	1.00	
Real Estate	–0.05	0.47	–0.14	0.03	0.05	1.00

Investors should proactively manage diversification from the market. Chapter 1 discusses how the Sharpe ratio adjusts returns for volatility to measure how efficiently risk has been deployed. However, just as investors should expect higher returns for higher volatility, investors should similarly expect higher returns for lower diversification or greater correlation. The BAVAR (***b**eta **a**nd **v**olatility **a**djusted **r**eturn*) ratio enhances the Sharpe ratio and also adjusts for market correlation. For example, if you already had exposure to the equity market through your traditional investments, which of the alternatives in **Figure 2.5** would be the most attractive investments?

The answer is that they are all equally attractive. The reason behind this and the BAVAR ratio is described in greater detail in the Appendix.

Investors should also seek diversification among the funds in their portfolio of hedge funds (as Chapter 14 discusses in detail). The key knowledge that the investor should develop is a comprehensive understanding of the risk exposures of each of his underlying funds so that he will be in a position to analyze cross-fund correlation.

FIGURE 2.5 Investment Alternatives with Similar Risk-Adjusted Profiles

FUND	ANNUAL RETURN	ANNUAL STANDARD DEVIATION	CORRELATION TO S&P 500
A	12%	18%	1.0
B	8%	18%	0.0
C	–2%	18%	–1.0

Hedge funds have a surprisingly high exposure to correlated risks. As a result, although a reasonably diversified portfolio of hedge funds will adequately diversify security-specific risks, a concentrated exposure to correlated risks often remains. For example, since early 2000 when the bull market came to an end, investors have been hurt by the correlated long bias of hedge funds to the underlying equity market. However, hedge funds may be even more sensitive to style biases because many hedge funds actively seek to hedge out market directional exposure (to be "market neutral") in favor of other risk exposures.

Systematic Biases

Equity long/short managers typically go long less liquid stocks and short more liquid stocks. For this reason, and others to be discussed, many equity hedge fund managers assume a significant correlated risk exposure to value and small-cap equity styles. For example, despite the overall poor performance of the equity markets from April 2000 to September 2002, value and small-cap stocks significantly outperformed on a relative basis over the previous several years, as **Figure 2.6** shows. In fact, small-cap value outperformed the S&P 500 by an astounding 93 percent over the period April 2000 through September 2002 (see "Beware of Systematic Style Biases," *Risk Magazine*, December 2002).

Many hedge fund investors had been drawn to the favorable returns of

FIGURE 2.6 **Cumulative Returns (April 2000–September 2002)**

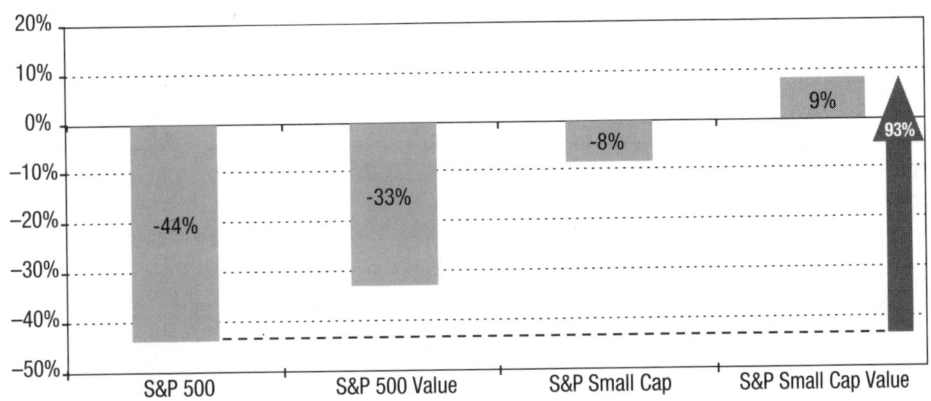

FIGURE 2.7 **Equity-based Strategies as a Percentage of Assets Under Management in HFR Fund Universe**

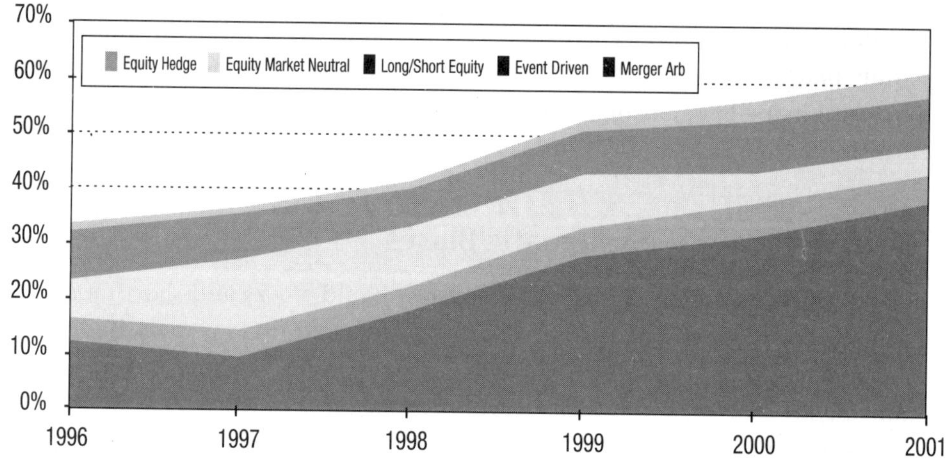

Source: HFR

FIGURE 2.8 **Relative Performance of S&P Growth versus Value**

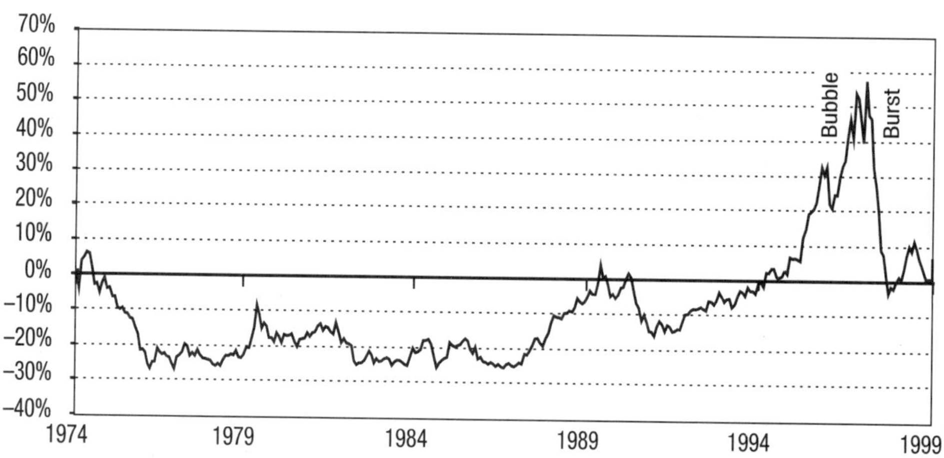

FIGURE 2.9 **Price/Forward Earnings Ratio**

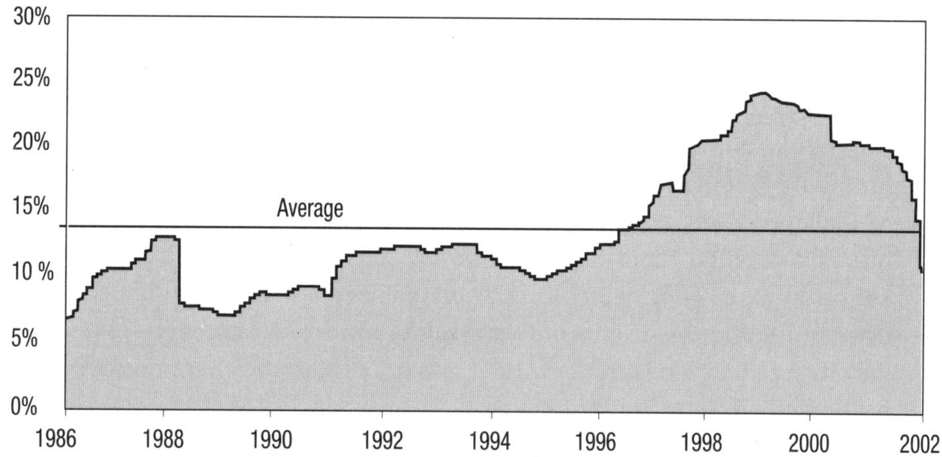

equity hedge funds in the late 1990s. Thus, the assets allocated to equity-based strategies had swelled, dramatically increasing hedge fund investors' exposure to equities (see **Figure 2.7**).

The relative performances of both value and small-cap styles have historically been highly cyclical with rapid reversals to growth and large cap (see **Figure 2.8**). One can see the dramatic outperformance of growth in the tech "bubble" followed by a mean reversion in the "burst."

Evidence suggested that we might have been nearing the end of the value/small-cap cycle toward the end of 2002. Price-to-earnings ratios had reverted from historic extremes to historical norms (see **Figure 2.9**). The reversion wasn't expected to happen immediately—it is extremely difficult to predict the precise timing of the pendulum swings of cyclical markets. Rather, the cycle would eventually turn, with many hedge fund investors unaware of their systematic exposure to a value/small-cap bias and of the favorable contribution of this bias to returns (despite the unfavorable returns of the underlying equity market). Although small cap did not outperform in the first half of 2003, the value/growth cycle did revert, and growth significantly outperformed value during this period.

If my thesis was correct—that the recent outperformance of value and small-cap styles might reverse—the obvious question then is: Would hedge funds respond? It seems logical that hedge funds would respond slowly, if at all, for the following reasons:

1 Historically, hedge funds have reacted slowly to a changing environment. Contrary to conventional wisdom, evidence suggests that many hedge funds are not nimble enough to respond when the market turns. During the bull market of the last decade, equity long/short managers generally had a substantial long bias and profited handsomely. However, since early 2000 when the bull market came to an end, equity long/short managers had generally not fared well despite holding themselves out as absolute return investments—either because they have failed to reverse their long bias or because they have not been adept at profiting from short positions.

There were 109 equity long/short hedge funds in the Hedge Fund Research (HFR) universe with records beginning in January 1997 and whose returns were positively correlated to the S&P 500 before the bubble burst in 2000. These funds realized an annualized return of 31 percent on average, from 1997 through the peak. Of these:

- 8 percent became short-biased (negatively correlated to the S&P 500) after the burst, generating compound annual returns of 9 percent since the peak.
- 18 percent remained long-biased (positively correlated to the S&P 500) but were able to earn returns exceeding the risk-free rate (through style bets or superior stock picking), generating 14 percent average annualized returns.
- 74 percent remained long-biased after the market peak, and achieved less than the risk-free rate. The funds in this category sustained average annualized losses of 14 percent since the peak.[1]

2 Hedge funds' value/small-cap bias is structural, not discretionary. The bias of hedge funds to value/small-cap stocks is a "structural" result of their investment process. Therefore, hedge funds are even less likely to modulate their value/small-cap bias as the value/small-cap cycle reverses than they were to change their long-market bias (which was not structural) as the bull market reversed. The previous point presented how few did respond to the reversal of the overall market.

- Hedge funds tend to go long less liquid stocks and short more liquid stocks, favoring small-cap and value stocks, especially in periods of stress.

- Hedge funds generally have an investable universe of more than 2,500 U.S. stocks, in contrast to the universe of 500 to 700 stocks typically considered by traditional money managers. The average market cap of this larger universe is significantly smaller than that of the S&P 500.
- Because hedge funds target underresearched stocks trading in less efficient markets, they are more likely to invest in a smaller-cap stock than a larger-cap stock. In contrast, traditional managers, typically measured against a market cap–weighted benchmark, are significantly more likely to invest in a larger-cap stock.
- Finally, statistically driven approaches used by many hedge funds tend to favor value-based valuations.

3 Equity hedge fund managers are often unaware of their "style bets." Most equity hedge fund managers are "stock pickers" or "traders" and not "style managers." Consequently, their bias to value/small-cap stocks is really inherent to their investment processes. The challenge in the equity long/short world is that it is extremely difficult to identify and assess risk exposures. In the long-only world, equity portfolios can be easily analyzed and categorized into "style buckets." Moreover, risk exposures are generally additive (that is, if you combine several value stocks in a portfolio, the portfolio will have a strong value bias). However, in the long/short world of hedge funds, this analysis is not valid. For example, you can construct a long/short portfolio with a significant small-cap behavior without investing in a single small-cap stock by going long medium-cap stocks and shorting large-cap stocks. It is difficult for managers who do not fundamentally consider their structural biases to proactively manage these biases.

Although it is difficult to quantify the degree to which hedge funds did respond to the shifting performance of both value and small cap, anecdotal evidence suggests that they did not. I believe this is a significant reason why equity long/short hedge funds (the HFR equity hedged index was up 7.2 percent) underperformed the S&P 500 (up 24.9 percent) in the first half of 2003. (Given the historical beta of 0.4 of this index to the S&P 500, the minimum return of the index that would be expected, assuming no contribution from exposures other than from the beta to the market, would be 10.0 percent. The actual 7.2 percent was significantly lower.)

FIGURE 2.10 **Impact of the Level of Diversification on the Correlation to the Equity Market**

	S&P 500	S&P SMALL CAP
Average of Individual Hedge Funds	0.41	0.45
Average of Individual Funds of Funds	0.37	0.48
HFR Fund of Fund index	0.56	0.69
HFR Composite index	0.72	0.85

Overdiversification

Finally, although diversification among funds is good, too much of a good thing can be bad. Overdiversifying results in diversifying away the valuable idiosyncratic risk and concentrating the equity exposure. The more diversified a portfolio of hedge funds gets, the greater the correlation to the equity markets —based on the HFR database (see **Figure 2.10**).

Consequently, a highly diversified portfolio of hedge funds has a 0.85 correlation with the equity market—approximating an expensive equity index option. The conclusion is that overdiversification destroys value.

Notes

[1]There are ninety-six equity long/short hedge funds in the HFR universe that were launched after the peak of the bubble that have at least a one-year history. Of these, 22 percent have had a negative correlation with the S&P 500 (significantly higher than the 8 percent of funds that launched earlier), achieving an average 8 percent annual return (similar to those with a negative correlation that launched earlier). The other 78 percent of funds have had a positive correlation to the S&P 500. They have realized average annual returns of 4 percent (significantly better than the –14 percent for funds that were launched earlier that were positively correlated with the S&P 500). This strongly suggests that new managers have been more cognizant of their market environment.

CHAPTER 3

Leverage

Archimedes reportedly said, "Give me a lever long enough and a fulcrum on which to place it, and I shall move the world." The Greek mathematician was one of the first people to fully recognize the immense power of leverage. He also recognized the risk of excessive leverage, stating that it could literally throw the earth off its course. As in mechanical systems, well-deployed financial leverage can greatly enhance performance. However, excessive leverage can be ruinous.

Risk leverage defines the sensitivity of the returns in a portfolio construction to those of the underlying market. If you remember your high school physics, there are multiple types of levers. Similarly, in the financial world, there are multiple forms of leverage. The three basic forms are:

- Financing leverage
- Construction leverage
- Instrument risk

Financing leverage is created through "borrowing leverage" and/or "notional leverage," both of which permit the fund to gain "cash equivalent" risk exposures greater than those that could be funded strictly through investing only the equity capital (the amount of capital shareholders invest) in cash instruments. Construction leverage is a manifestation of how the securities are combined in a portfolio construction. Instrument risk reflects the intrinsic risk of the specific securities selected (for example, an equity option on Cisco is significantly more risky than an equally sized investment in a 1-year Treasury bond).

This chapter explores all of these forms of leverage in greater detail. All combine to create the ultimate measure of leverage:

$$\text{Levered Risk} = \frac{\text{Risk}}{\text{Equity Capital}}$$

Levered risk defines the aggregate level of risk an investor should anticipate per dollar of capital invested. Remember that risk derives from volatility, the fact that returns are uncertain. As risk comes from uncertainty, it is by definition not well-behaved or easily described. Therefore, there are a wide variety of ways to measure risk (such as standard deviation, semi-deviation, drawdown, and VaR). The hedge fund industry has generally focused on the annualized standard deviation of monthly returns as a percent of equity as the most common metric of risk. However, managers should fully understand the risk of a fund, including that of greatest decline and behavior of the "tails" of the distribution (best characterized by VaR).

Let's start off exploring levered risk with an example of how portfolios with very different types of leverage can have the same aggregate risk. Which of the following four portfolios has the greatest risk?

1 A portfolio that is long a stock with a beta of 2
2 A portfolio whose borrowings are equal to equity capital and all its invested capital is invested in a stock with a beta of 1
3 A portfolio that is long a single stock future with a beta of 1 and that is 50 percent cash funded and 50 percent notionally funded
4 A portfolio that is long a stock with a beta of 3 and short a stock with a beta of 1

The answer is that they all have the same risk. Each portfolio has an aggregate beta of 2. The first portfolio achieved this through selecting risky securities, in this case securities with high internal leverage. The second portfolio achieved this through borrowing leverage, the third through notional funding leverage, and the fourth through construction leverage. No one method of introducing leverage is inherently better than the others—they are just different.

Let's look at a fixed-income example. Which portfolio has the greatest risk?

1 One that is long a 1-year zero-coupon Treasury bond levered 30 to 1
2 One that is long a 3-year zero-coupon Treasury bond levered 10 to 1
3 One that is long a 10-year zero-coupon Treasury bond levered 3 to 1

4 One that is long a 30-year zero-coupon Treasury bond
5 One that is long a swap on a 1-year zero-coupon Treasury bond with a margin requirement of 3 percent

Again, one can achieve the same aggregate risk by varying the application of component leverage. The first four ways are through varying levels of borrowing leverage, and the fifth is through notional leverage.

Having demonstrated that there are many ways that risk can be levered, let's explore how the many components of levered risk fit together. Levered risk is the combination of financing leverage and unlevered risk:

Levered Risk		**Financing Leverage**		**Unlevered Risk**
$\dfrac{\text{Risk}}{\text{Equity Capital}}$	=	$\dfrac{\text{Cash Equivalent}}{\text{Equity Capital}}$	X	$\dfrac{\text{Risk}}{\text{Cash Equivalent}}$

Financing Leverage

Financing leverage is the combination of borrowing leverage and notional leverage, plus one (representing the equity capital):

$$\text{Financing Leverage} = 1 + \text{Borrowing Leverage} + \text{Notional Leverage}$$

Borrowing Leverage

Borrowing leverage is the first form of leverage that typically comes to mind when one speaks of leverage. It is the leverage created by augmenting the equity capital invested in the fund by borrowing at rates relatively close to the risk-free rate. The invested capital is the sum of the absolute value of the market value plus the margin value of futures (to be discussed later) of all the positions in the construction. The invested capital is also equal to the equity capital plus the borrowed funds. Therefore, the borrowing leverage is the difference between the invested capital as a percent of equity capital minus 1 (representing equity capital), or:

$$\text{Borrowing Leverage} = \frac{\text{Invested Capital}}{\text{Equity Capital}} - 1$$

- If no funds are borrowed, the invested capital equals the equity capital and the borrowing leverage is zero.
- If the fund is not fully invested, the invested capital is less than the equity capital and the borrowing leverage is negative (net cash position).
- If the fund does borrow funds, the invested capital will be greater than the equity capital and the borrowing leverage is positive.

The typical borrowing leverage will vary significantly depending on the risk of the asset (see **Figure 3.1**).

Notional Leverage

Some financial instruments permit investors to assume risk without investing the full amount that an equivalent cash investment would require. These instruments are listed in **Figure 3.2**.

Notional leverage is a combination of option leverage, futures leverage, and swap leverage:

$$\text{Notional Leverage} = \text{Option Leverage} + \text{Futures Leverage} + \text{Swap Leverage} = \frac{\text{Cash Equivalents}}{\text{Equity Capital}} - \frac{\text{Invested Capital}}{\text{Equity Capital}}$$

FIGURE 3.1 **Leverage Ranges by Asset**

ASSET	TYPICAL BORROWING LEVERAGE
Equities	0 to 1
Treasuries	10 to 20
Corporate Bonds	Investment Grade (5 to 10) Noninvestment Grade (1 to 5)
Mortgage-Backed Securities	Agencies (5 to 20) Non-Agency (1 to 5)
Futures	20 to 100
OTC Derivatives	50 to 100+

FIGURE 3.2 **Notional Leverage Instruments**

Exchange-Traded Options	Exchange-traded securities that provide the right but not the obligation of buying or selling a security at a specified time at a specified price
OTC Options	OTC-traded securities including swaptions (options on swaps) and caps and floors. The amount of these are expressed as the notional value.
Futures	Exchange-traded securities that provide exposure to equities, fixed-income instruments, currencies, or commodities by depositing a relatively small margin requirement
Forwards	OTC instruments that provide exposure to equities, fixed-income instruments, currencies, or commodities by depositing a relatively small margin requirement
Swaps	OTC instruments, with customized negotiated terms, traded in a market governed by International Securities Dealers Association

Notional leverage is also equal to the difference between the cash equivalents (the market value of cash instruments that would represent the equivalent risk exposure) minus the invested capital.

Option leverage. Options (including swaptions) can create a significant amount of option leverage. Option leverage results from the fact that options can provide exposure to the underlying security, per dollar of invested capital, that is significantly greater than that provided by investing in the cash security. The option leverage is the difference between the market value of a "delta equivalent exposure" to the underlying security (the cash equivalent value) to the market value (premium) of the option (the invested capital). Delta expresses how much the value of the option will change as a result of changes in the value of the underlying security.

$$\text{Option Leverage} = \frac{\text{Delta Equivalent Market Value}}{\text{Equity Capital}} - \frac{\text{Option Market Value}}{\text{Equity Capital}}$$

When an investor shorts options, the exposure to the underlying security is similarly significantly greater than an equivalent amount of capital invested in the cash instrument. Figure 3.3 shows some typical option leverages.

FIGURE 3.3 **Common Option Leverages**

INSTRUMENT	INVESTED CAPITAL MARKET VALUE	NOTIONAL VALUE	DELTA EQUIVALENT	OPTION LEVERAGE
IBM at the money put	$10	$80	$40	$30/$10 = 3
IBM in the money call	$25	$80	$75	$50/$25 = 2
Gold out of the money call	$5	$300	$60	$55/$5 = 11

Futures leverage. Futures and forwards can create a high level of futures leverage. Futures are exchange-traded instruments in which one agrees to pay a specific price in the future (hence the name) for some underlying instrument. The underlying instrument can be:

- An equity (single stock futures were recently introduced)
- An equity index
- A bond
- An interest rate
- An exchange rate
- A physical commodity

One earns profits if the future price is less than the value of the underlying instrument at the time the future expires. One sustains losses if the future price is greater than the value of the underlying instrument at the time the future expires. The "notional" value of the future is the current value of the underlying instrument. This is the amount of invested capital an investor would have to commit were the investment made in the cash market. Although one does not have to commit the invested capital that would be required were the investment cash funded, an investor is required to commit the "margin" requirement, a relatively small percent of the notional value of the future. The exchange sets the margin requirements for each contract. The balance is "notionally funded." This is the source of futures leverage.

$$\text{Future Leverage} = \frac{\text{Future Notional Value}}{\text{Equity Capital}} - \frac{\text{Future Margin Requirement}}{\text{Equity Capital}}$$

Figure 3.4 shows examples of futures leverage.

FIGURE 3.4 **Examples of Futures Leverage**

INSTRUMENT	INVESTED CAPITAL (MARGIN)	NOTIONAL VALUE	NOTIONAL LEVERAGE
S&P 500 future	$12,000	$250,000	$238,000/$12,000 = 20
LME copper future	$1,500	$45,000	$43,500/$1,500 = 29
5-year Treasury future	$1,150	$112,000	$110,850/$1,150 = 96

Forwards are the equivalent of futures but issued over the counter (OTC). In contrast to futures, where the exchange sets the margin requirements, the issuing party sets the margin requirements for forwards.

Swap leverage. Swaps are OTC instruments issued by broker dealers. The most common swaps are interest rate swaps, in which the dealer, acting as counterparty, agrees with the client to swap one cash stream for another. The parties typically agree to swap the coupon from a fixed-rate bond to one with variable rates. For example, a five-year swap pays out a fixed rate of the current five-year swap rate (the equivalent cash flows of the coupons of a 5-year Treasury plus a spread) and receives the LIBOR floating rate that would be current at the time of each of the payments (in fact, there are many alternative mechanisms for the variable rate to reset). The risk of a swap is approximately equivalent (there is a relatively small amount of credit risk) to repoing (the practice of purchasing a security by using the security as collateral to borrow money) a Treasury bond. As swaps are generally 100 percent notionally financed at the time of issue, they result in a significant amount of swap leverage.

There is an increasing use of credit default swaps in the financial markets. These are instruments in which a counterparty seeking credit protection agrees to pay a premium to the protection seller for the right to be compensated in the case of a default of the reference issuer.

Swap leverage is the difference between the notional value of the swap minus the market value, or:

$$\text{Swap Leverage} = \frac{\text{Notional Value of Swap}}{\text{Equity Capital}} - \frac{\text{Market Value of Swap}}{\text{Equity Capital}}$$

The fixed rate at the time of issue will typically be established such that the market value of the swap is zero.

Unlevered Risk

Unlevered risk is a combination of instrument risk and construction leverage:

Unlevered Risk		Instrument Risk		Construction Leverage
$\frac{\text{Risk}}{\text{Cash Equivalent}}$	=	$\frac{\text{Gross Risk}}{\text{Cash Equivalent}}$	x	$\frac{\text{Risk}}{\text{Gross Risk}}$

Instrument Risk

Instruments (that is, securities plus OTC derivatives, which are technically not securities) have significantly different levels of internal leverage. When managers think about internal security leverage they are typically interested in the sensitivity of the performance of the specific security to changes in the broad market. For example, in the equity world, managers speak of the beta to the market. In the fixed-income world, managers speak of "duration" (the sensitivity of the price of a bond to a change in interest rates). Risk does not directly tie to cash equivalent exposure. For example, a $1,000 investment in a 30-year zero-coupon bond may have thirty times the duration of an investment of the same $1,000 in 1-year zero-coupon bonds, despite the fact that the size of the investment is the same. Similarly, an investment in a high-beta stock such as Cisco (with a beta of 1.6) will represent significantly greater market risk than an investment of the same size in Cinergy (with a beta of 0.6). This means Cisco's performance will be significantly more volatile than that of Cinergy.

The instrument risk is the ratio of the gross risk (the weighted average volatility of the holdings in the portfolio ignoring any diversification/hedging benefit) divided by the cash equivalent value (the sum of the absolute value of the cash equivalents). Therefore, a stock with a beta of 1.5 will have three times the risk leverage of a stock with a beta of 0.5 (ignoring the non-market components of risk).

Construction Leverage

If there were no diversification in a portfolio, the risk of the portfolio would equal the sum of the risks of the individual positions (if there were no diversification the correlation among all the positions would be 1, and there effectively would be only one position). Because of a combination of diversification and the fact that short positions naturally hedge long positions, the risk of the

FIGURE 3.5 **Example of Construction Leverage**

PORTFOLIO	RISK (WEEKLY STANDARD DEVIATION)
Long ExxonMobil Long ChevronTexaco	2.2%
Long ExxonMobil Short ChevronTexaco	0.8%

portfolio will typically not equal the sum of the risk of the individual positions. This phenomenon is construction leverage. Construction leverage is the ratio of the risk of the portfolio construction (the risk of the portfolio given the actual diversification/hedging) divided by the gross risk (the risk were there to be no diversification/hedging benefit).

Recall from Chapter 2 that diversification is good, as it reduces risk without reducing returns. Furthermore, it is good to target idiosyncratic risk, often by hedging long positions with short positions. These two hedge fund practices can significantly reduce the overall portfolio risk of a portfolio. For example, both of the portfolios in **Figure 3.5** combine equal exposures to two oil companies. In the first portfolio, both positions are long positions. The second portfolio combines a long position in ExxonMobil with a short position in ChevronTexaco. The risk of the first portfolio is almost three times that of the second because of construction leverage.

What Is the Right Amount of Leverage?

There is no simple answer to this tough question. A fixed-income relative value strategy that takes highly diversified "micro" plays with 25 times leverage can be less risky than a long-biased biotech equity fund with a gross exposure of 0.7 of invested capital (borrowing leverage of less than 1 but extremely high internal security leverage and construction leverage). The ultimate measure of leverage is the overall relationship between risk and equity capital. Although managers should disaggregate this risk into its component parts, naïvely establishing rigid limits for one component of total leverage is not constructive (excuse the pun).

Another cautionary note is that many equity managers spooked by two years of poor returns subsequently reduced the risk of their portfolios by putting significant amounts of equity capital in cash. This was driven by the fact that most investors in these funds have been retail investors for whom the managers believe they must mute risk. Holding cash is an extremely inefficient approach to risk management, however. Equity deployed in cash destroys value. In early 2004, cash was potentially earning 75 basis points (bps) in current markets. After paying performance fees of 15 bps (small because of the extremely low interest rate) and management fees of potentially 150 bps, each dollar of capital invested in cash loses 90 bps. If funds do not have investments that can earn an acceptable return, they should distribute excess cash to their shareholders. Although this will unquestionably increase the volatility of the fund, the investor can respond to this by reducing the exposure to the fund as part of his overall portfolio (the distribution of excess cash would have already accomplished this). You do not need to destroy value to manage risk!

CHAPTER 4

Illiquidity

The *Titanic* was built to navigate the world's waters. When a relatively small fraction of these waters became illiquid (froze), this illiquid instrument (the iceberg) became the cause of one of the world's greatest catastrophes. The designers of the world's grandest ship had so arrogantly ignored the possibility of such an event that they had never developed an appropriate escape plan. Tragically, there were only enough lifeboats for fewer than half of the passengers on the ship. The key lesson learned is: Develop an escape plan before the alarms sound.

Although icebergs are extremely treacherous, vigilant observation can spot them in time to avert a disaster. When the captain sees "the tip of the iceberg," he should assume that there is significant risk beneath the surface and that he can't simply cruise through the perilous waters.

Planning in Case of Crisis

The value of having a good escape plan is proven time and time again. The vast majority of residences have alarms. Some of them are very basic, such as smoke detectors. Some have extremely sophisticated integrated systems with central station monitoring. Whatever alarms they have, however, most of these households have not developed an adequate escape plan. If people devoted more time to figuring out how to escape in case of an emergency, significantly fewer catastrophes would occur.

Similarly, most hedge funds have risk alarm systems. Some of these are very basic, such as stop-losses. Some have extremely sophisticated statistical systems with third-party monitoring. Whatever alarms they use, however, the vast majority of hedge funds have not developed an adequate response plan. If managers devoted more time to planning a remedial program in the case of a crisis, significantly fewer catastrophes, both financial and others, would occur.

We have already spoken about leverage. Although a fund without financing leverage can lose money, it cannot "blow up." This is because 100 percent of such a fund is financed by equity capital and there cannot be a run on the bank in the case of poor performance. However, financing leverage can result in a blow-up if the fund fails to satisfy its financing obligations. Both components of financing leverage—borrowing leverage and notional leverage—can result in liquidity problems. Here's how:

- ***Borrowing leverage.*** Borrowing leverage can result in a liquidity crunch if the investment sustains a loss (short an inflating asset and/or long a declining asset). The fund can be squeezed by the requirement to finance losses. Furthermore, brokers can increase "haircuts" as financing rolls over, and funds can be squeezed by the requirement to maintain larger haircuts. (A haircut is the difference between the value of the security and the amount that one can borrow using the security as collateral.) It was this phenomenon that resulted in many of the hedge fund financing crises in the fall of 1998, such as that of Long-Term Capital Management (LTCM). Many funds have become more creative in their financing, entering into multiple financial arrangements with rolling expiration dates and evergreen financing so that the fund will not be required to increase the margin.
- ***Option leverage*** (if short). Options can increase in value at an extremely rapid rate. If an investor is short the option, the need to finance his losses (resulting from being short a rapidly inflating asset) can result in a cash crunch.
- ***Future leverage.*** Notional funding is provided in exchange-traded futures. In this case, the risk represented is significantly greater than the margin requirements established by the exchange. Therefore, if the fund sustains a loss, it must finance this loss. The need to fund these losses can result in a financing crunch for the fund. However, futures are extremely liquid, so losses can typically be funded by liquidating holdings.
- ***Swap leverage.*** Notional funding is provided on OTC-issued swaps. The risk represented is significantly greater than the margin requirements established by the issuing counterparty. Therefore, if the fund sustains a loss, it must fund this loss. The need to fund these losses can result in a financing crunch for the fund. Although swaps are extremely liquid, they are strictly notional instruments, and monetizing will not generate adequate capital to fund the loss.

The Size Factor

An important factor related to illiquidity is the size of the fund. Whereas some securities are extremely illiquid in general, the liquidity of other securities depends on the size of the position. The size of a holding depends on the weight of the security in the fund, the equity capital of the fund, and the borrowing leverage (the equity capital and borrowing leverage jointly define the invested capital). Consequently, the greater the assets under management (AUM), the greater the exposure to illiquidity. This balance will be driven not by the AUM of a particular fund, but rather by that of all funds and separate accounts managed on a pari passu (or very similar) basis. Many hedge funds deal with this by limiting their size. Consequently, many funds with good track records are closed to new investors (soft close) or closed to new money (hard close).

Many investors believe that they have minimized their liquidity risk by investing in funds with monthly redemptions. This is naïve! Liquidity risk is minimized only if the fund has appropriately matched the liquidity it is providing to its investors with the liquidity of the fund's underlying holdings. Many investors who believed they were adequately protected have been shocked to discover that almost all hedge funds have the right to halt redemptions if the fund is in a liquidity squeeze. This is equivalent to saying that the fund is very liquid unless it is in a liquidity crisis, in which case this redemption "right" evaporates. Consequently, even though the fund may tout monthly liquidity, investors should not be so sanguine; they should make sure they understand the liquidity of the fund's underlying holdings and should "stress test" the liquidity of those holdings in a crisis. Hedge funds frequently go long the less liquid security and short the more liquid security. This leads to a net exposure to illiquidity. Liquidity often becomes the biggest issue during a crisis, when there is a general "flight to quality" and therefore a simultaneous drying up of liquidity across all markets.

Elements in an Escape Plan

A comprehensive escape plan should include the following considerations:

Financing plan. Hedge funds should have a financing strategy that provides flexibility. Much has been learned since the LTCM debacle. Funds have established repos (the structure used to borrow in the OTC market where the specific security is used as collateral against which a loan is made) with revolving expiration dates and evergreen relationships (relationships that remain in place perpetually until cancelled) to limit the risk of a synchronous run on the bank.

Cash reserves. Hedge funds should have an explicit target for the amount of cash held. This must take the fund's financing and liquidation strategies into account and must be based on the level of risk in the portfolio—not on the amount of leverage. That is because it is risk that dictates the likelihood of triggering an event that requires this reserve. For example, a fund that is long $100 million of 30-year Treasuries will have significantly greater risk than a fund that is long $300 million of 24-year Treasuries and short $300 million of 23-year Treasuries (even though the first fund has a gross long position of $100 million and the second fund has a gross position of $600 million).

The question is, what is the appropriate level of cash reserves? Unfortunately, there is no simple answer. Furthermore, the amount of cash reserves is highly dependent on the fund's financing plan and its liquidation plan. Therefore, rather than a magic formula, there is a methodology of how to think through this complex question. The fund manager must first determine the length of the period during which the fund will have to finance losses from cash reserves rather than through liquidating assets. This is clearly dependent on the liquidity of the underlying assets. Significantly greater cash reserves are required for less liquid investments.

The manager must then establish a level of confidence that cash reserves should cover losses during this period. This is equivalent to a VaR confidence limit. In the financial markets, as in all other worlds, there is no sure thing, so the manager must realistically accept some level of risk and plan accordingly. Given this level of confidence, the fund manager should utilize the actual distribution of returns to determine the cash reserves that would be required to achieve this level of confidence.

As managers are concerned with blow-up risk, it is critical to understand the potential behavior of the fund in extreme events. Therefore, it is critical to utilize the actual distribution with the full set of fat tails and asymmetries rather than oversimplifying the analysis by assuming that returns will be normally distributed. Finally, the fund should consider how cash-generative the underlying securities in the fund are. Cash-generative securities, such as IOs (mortgage-backed interest only derivatives that amortize at a rapid rate), can partially substitute for cash reserves.

Liquidation plan. Hedge funds should plan the sequence in which assets would be liquidated with a detailed understanding of how much and how quickly cash could be raised (including an outlook on the penalty that could be incurred). Some securities (such as Treasuries) are highly liquid and could be monetized within hours. However, the haircuts are extremely small. Therefore, the amount of cash raised by liquidating them can be extremely limited. Do not assume that, just because such securities can be rapidly liquidated, they will raise a commensurate amount of cash.

As previously stated, hedge funds are generally long the illiquid instrument and short the liquid instrument. This should be explicitly recognized in developing a liquidation plan. When this is the case, funds will typically be able to unwind their short holdings more rapidly than they can sell their long positions. If the short holdings are acting as hedges to the long holdings, this can significantly increase risk while reducing gross investments. The liquidation plan should be developed to synchronize the unwinding of both long and short positions.

The Cost of Illiquid Redemption Policies

To understand the opportunity costs associated with hedge fund redemption policies, consider the following question. There are two roadside fruit stands near your house. Both sell a crate of apples for 60 cents per pound. Neither lets you open the crate to see if the apples have spoiled, but one permits you to return the opened crate if they are not good while the other does not. You have bought from these stands for a long time and you know that there is a 25 percent chance that the crate will be spoiled. Which stand would you buy from? The answer is obvious. You would buy from the stand that permitted you to return the crate if the apples are spoiled.

Now suppose that the stand that did not permit returns dropped its price to 45 cents per pound. Which stand would you buy from now? The answer is not as obvious. The astute buyer would be indifferent because the 15 cents per pound price differential represents exactly 25 percent of the original 60 cents per pound price, fully compensating you for the 25 percent probability that the crate of apples that was selected will be spoiled. Therefore, the value of being able to return the crate, a "price tag on liquidity," is 15 cents per pound. In this example, the appropriate price tag for liquidity is exactly equal to the "expected cost" of not having the flexibility to return the crate of apples.

Choosing among Alternatives

Now let's apply these lessons learned in the fruit markets to the financial markets. From a perspective of liquidity, which alternative investment (excuse the double entendre) would you choose (assuming that you were indifferent among the alternatives based on your ***expectations*** of risk-adjusted returns and diversification)?

1 An alternative investment that provides daily liquidity (e.g., managed futures)
2 An alternative investment that permits redemption on a monthly basis with 10 days notice (40-day liquidity)
3 An alternative investment that permits redemption on a quarterly basis with 60 days notice (150-day liquidity)
4 An alternative investment with annual liquidity (such as a venture capital fund)

Being a knowledgeable investor, one who appreciates the value of liquidity, you would rationally pick the first alternative. Let's explore why you should value liquidity. The fundamental reason is that there is a risk that a specific investment will not achieve your performance expectations. In fact, no matter how skilled an investor you are, there is a 50 percent probability that the actual performance of any investment will be inferior to your expectations (matched with a 50 percent probability that the performance will exceed your expectations). If all investments exactly achieved your expectations, then there would be no opportunity cost of illiquidity, because there would be no reason to redeem.

The opportunity cost of illiquidity results from the delay in liquidating your investment after you have concluded that an investment is not meeting your expectations. The longer the liquidity period, the longer you must expose yourself to inferior returns (the term *opportunity cost* is used because it represents the lost opportunity of redeploying the capital in an investment that can achieve your investment expectations, even though you may still be generating positive returns in the interim period).

Calculating the Opportunity Cost of Illiquidity

Now comes the tough question. How much greater must your expectation of risk-adjusted returns for each of the other three above alternatives be to make you indifferent to the lower liquidity provided? In other words, how would you go about putting a price tag on liquidity? What follows below both:

- Presents a methodology for rationally putting a price tag on hedge fund liquidity
- Calculates the appropriate price tag based on actual industry data.

The overly simplistic example of the apples actually provides significant insight as to how a price tag on liquidity should be established. One can conclude from that example that the price tag should equal the expected value of any cost arising from any constraints on liquidity. In the original example, the fruit stands either permitted or forbade returns. In hedge funds the relationship is more complicated. All hedge funds permit redemption, however with significantly varying liquidity periods (the liquidity period is the sum of the notice period and the redemption period). Because the illiquidity penalty occurs over periods of variable length in hedge funds, the expected cost of illiquidity is the combination of two factors:

1 The expected monthly cost of investing in an underperforming fund
2 The liquidity period, or the number of months during which you must remain invested in a fund after you have decided to redeem

In the example of apples, the outcome was binary (the apples were good with 75 percent probability and spoiled with 25 percent probability), and the expected cost of illiquidity is simply calculated by multiplying the probability of the apples being spoiled (25 percent) by the consequent cost (60 cents per pound). In contrast, hedge funds display a complex distribution of potential returns. Not only is the distribution of hedge fund returns not binary, hedge fund returns are not even normally distributed. As most investors know, hedge fund returns demonstrate "fat tails" and "skew" (discussed in Chapter 1). Therefore, one can only calculate the expected monthly cost of investing in an underperforming fund by determining the magnitude of the underperformance of each underperforming fund and averaging the gap (no assumption on the distribution is required).

Now let's segue from theory to practice and apply this methodology to actual hedge fund data. **Figure 4.1** shows the actual distribution of hedge fund risk-adjusted returns (Sharpe ratio) for 1,214 funds in the Hedge Fund Research (HFR) database for which there was a minimum of two years of data. The mean Sharpe ratio was 0.36 (the mean annualized standard deviation of returns was 12.4 percent and the mean annual return was 9.46 percent). For the 50 percent of funds that have Sharpe ratios below the mean, the average gap between each fund's Sharpe ratio and the mean was 0.85.

FIGURE 4.1 **Distribution of Hedge Fund Sharpe Ratios**

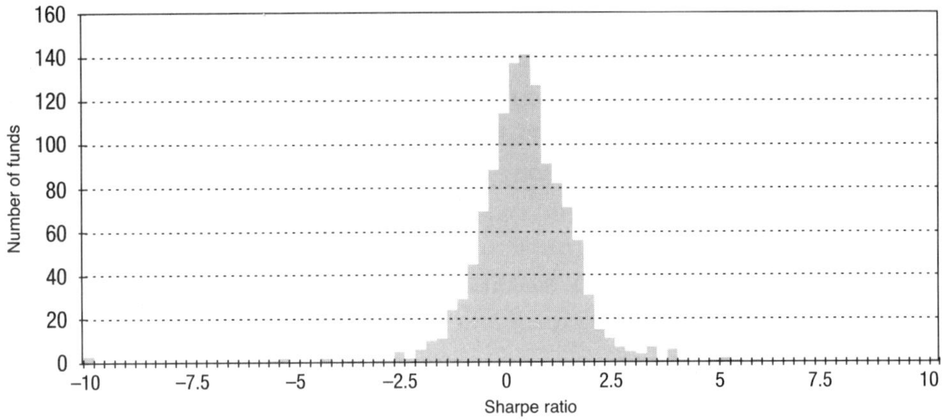

This expected underperformance of the Sharpe ratio (the Sharpe ratio was chosen rather than returns because it permitted funds of varying volatilities to be rationally combined) equates to an underperformance in annual return (based on an average annualized standard deviation of 12.4 percent) of 10.5 percent or an underperformance in monthly return of 84 bps. Since a fund has a 50 percent probability of underperforming the mean, this should be weighted by a 0.5, resulting in a 42 bps expected opportunity cost for each month that a fund cannot be liquidated. Assuming that the average period required to determine that a fund is underperforming, and for the investor to divest of it, is 12 months,

FIGURE 4.2 **Liquidity Period**

LIQUIDITY PERIOD	OPPORTUNITY COST OF ILLIQUIDITY
0 days	N/A
30 days	42 bps
60 days	84 bps
90 days	126 bps
120 days	168 bps
180 days	252 bps
360 days	504 bps

FIGURE 4.3 **Hedge Fund Liquidity Policies**

REDEMPTION PERIOD	NOTICE PERIOD	LIQUIDITY PERIOD	PERCENT	CUMULATIVE PERCENT
Daily	0	1	3%	3%
Weekly	0–30	7–37	4%	7%
Monthly	5–7	35–37	4%	11%
Monthly	10–15	40–45	10%	21%
Monthly	30	60	20%	41%
Monthly	45	75	2%	43%
Monthly	60	90	2%	45%
Quarterly	10–15	100–105	2%	47%
Monthly	90	120	2%	49%
Quarterly	30	120	20%	69%
Quarterly	45	135	7%	76%
Quarterly	60	150	7%	83%
Quarterly	90	180	4%	87%
Semi-Annual	0–60	180–240	4%	91%
Semi-Annual	90–180	270–360	1%	92%
Annual	0–60	360–420	6%	98%
Annual	90–180	450–540	2%	100%

the expected opportunity cost for each month an underperforming fund is held is 42 bps. **Figure 4.2** shows the price tags that can be placed on funds of varying liquidity periods, reflecting the risk of having to stay in an underperforming investment for longer than you would choose.

The liquidity policies of alternative investments range from daily for most CTAs or managed futures to multiple years for venture capital or real estate. **Figure 4.3** displays the distribution of liquidity policies for hedge funds (excluding CTAs) based on the HFR universe. More than 50 percent of hedge funds in the HFR universe have liquidity periods of greater than 105 days. As has already been presented, illiquidity comes with a significant penalty. Investors must be aware of the cost of illiquidity and appropriately factor it into their investment decisions.

II

Part Two

Market Risk Management

CHAPTER 5

Measuring Risk

This chapter and the following one focus on two interrelated but significantly different processes. This chapter focuses on measuring risk, that is, quantifying the aggregate amount of risk in the portfolio. The next chapter focuses on understanding the source of this risk. I first review the risk management practices of the sell-side, which are significantly more advanced than those of the buy-side, to learn from their experience. Sell-side risk management organizations focus on measuring risk by employing a common reporting framework across the diverse asset classes they hold. (The trading desks use specific tools to understand the unique risks of their specific asset class.) Although monitoring risk is an important process in the buy-side, the buy-side focuses on fundamentally understanding the sources of risk. This understanding is critical for portfolio managers to make informed portfolio decisions that efficiently deploy risk.

Sell-Side Heritage

The sell-side (banks and broker-dealers) implemented extensive risk management infrastructure years ago in response to government regulations. The Bank for International Settlement (BIS) established guidelines for banks globally, first for developed market banks (1993) and subsequently for broker-dealers and developing/emerging market banks (1997). These guidelines are defined in the Basel Accord. The Accord defines how risk is to be measured and establishes standards on which a bank's capital requirements are set. These standards are based on each bank's Value at Risk, or VaR. VaR is a statistically based generic tool that measures aggregate risk in a large and complex organization and permits independent, third-party monitoring of this risk.

It's time to demystify VaR. VaR is simply a method to describe the distribution of profits and losses related to a portfolio. The inherent advantage of VaR is that no assumption on the distribution of returns need be made (although many VaR systems do make such simplifying assumptions). For example, if you assume that the returns are normally distributed, the full distribution of returns can be completely characterized by the mean and standard deviation. The two values are adequate information to calculate any measure such as the likelihood of the return being less than a specified amount, the expected amount by which the return would exceed a specified amount, and the like. Although this is attractively simple, if the returns are not normally distributed, it is not accurate.

VaR is defined as the maximum amount at a specified level of confidence that could be lost over a defined period based on historical market behavior. The VaR is calculated by taking the current holdings and simulating what the profit and loss would have been given history. This will differ from the actual profit and loss (P&L), which is calculated as the profits and losses of the actual holdings as they change over time, rather than a simulated P&L of the current holdings.

The Basel Accord establishes the standard as the maximum amount that could be lost over a ten-day holding period at a 99 percent confidence level—that is, the probability of losing more than this amount is equal to approximately 1 percent. The historical time horizon is focused on the recent past, generally a couple of years or less (although the Accord establishes one year as the minimum historical period that can be used to calculate VaR). Furthermore, banks and broker-dealers are trading oriented, and, consequently, the ten-day holding period was selected because most holdings on the sell-side can be unwound within a couple of weeks. The required capital is then established as a multiple of the bank's VaR. Consequently, the Basel Accord places a clear price tag on taking risk, that is, the cost of the required capital.

Although capital requirements are established based on VaR, the Accord actively promotes stress testing as another important analysis. The Accord recognized that the world does not neatly follow a normal distribution but that ten standard deviation events, events that statistically should not have taken place, repeatedly occur—although the underlying cause, and consequently the financial dislocation, varies across crises. The Basel Committee suggests a battery of stress tests (primarily based on historical crisis scenarios), but no standards have been established. As a result of these requirements, banks and broker-dealers, on a global basis, have all implemented complex risk management systems.

Normal Market Behavior

There are two methods used to calculate the risk of hedge funds in normal markets. The first is based on the actual monthly fund returns. The second uses simulated returns based on the current construction (similar to the sell-side's calculation of VaR) and actual market returns. Three alternative approaches exist for calculating simulated returns. The text that follows addresses the strengths and weaknesses of each and ultimately recommends risk statistics based on historical simulation be used for hedge funds. However, both methods attempt to predict future risk based on history. Before reviewing these methods, let's first look at how relevant risk history is to future outcomes.

Will History Repeat?

The complaint most frequently raised about statistical risk management is that it is backward looking. Before defending the value of a backward-looking view of risk, it is useful to present empirical research on the sustainability of hedge fund returns and risk.

In January 1997, the National Bureau of Economic Research (NBER) in Cambridge, Massachusetts, wrote, "We find no evidence of performance persistence in raw returns or risk-adjusted returns, even when we break funds down according to their returns-based style classifications ... In contrast to the mounting evidence of differential skill in the mutual fund industry, the hedge fund arena provided no evidence that past performance forecasts future performance" ("Offshore Hedge Funds: Survival and Performance 1989–1995," NBER Working Paper Series). In May 2002, the International Securities Market Association (ISMA) Center at the University of Reading, U.K., wrote, "We find little evidence of persistence in mean returns but do find strong persistence in hedge funds' standard deviations and their correlation with the stock market" ("Persistence in Hedge Fund Performance: The True Value of a Track Record," ISMA Working Paper). Although the research analyzing the persistence of hedge fund performance behavior is limited, the research that has been published broadly supports that differential returns do not repeat. However, the research concludes that risk, both volatility and correlation, does tend to repeat.

The following analysis expands on this body of research. Kenmar analyzed the year-to-year relationship of the behavior of hedge funds (1997 through 2002) based on the Hedge Fund Research (HFR) database. This provided almost 7,000 data points. In contrast to prior research, this analysis identified a minimal persistence in returns:

- 59 percent of funds that had performed in the bottom half of returns in the prior year performed in the bottom half the subsequent year.
- 57 percent of funds that had performed in the top half of returns in the prior year performed in the top half the subsequent year.

If there were no relationship, these statistics would be 50 percent, so these statistics suggest a minimal, though not statistically significant, level of return persistence. In contrast, volatility demonstrated a high level of persistence:

- 91 percent of funds that had performed in the bottom half (highest) of volatility in the prior year performed in the bottom half the subsequent year.
- 93 percent of funds that had performed in the top half (lowest) of volatility in the prior year performed in the top half the subsequent year.

Now, let's begin the debate of the value of a backward-looking analysis of risk. Detractors argue that a backward-looking analysis of risk is equivalent to steering a vehicle using a rearview mirror. I agree that if the objective were to predict what returns would be in the future (the equivalent of driving the car down the road), then a backward-looking view is of questionable value. Just as you would not know which way to turn the steering wheel on a curvy road by only looking at the rearview mirror, you do not know what directional bets to make by exclusively looking at history.

Risk management, however, does not attempt to predict markets. Rather, it attempts to quantify the level of risk related to a strategy. This is equivalent to keeping statistics on what percentage of cars drove off a particular stretch of road to understand what the risk is of there being an accident on that stretch in the future. Although the backward-looking view through the rearview mirror will not keep the vehicle on course, maintaining statistics on the frequency of vehicles careening off the road will provide an understanding of how risky the road is—whether the car is on a risky (curvy and narrow) road or on a relatively safe (straight and wide) highway.

Just as retrospective statistics on vehicular accidents are a meaningful measure of future driving risk, projecting the performance of an investment vehicle, in this case a hedge fund, in historical markets is a meaningful measure of future investment risk. This is particularly valid given that research concludes that risk (volatility and correlation) tends to repeat. Although the research suggests that history does not represent a statistically significant indicator of future alpha generation, a backward-looking measure of how the portfolio would have performed in various historical markets is a valid and useful measure of risk. However, as Chapter 10 discusses, the historical risk relationships should be combined with a prospective return outlook to drive the portfolio construction. As the saying goes, "He who does not learn from history is doomed to repeat it."

FIGURE 5.1 **Risk Measures**

BEHAVIOR	MEASURE
Volatility	Standard Deviation Semi-Deviation Downside Deviation
Crisis Behavior	Worst Drawdown Longest Drawdown
Risk-Adjusted Return	Sharpe Ratio Sortino Ratio
Diversification	Correlation to Indices

Risk Measures Based on Actual Fund Returns

The most typical approach to measuring risk in hedge funds is based on actual monthly fund returns. These returns are used to calculate a variety of risk statistics, shown in **Figure 5.1**.

The major advantage of risk statistics calculated based on actual fund returns is that only fund return data are required. In addition, they are simple to calculate. However, there are a variety of related problems:

Short history. Funds have varying lengths of history. Unfortunately, when you are comparing funds, the relevant data are limited to the common history. Therefore, in analyzing a portfolio of funds, the analyses can be uniformly performed only over the period defined by the fund with the shortest history. This limitation often eliminates crisis periods, extremely important periods on which one would want to focus. In markets that are often cyclical, short histories can have significant biases. For example, funds with short histories that were value oriented demonstrated superior risk-adjusted returns in mid-2002, and funds with short histories that were credit focused demonstrated superior risk-adjusted returns in mid-2003. It is likely that neither group of funds will demonstrate superior returns or equally low risk going forward.

Valuation flexibility. As Chapter 13 discusses, price discovery of illiquid securities, which can represent a significant percent of a hedge fund, is limited. By necessity, valuations are often based on dealer quotes. For some securities (such as mortgage-backed derivatives), quotes can vary by 30 percent. For other securities, it is all but impossible to obtain more than one quote (in these cases the quote will come from the issuer of the security). Even with the best of intentions, there is a lot of subjectivity in valuing such securities.

Over an extended period of time, reported returns will not be influenced as month-to-month flexibility in valuation averages out. Measures of risk, however, can be dramatically distorted. Volatility can be dramatically understated. Some of this may be intentional—it is human nature to dampen volatility when one cannot accurately measure it. Furthermore, correlations can be similarly distorted. For example, a manager of a Reg D fund (a fund invested in private placement offerings) boasted of a 0.13 correlation to the S&P 500. An analysis of the fund's returns, however, showed that although the fund did have a 0.13 correlation on a monthly basis, it had a 0.84 rolling 12-month correlation to the S&P 500. The fund's monthly valuation had masked the true underlying correlation, whereas the longer term statistic revealed the underlying relationship.

Changing portfolio. The average holding period of a hedge fund is approximately one month, although with significant variations across funds. Therefore, if a fund had a three-year return history, only 3 percent of this history would be based on holdings currently in the fund. Because hedge fund strategies can be very dynamic, the remaining 97 percent of the data may not represent the behavior of the current portfolio.

Limited data. Even with a reasonably long history, monthly data provide limited data from a statistical perspective. For example, a fund with a three-year history would have only thirty-six monthly data points. If you were to perform a sensitivity analysis to determine the relationship between the fund and various indices, utilizing more than three or four factors (equity index, government bond index, credit bond index, commodity index, exchange rate, etc.) would not be statistically significant.

Consequently, statistics based on monthly fund returns do not meaningfully measure the risks of hedge funds.

Risk Measures Based on Simulated Fund Returns

Using simulated fund returns to calculate risk measures solves the many problems related to risk statistics based on actual fund returns:

- The simulation is exclusively based on the current portfolio construction
- An extended simulated history can be calculated (earlier than the inception of the fund's valuation)
- The volatility is based on independent market data and cannot be influenced by the fund

FIGURE 5.2 **The History of Market Returns Drives Simulated Returns**

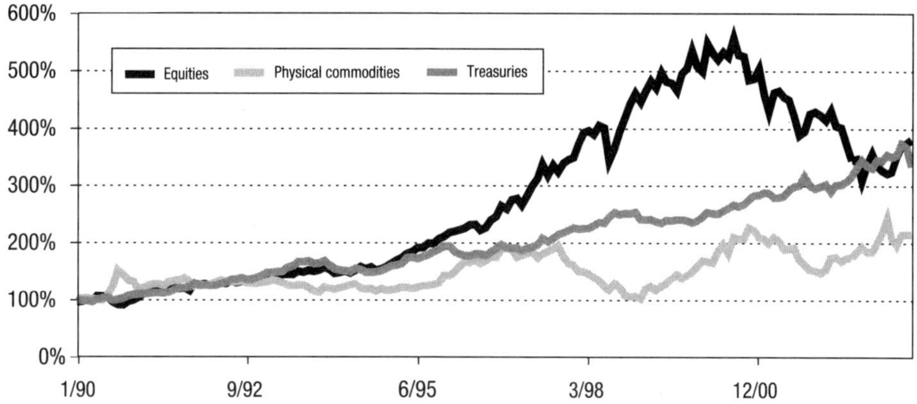

- There is a significant amount of data as simulated P&Ls can be calculated on a weekly or even daily basis

The only disadvantage of using simulated fund returns is that the position data must be processed through a system to generate the simulation. Although this is certainly possible, it does require some effort. **Figure 5.2** shows the historical returns of market risk factors (including U.S. equities, physical commodities, and Treasuries) that drive the historical simulation.

There are three techniques used to create simulated returns in "normal" markets:

1 ***Historical simulation.*** The historical simulation, which is the best technique to apply to hedge funds, replicates how the current portfolio construction would have performed in each historical period.

2 ***Parametric model.*** The parametric model synthesizes history into a variance and covariance matrix that is used to drive a closed-form analytic calculation of risk.

3 ***Monte Carlo simulation.*** The Monte Carlo simulation is similar to the parametric model in that it synthesizes history into a variance and covariance matrix. However, it is even more complex. This matrix is used to iteratively create hypothetical scenarios by using a random number generator to transform the variance/covariance into stochastic series.

All three approaches combine the current portfolio construction with historical market data to project how today's construction would have performed in yesterday's markets. However, historical simulation is the best alternative for analyzing the behavior of hedge funds in normal markets for the following reasons:

Historical simulation is easy to understand. Historical simulation is by far the easiest methodology to understand as it simply recreates how a current portfolio would have performed given the historical market movements. The variance/covariance approach used by the parametric model and Monte Carlo simulation are too complex to describe in this book. The Monte Carlo simulation ups the level of complexity by a giant step, overlaying a transformation of this variance/covariance matrix by selecting path-dependent random numbers and itteratively creating hypothetical scenarios of the behavior of each security.

Historical simulation uses actual volatilities. The parametric model and Monte Carlo simulation generally assume returns are normally distributed. However, this simplification does not accurately capture the typical return behavior of hedge funds. Hedge funds generally demonstrate fat tails and skew as compared to the assumed normal distribution. Historical simulation uses the actual return distribution, explicitly incorporating fat tail behavior into the analysis.

Historical simulation uses actual idiosyncratic correlations. The parametric model generally assumes that all idiosyncratic or security-specific returns (the residuals after removing the behavior explained by risk factors) are independent of those of all other securities. If the risk factors had successfully captured all systematic behavior this would be a logical conclusion. However, this is typically not the case. The Internet bubble was a concrete example of this. Prior to and well into the bubble, existing risk factors did not recognize the unique behavior of the Internet sector. Therefore, they ignored correlation across Internet stocks as it was assumed to be independent security-specific behavior. The returns of Internet stocks, however, proved to be highly correlated, and the consequent risk of a concentrated portfolio of Internet stocks proved to be dramatically greater than was calculated assuming independent security-specific returns.

Historical simulation can use a flexible historical period. The parametric model and Monte Carlo simulation generally utilize preprocessed return distributions that have been based on a preestablished historical time horizon. Historical simulations are generally flexible in the selection of a historical time horizon.

Historical simulation handles basic options. The parametric model can handle equity equivalent (delta) risk of an option but cannot handle the sensitivity to volatility (vega) and the convexity (gamma) of an option. Both historical and Monte Carlo simulations can analyze all the risks of a basic option.

Historical simulation handles serial correlations. As has been noted, both the parametric model and Monte Carlo utilize a single variance/covariance matrix. This assumes that the movements across periods are independent. However, markets often demonstrate significantly correlated behavior across periods (called serial correlation). That is, it is more likely that the returns of a period will be positive if the returns of the prior period are positive. To the extent that behavior is serially correlated, it will differ from the averaged relationships and will ignore these extremes. Historical simulation utilizes the actual history; therefore, serial correlation will not be masked by averaging.

Historical simulation handles shifting correlations. The single variance/covariance matrix utilized by the parametric model and Monte Carlo simulation tends to average the relationships over the historical period selected. To the extent that correlations shift and the behavior before and after the shift differ significantly, averaging the behavior masks the relationships. Historical simulation recreates the full history; therefore, averaging will not mask shifting correlations.

Historical simulation supports risk factors. Both the parametric model and the historical simulation can incorporate a risk-factor framework. The Monte Carlo simulation cannot incorporate a risk-factor framework.

Historical simulation is responsive and structural. The goal is to be simultaneously responsive to current market conditions while capturing long-term, structural relationships. The historical simulation can combine sensitivities to risk factors calculated based on recent history with long-term risk factor returns to project how a current portfolio with today's risk-factor sensitivities would have performed over a long-term risk-factor history. Neither a parametric model nor Monte Carlo simulation permit current sensitivities to be combined with long-term market behavior.

There are two considerations in selecting a VaR methodology that are not currently relevant to hedge funds:

The ability to handle complex options. Monte Carlo simulations are superior in analyzing complex and exotic options, which cannot be analyzed using a closed-form model. These options include those with multiple path dependencies, knockouts, and the like. Being able to handle complex options is a requirement for the custom-structured products issued by the sell-side. However, this is not required for hedge funds.

FIGURE 5.3 **Comparison of VaR Techniques**

	FACTOR	IMPORTANCE	PARAMETRIC	HISTORICAL SIMULATION	MONTE CARLO
1	Is easy to understand	Very	Bad	Good	Bad
2	Uses actual volatilities	Very	Bad	Good	Partial
3	Uses actual idiosyncratic correlations	Very	Bad	Good	Partial
4	Uses flexible historic period	Very	Bad	Good	Bad
5	Handles basic options	Very	Bad	Good	Good
6	Handles serial correlations	Very	Bad	Good	Bad
7	Handles shifting correlations	Very	Bad	Good	Bad
8	Supports risk factors	Very	Good	Good	Bad
9	Is responsive and structural	Very	Bad	Good	Bad
10	Handles complex correlations	Minimal	Bad	Bad	Good
11	Is computationally efficient	Minimal	Good	Bad	Bad

☐ Bad ■ Partial ■ Good

Computational efficiency. Computational efficiency used to be an important consideration in the 1980s and early 1990s. However, driven by Moore's Law (the law originally stated by the founder of Intel that the cost of computers will decline by 50 percent every eighteen months), the price of computers has declined exponentially, so this is no longer a material consideration.

Figure 5.3 grades the ability of each alternative approach to analyze the behavior of hedge funds in normal markets.

Crisis Market Behavior

As **Figure 5.4** shows, market dislocations are occurring with ever-increasing frequency. There are two tools used to analyze the potential behavior of a portfolio in a crisis market environment:

- Historical crisis scenarios
- Hypothetical stress scenarios

Performing these analyses is particularly important for hedge funds, as compared to traditional investments, because of the significant level of convexity that often exists in hedge funds, as previously discussed. In traditional invest-

FIGURE 5.4 **Crisis History**

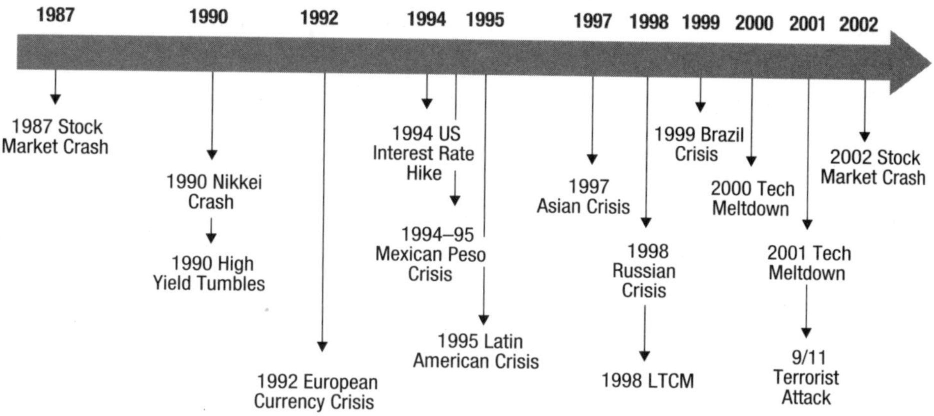

ments, if the market's returns in a period are double those of another period, typically the portfolio's returns during the period will be roughly double those of the other period. However, convexity undermines this simple linear relationship. The returns of hedge funds during the period when the market returns are double could be significantly less than or greater than double those of the first period.

The first tool examines how the portfolio would have behaved in historical crisis scenarios. This is accomplished by selecting these periods and isolating the historical simulation results during them. Figure 5.5 shows some of the historical crisis scenarios that you would want to routinely use.

The second analytic tool subjects the portfolio to a battery of stress scenarios, standard hypothetical extreme scenarios. This should be separately performed for each of the six primary market exposures.

FIGURE 5.5 **Standard Historical Crisis Scenarios**

	1994	1997	1998	2000–2001	2001
	Bond Crash	**Asian Flu**	**Fall 1998**	**Meltdown**	**9/11**
BEGIN	February 1994	July 1997	August 1998	April 2000	September 2001
END	April 1994	December 1997	October 1998	September 2001	September 2001

History has proven that markets tend to behave synchronously (that is, they become significantly more correlated) in a crisis. This is because in times of crisis there is a similar "flight to quality" across all markets. Therefore, having analyzed the independent behavior of a portfolio to potential extreme dislocations of each of the six primary risk exposures, it is critical that the potential behavior of potential simultaneous extreme market moves be analyzed.

As previously discussed, risk is generally best measured on a relative basis. It is all but impossible to look at the stress test results of a single portfolio and assess the inherent risk. However, if you compare the results to those of previous constructions or to the results of other portfolios subjected to the same scenarios, they become meaningful. Therefore, for stress tests to be most valuable, you must consistently apply a standard battery of scenarios. This makes the results both comparable and easy to aggregate.

CHAPTER 6

Understanding the Source of Risk

A variety of approaches are used by the traditional buy-side to quantify and explain the source of risk:

- "Slicing and dicing" or "bucketing"
- Index-based benchmarks
- Value at Risk (VaR)
- Risk-factor framework

The first three do not represent statistically significant tools to understand the risks inherent in hedge funds. However, the fourth tool, a risk-factor framework, can simultaneously provide both a holistic approach to measuring risk and a fundamental understanding of the source of risk. Furthermore, as is discussed in later chapters, such an approach provides an additive framework that can permit risk transparency on a structural level without requiring the disclosure of specific holdings.

Slicing and Dicing or Bucketing

In the long-only traditional investment world, risk can be meaningfully characterized by simply slicing and dicing positions into buckets. For example, simply grouping the positions into industry sectors provides a significant amount of information. Managers have an understanding of the behavior of each sector (for example, basic materials is a value sector, technology is growth). Portfolios can be sliced and diced by:

- Industry groupings
- Exchanges
- Credit ratings
- Maturity
- Countries/regions
- Market cap groupings

However, slicing and dicing is significantly less effective in characterizing a portfolio that includes both long and short positions. Let's consider a portfolio that has equal long and short exposures to the tech sector. In this case the net exposure to the sector will be zero. However, the risk of the portfolio will vary dramatically if:

- The portfolio is long biotech stocks and short semiconductors
- The portfolio is long software companies and short pharmaceuticals

In neither case will the returns be adequately represented by the index returns of the tech sector.

Now let's add the complication that hedge fund exposure need not be cash funded. For example, hedge funds can gain highly levered exposure to risk through options, futures, or swaps (see Chapter 3). Inherent in the slicing and dicing is that there is a common denominator that can be sliced. In the traditional world all instruments are cash funded, and one can use the cash value of the instrument as a common basis. This is not feasible in hedge funds. Consequently, slicing and dicing or bucketing does not meaningfully explain the sources of risk in hedge funds.

Index-Based Benchmarks

In the long-only world, indices are used as benchmarks against which to measure both risk and return of portfolios. As Chapter 1 discusses, the measurement of the performance of traditional managers relative to these indices represents a force that pulls the behavior of these managers toward their respective index. Hedge funds, however, are focused on absolute, not relative, returns, and no such gravitational force exists. Consequently, hedge fund style categorizations are not statistically significant classifications of funds, so style indices do not meaningfully explain the behavior of individual funds.

For example, the average correlation of each of the hedge funds in the Hedge Fund Research (HFR) universe to their respective style index is no greater than the average of the correlation of that fund to the HFR composite index or various equity indices (see **Figure 6.1**).

The fundamental issue is that hedge fund styles do not define a homogeneous strategy. This is because the performance of funds within a style grouping are so disparate that the ability of the related style index to explain their behavior is not meaningfully greater than that of the hedge fund composite index. For example, a convertible arbitrage fund can be long or short interest rates, credit,

FIGURE 6.1 **Average Correlation of Individual Hedge Fund to Its Style Indices and Other Indices**

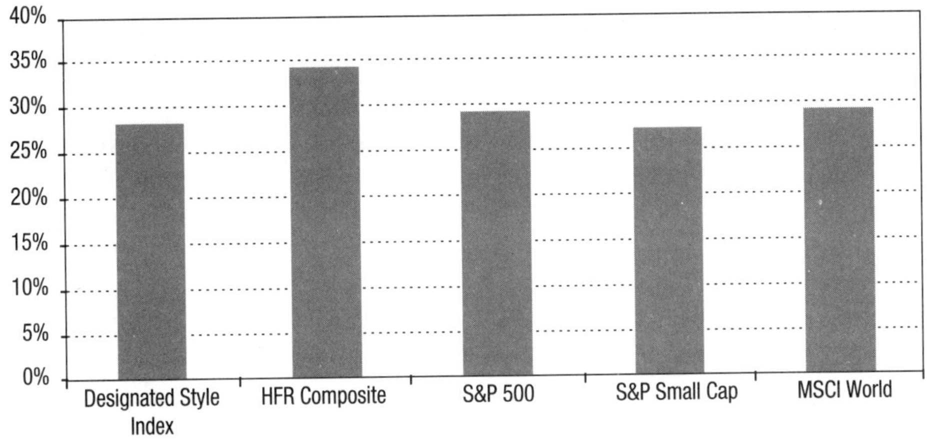

volatility, the underlying equity, or liquidity. Furthermore, "busted converts" introduce event risk. The behavior of individual convertible arbitrage funds will vary dramatically depending on what exposures the specific fund has. In other words, the style indices do not explain the behavior of each of the funds in their respective sub-universes better than generic hedge fund and equity indices do. Consequently, hedge fund indices do not meaningfully explain the sources of risk in hedge funds.

Value at Risk (VaR)

Previous chapters have already discussed Value at Risk (VaR) in some depth. VaR has been universally adopted on the sell-side as a measure of aggregate risk because it is a *simple, unidimensional measure that is applied consistently across all asset classes.* VaR's greatest strength in measuring risk is its greatest weakness in explaining the source of risk. VaR fails to identify the source of risk because it is a *simple, unidimensional measure that is applied consistently across all asset classes.*

For example, if each of two funds has a single holding, IBM, and one fund is long 100 shares and the other fund is short 100 shares, their VaRs would be roughly equivalent. That is because VaR shows aggregate risk and not directionality or causality. If either were the only fund in which you invested, the risk would be approximately equal and this representation of risk would be accurate. However, if you invested in both funds and were given only a VaR statistic for each, you would not know whether either fund was long or short, you would not know that the reason they have the same VaR is that they both invested in IBM, and you would not know whether the risk of these two funds is concentrating or diversifying.

The most significant problem is that VaR is not additive. If an investor is given a VaR by each of her funds, she would have no basis to determine what the VaR of her portfolio of funds would be and how efficiently the risks of each of the individual funds combine in the portfolio.

Risk-Factor Framework

A risk-factor framework has proven to be extremely valuable in explaining the sources of risk on the traditional buy-side. The standard systems that utilize such a framework include BARRA, Wilshire, Zephyr, and Northfield. However, as is discussed in Chapter 1, significant differences exist in the types of risk exposure between hedge funds and traditional investments. Consequently, the risk-factor frameworks used in the latter environment do not adequately support hedge fund strategies. The fundamental shortcomings of these systems for hedge funds are the following:

- The risk factors are typically calculated using a relatively long period of monthly data. This is not responsive to hedge fund "trading-oriented" strategies.
- Such systems primarily focus on the parametric approach (see Chapter 5) that ignores the more complex behavior of hedge fund strategies, such as convexity, fat tails, and asymmetries.
- Such systems assume that the idiosyncratic, or security-specific, risk is independent and normally distributed.

A risk-factor framework specifically designed for hedge funds, on the other hand, can be an extremely valuable tool in understanding their risks.

A risk-factor framework can provide a complete picture of the sources of risk. Risk is inherently nonadditive and multidimensional. This makes it complex and difficult to understand. However, a risk-factor framework can communicate risk in a relatively simple and straightforward additive framework.

The relationship that ultimately defines the behavior of a hedge fund is its sensitivity to the markets. An understanding of the unique market risk exposures of a fund is required to explain the behavior of that fund. The section of this chapter on index-based benchmarks gives the example of why the behavior of convertible arbitrage funds is not homogenous, the unique behavior being driven by whether the fund is long or short interest rates, credit, volatility, the underlying equity, or by illiquidity. These are the primary market factors, which are called risk factors. Consequently, the behavior of a hedge fund is dependent on the fund's sensitivities to risk factors.

Risk factors are a set of indices that permit one to describe the risk of a holding. For example, the risk factors related to equities include:

- The general returns of the equity market (such as the S&P 500)
- Style factors such as value versus growth and large-cap versus small-cap exposures
- Industry factors such as technology, financial, etc.
- Stock-specific risks

Similarly, fixed-income assets are exposed to a set of interest rate risk factors (in addition to a separate set of credit risk factors):

- The general movement of interest rates (duration)
- The relative movement to specific points on the curve (partial duration)
- The relative movement across basis (geographic, cash/bonds/swaps/futures, etc.)
- Bond-specific risk

Risk can be communicated through the relationship of how much the value of the instrument will change as a result of a change in the value of the risk factor. This is called the risk-factor "sensitivity." The most common risk-factor sensitivities are the beta to the equity market and the interest rate duration. For example, a stock that has a beta of 1.3 to the S&P 500 is on average expected to increase by 1.3 percent when the S&P 500 increases by 1 percent. Similarly, a bond that has a duration of 2 is anticipated to increase by 2 percent in value when interest rates decline by 1 percent.

However, an instrument could have sensitivities to multiple risk factors. For example, Microsoft is sensitive to:

- The broad equity market
- The relative performance of growth stocks
- The relative performance of large-cap stocks
- The relative performance of technology stocks

FIGURE 6.2 **Market Risks**

PRIMARY MARKET RISK	MEASURE
Equity	S&P 500
Interest Rate	Curve shift
Credit	Spread shift
Commodity	Goldman Sachs Commodity Index
Currency	US Dollar Index (DXY)
Real Estate	National Council of Real Estate Investment Fiduciaries (NCREIF)

In this simple example, there are interdependencies across these various risk factors. Growth stocks tend to outperform when large-cap stocks do. The relative performance of technology stocks tends to be correlated with the performance of both growth and large-cap stocks. It is possible to create risk factors that are "orthogonal," that remove the interrelationships among risk factors and create an independent and additive set of risk factors. This is discussed below and again in detail in Chapter 18.

There are three broad types of risk factors: market, secondary, and idiosyncratic.

Market risk factors. Market risks are the systematic risks that cannot be diversified away in a long-only portfolio. **Figure 6.2** shows six primary market risks.

Secondary risk factors. Secondary risks are the correlated risks across multiple securities that could be diversified away in a long-only portfolio. For example, an exposure to value stocks can be diversified away through an exposure to growth stocks. Other such factors are shown in **Figure 6.3**.

Idiosyncratic risk factors. Idiosyncratic risks are risks that are unique to a specific holding. For example, IBM's precipitous decline in 1992 was an idiosyncratic risk attributable to its decision to move away from mainframe computers (or the market's forcing it to do so), and its subsequent recovery due to the success of its service business.

Traditional risk factors assume that all idiosyncratic or security-specific risk is normally distributed and independent of that of all other positions. This is an acceptable simplification in traditional, long-only portfolios. However, as previously discussed, hedge funds target relative value strategies, resulting in a significantly greater percent of risk being idiosyncratic. Consequently, it is critical to

FIGURE 6.3 **Secondary Risks**

PRIMARY MARKET RISK	SECONDARY RISK	MEASURE
Equity	Style	Large Cap/Small Cap* Value/Growth*
	Industry	GICS Groupings
	Volatility	Equity Volatility
Interest Rates	Rate Curve	Curve Twist Curve Butterfly
	Volatility	Rate Volatility
Credit	Credit Spreads	Spread Twist Spread Butterfly
	Credit Quality	High-Grade Spread Junk Spread
	Volatility	Credit Volatility
Commodity	Group	Agricultural Base Metals Energy Livestock Precious Metals
	Commodity	Gold* Crude* Wheat*
	Volatility	Commodity Volatility
Currency	Currency	Currency
	Volatility	Currency Volatility
Real Estate	Type	Region Property Type

*Partial list

capture the true idiosyncratic risk behavior and understand how much of it is correlated across positions versus how much is truly independent. For example, if you were long the SPA share class of Fiat and short the RNC class, the resulting actual standard deviation of the portfolio (0.26 Euro) would differ from that which would have been calculated assuming they were statistically independent (0.78 Euro) by a factor of three (see **Figure 6.4**).

FIGURE 6.4 **Fiat Example**

	PORTFOLIO	DAILY STANDARD DEVIATION
Individual Stocks	Long Fiat SPA	0.53 EUR
	Long Fiat RNC	0.57 EUR
Actual Correlation	Long Fiat SPA Long Fiat RNC	1.05 EUR
	Long Fiat SPA Short Fiat RNC	0.26 EUR
Assumption of Independence	Long Fiat SPA Long Fiat RNC	0.78 EUR
	Long Fiat SPA Short Fiat RNC	0.78 EUR

A benefit of presenting risk as a sensitivity to risk factors is that such sensitivities are additive. If you combine a portfolio with a duration of 0.2 and another portfolio of equal size with a duration of 0.6, the combined portfolio would have a duration of 0.4 (the average of 0.2 and 0.6). Similarly, if you combine two portfolios of equal size, the first having a beta to the market of 0.6 and the second a beta of –0.2, the combined portfolio will have a beta to the market of 0.2 (the average of 0.6 and –0.2).

Equity risk factors can be calculated by creating indices of stocks displaying specific behaviors and then using sensitivity analysis (multiple regression) to determine the sensitivity of the security to each of the risk factors. There is a significant amount of correlation among risk factors (multicolinearity). For example, small-cap stocks tend to be value- (versus growth-) oriented. This correlation (colinearity) can be removed through a process called orthogonalization. Orthogonalization effectively takes the large-cap/small-cap behavior out of the value/growth risk factor so that the residual risk factor measures the incremental returns of value (relative to that of large cap).

As in any decomposition, you must select the sequence in which you attribute joint exposures. The objective in orthogonalizing is to identify as much risk as is possible in the most common form. Therefore, equity risk factors should be calculated in the following sequence:

- Market
- Style
- Industry

In this way, if a portfolio is long banks (a value industry) and short technology (a growth industry) the offsetting sensitivity to value/growth will be recognized, and only the residual industry-specific risk will be represented by the industry risk-factor exposures.

Note that risk factors are separate from instruments. The following is a categorization of instruments:

- ***Cash instruments***—Including equities, bonds, and cash holdings of physical commodities and currencies.
- ***Futures***—Including exchange-traded futures and forwards, the equivalent of futures traded in the OTC market.
- ***Options***—Including exchange-traded options, rights, and warrants.
- ***OTC derivatives***—Including interest rate and credit default swaps, swaptions, caps, floors, etc.

Let's use equities as an example of the difference between risk-factor exposures and instruments. You can gain equity risk exposure through cash positions in equities, single stock or equity index futures, and equity or equity index options. Consequently, you can gain exposure to the equity markets through multiple instruments.

Similarly, you can gain access to interest rate exposure by investing in cash instruments (bonds, asset-backed, mortgage-backed), by investing in either bond or interest rate futures or options on them, or by purchasing OTC derivatives. Again, interest rate exposure can be achieved through a variety of instruments.

Marginal Risk Measures

The value of risk factors can be enhanced through marginal measures of risk. As discussed earlier in this chapter, risk factors related to a particular set of risks (such as equity risks and interest rate risks) can be constructed to be orthogonal, or independent of each other. However, there are correlations across primary market risks that must be explicitly measured to fully understand risk. This results in there being interdependencies within a risk-factor framework. Marginal risk measures represent an additive framework that can be extremely useful. This is because when you add a pro rata amount of each marginal risk, the result is an investment with an equivalent amount of risk. This additive framework permits you to decompose (disaggregate) risks to their root sources. Although any measure of marginal risk can be used, the following have proven to be very valuable:

- Marginal standard deviation
- Marginal drawdown
- Marginal VaR

The use of marginal measures of risk are particularly useful because of correlation among risks. Although the six sets of risk factors for each of the primary markets (equity, interest rate, credit, commodity, currency, real estate) can be individually orthogonalized, correlations among these orthogonalized sets of risk still exist (see Chapter 2). A common example of this is the correlation between the credit and equity markets. This correlation is more than coincidental. It results from the fact that corporate bondholders have the first claim and stockholders have the subordinated claim to a company's earnings; however, if the earnings outlook for the company changes, both stakeholders will be similarly affected. When you analyze a portfolio of funds, these relationships across risk factors should be integrated into the analysis. Marginal risk permits risk that is inherently nonlinear and nonadditive to be viewed on a linear and additive basis.

Marginal risk measures permit an investor to understand the impact of adding an extremely small amount of risk to each risk factor. The marginal risk calculation is sensitive to the risk inherent in the overall portfolio, and will change as the construction of the portfolio changes. As you increase the exposure to a position, the marginal risk of that position will increase, as the diversification benefit decreases.

Marginal risk integrates both volatility and correlation. **Figure 6.5** shows, for three scenarios, the relationship of the marginal risk of two hypothetical positions to a portfolio based on varying assumptions of the relative volatility and correlation to the portfolio.

- If both positions have the same correlation to the existing portfolio, the marginal risk of the position with five times the volatility of the other would be approximately five times greater.

FIGURE 6.5 **Marginal Risk—Ratio of Risk Measures between Two Hypothetical Positions**

	VOLATILITY	CORRELATION	MARGINAL RISK
Scenario 1	5x		5x
Scenario 2		5x	5x
Scenario 3	5x	5x	25x

- If both positions have the same volatility, the marginal risk of the position with five times the correlation to the existing portfolio would be approximately five times greater.
- Finally, the marginal risk of the position with both five times the volatility and five times the correlation to the existing portfolio would be approximately twenty-five times that of the other.

As complex as risk is, a combination of the methods described in this chapter can provide a comprehensive understanding of the sources of risk in a fund, or as discussed later, in a portfolio of funds.

CHAPTER 7

Risk Visualization and Articulation

Risk is both very difficult to visualize and extremely challenging to describe. It is both nonlinear and nonadditive. Furthermore, the risk of a single position cannot be independently quantified but can be properly measured only in the context of an overall portfolio. What may represent a risk-mitigating hedge in one portfolio can represent an extremely risky position in another.

Comparative Statistics

Because risk is extremely difficult to understand and communicate on an absolute or isolated basis, it is typically best communicated on a comparative basis. The two primary dimensions of presenting risk on a comparative basis are:

Across time. The primary cause of unanticipated hedge fund behavior is probably "style drift." As Chapter 8 will discuss, style drift is difficult to define and identify, because investors in hedge funds seek managers who are nimble and creative. There is a fuzzy line between being flexible and being undisciplined. However, although investors should not seek to establish rigid mandates for hedge funds (hedge fund managers will not accept them), investors should track the progression of a fund over time to ensure that they are comfortable with the path along which the manager is taking the portfolio. For example, although hedge fund investors may look unfavorably upon a fund that is consistently long the underlying equity market, they should seek managers who can generate returns by nimbly moving between long and short market exposures as part of their strategy. If you look only at a snapshot of risk you cannot determine whether a fund's management of its equity market exposure is passively long-biased or actively moving between long and short biases. Tracking a fund's bias to the market over time provides this information.

If you are told that the annualized volatility of a fund is 11 percent or that the Sharpe ratio is 0.45, it is extremely difficult to internalize what this represents

FIGURE 7.1 **Profile of the Largest Positions**

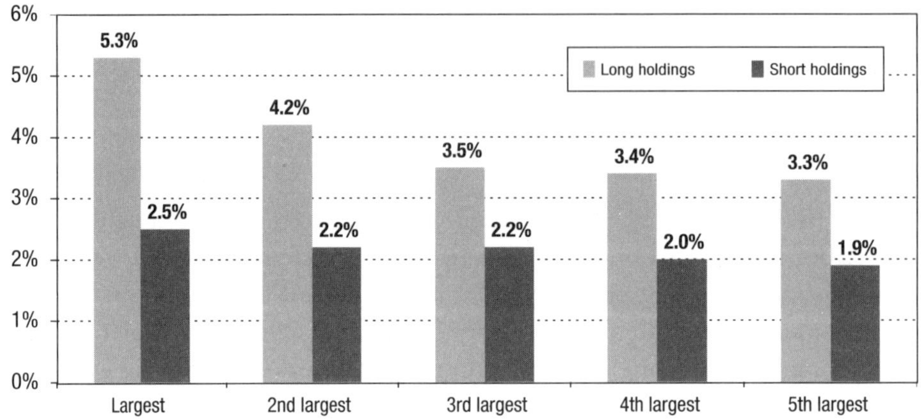

on an absolute basis. However, if you are also told that the annualized volatility of the fund has ranged from 2 percent to 7 percent over the past twelve months, the current level of 11 percent would raise some questions.

Compared to peers. Comparisons of specific risk measures of a fund to those of its peers serve to explain performance relative to a "norm." As with most other measures, risk measures have meaning only in context. The simplest comparison is to an index that is constructed as the average of the peer group. This shows how a fund compares in a specific measure to the average, but not where it ranks. Therefore, a very useful statistic is the fund's percentile ranking based on a specific measure within some (preferably homogeneous) group of funds or within the full universe of funds. This truly presents comparative performance.

You might not know how to interpret the fact that a specific equity fund could liquidate 95 percent of its portfolio in thirty days. However, if you were also told that the average time for similar funds to liquidate 95 percent of their portfolios was ten days you would have a significantly better context. Furthermore, knowing that a fund's time to liquidate 95 percent of its portfolio was in the 30th percentile of all similar funds would be extremely useful information.

FIGURE 7.2 **Profile of the Time to Liquidate**

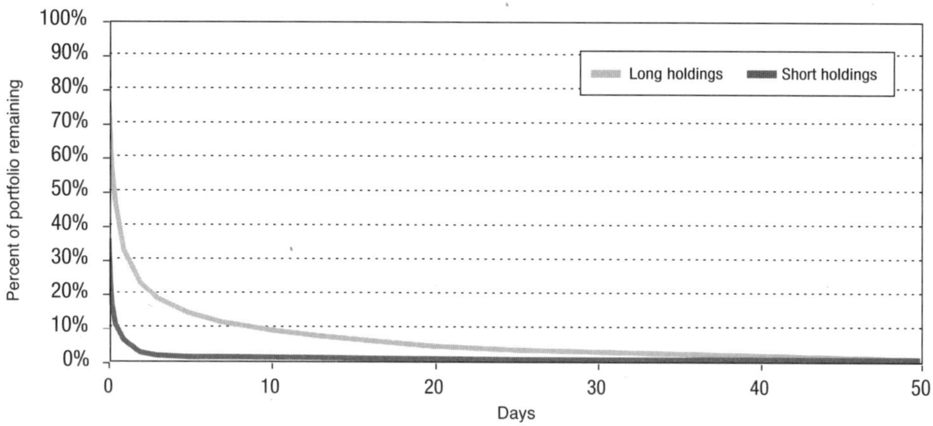

Risk Visualization Techniques

A key component of understanding risk is "risk visualization." As the old adage goes, "one picture is worth a thousand words" (or in the case of risk, a thousand numbers).

Imagine asking someone to describe a spiral. It is extremely difficult to describe it in words. Almost everybody resorts to using his hands to demonstrate the shape. Risk is even more difficult to describe in words. Therefore, presenting risk visually can be extremely powerful. The most useful visualization techniques are as follows:

Profiling. Graphically profiling the risk of a fund can be very valuable. For example, **Figure 7.1** presents the concentration of a fund's largest long and short holdings.

Similarly, graphically profiling the days to liquidate the fund provides a clear picture of the underlying liquidity of the fund, as shown in **Figure 7.2.**

Style drift analysis. Viewing the progression of each fundamental risk measure over time is extremely useful. **Figure 7.3** shows how trend-line risk measures such as volatility (measured as annualized standard deviation) are the primary way to identify style drift.

Attribution/decomposition. Trending the source of risk over time provides insight as to the primary risks that a fund has been taking, as shown in **Figure 7.4.**

FIGURE 7.3 **Style Drift Analysis of Volatility**

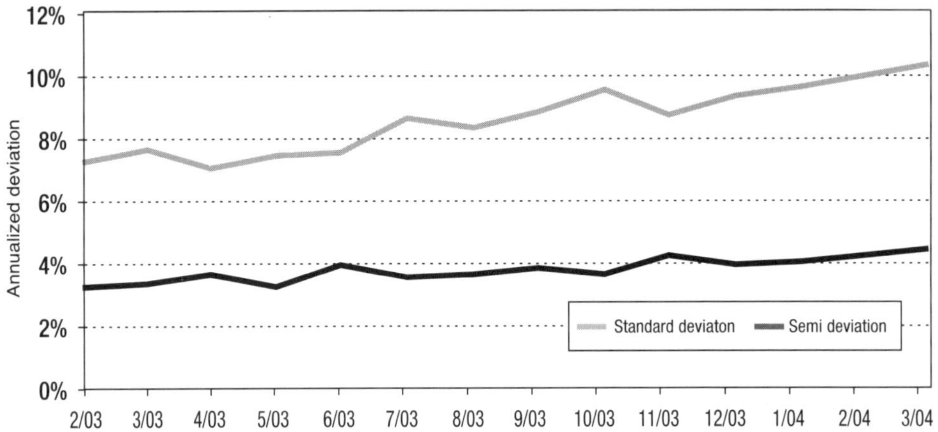

FIGURE 7.4 **Trending the Source of Risk (Attribution)**

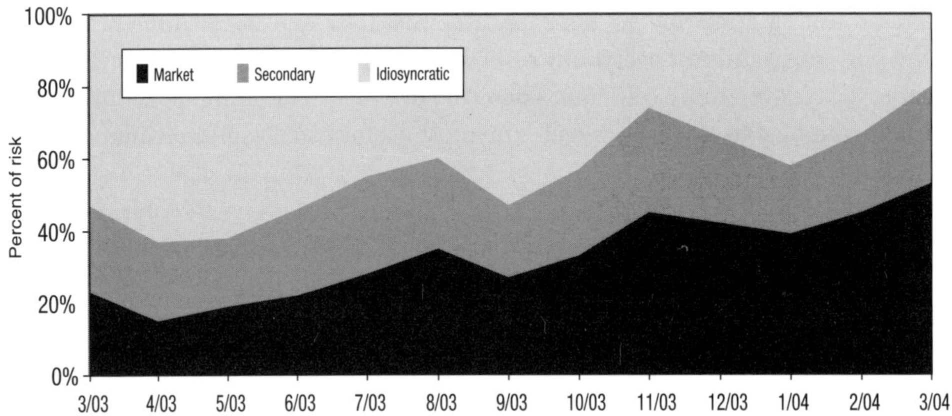

FIGURE 7.5 **Large Position Concentration Compared to Historical Norms**

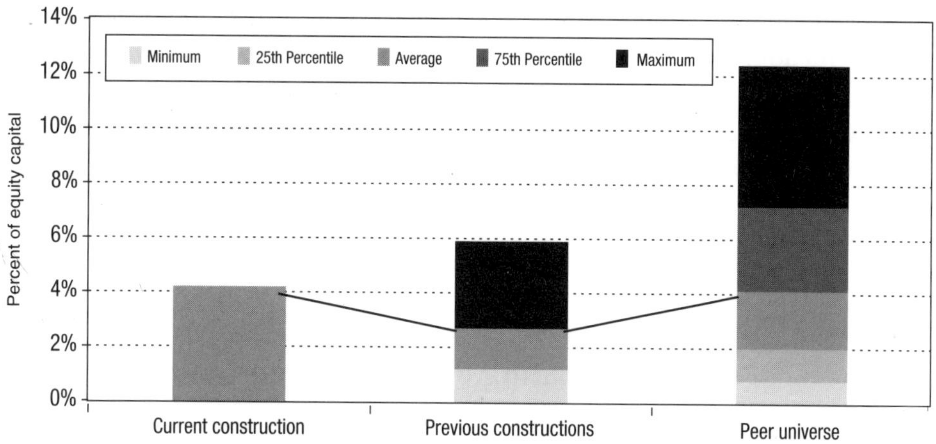

FIGURE 7.6 **Leverage Peer Comparison**

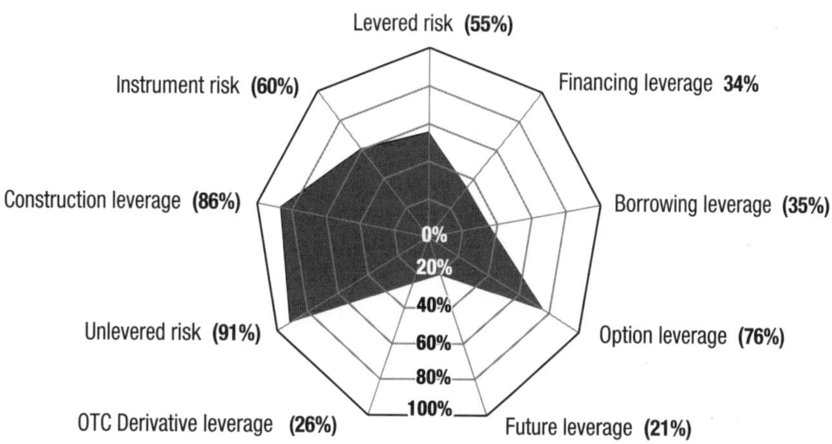

Comparison to historical norms. Comparing specific risk measures of the current construction with comparable statistics of prior constructions provides a picture of consistency and normalcy. For example, whereas the profile of the concentration of large holdings in Figure 7.1 provides a snapshot of the current construction, **Figure 7.5** shows how comparisons with the minimum, maximum, and average of prior constructions provides valuable insight.

Comparison to peers. Of equal value to comparisons across time are comparisons across funds. For example, presenting the leverage for an equity long/short fund along with the norms for its peer universes provides an understanding of the comparative behavior of the specific fund, as shown in **Figure 7.6.**

Communicating Risk in "Hedge-Speak"

The Rosetta stone, discovered in 1799, is a stone that contains the same passage written in both hieroglyphics (a language that at the time had not yet been deciphered) and Greek. The stone provided the basis to decipher ancient Egyptian hieroglyphics.

Similarly, if transparency is to take hold in the hedge fund industry, the measures of risk must be presented in the language of hedge funds. It is critical that fundamental risk measures, traditionally expressed in the language of financial engineering (financialese), are translated and presented in "hedge-speak." **Figure 7.7** is the financialese/hedge-speak Rosetta stone.

Quality risk reporting should be bilingual. It should be presented in both:

Financialese. This is the language currently spoken by traders and financial engineers. As hedge fund strategies tend to be divided into independent silos (such as equity long/short and volatility arbitrage), there are many dialects. For example, equity long/short managers speak about beta to the market, value versus growth, large versus small cap, and sector exposures. Relative value arbitrage players

FIGURE 7.7 **Translation Table**

FINANCIALESE	HEDGE-SPEAK
Stress test results	Drawdown
Serial correlation	Worst month, quarter, year
Short volatility	Liquidity supplier
Kurtosis	Fat tails
Illiquidity	Blow-up risk
Risk-adjusted returns	Sharpe ratio
Correlation	Beta

speak of duration, partial duration, twists, and shifts. Funds utilizing option-based strategies talk of implied volatility, delta, gamma, theta, and the like.

Hedge-speak. This is the language currently spoken by investors in hedge funds. It includes jargon such as drawdowns, fat tails, and Sharpe ratios.

CHAPTER 8

Risk Culture

The traditional role of risk management in investment banks, the creators of the function, was that of a "risk cop." It was a control function that policed traders so that they remained within their risk limits. Risk managers operated as third-party oversight rather than as a team with the trading desks. They were guided by rigid constraints (dogma) rather than a shared goal. Over the years, risk management in these organizations has advanced from being a policing function to being an active participant in decision-making. The risk management functions within these organizations have grown to be "risk strategists." In this capacity, they serve as active participants in formulating decisions that rationally balance the potential returns and risks of alternative investments.

THE RISK COP

The objective of risk management in hedge funds should similarly be to rationally balance the potential returns and risks. As hedge funds have become institutionalized, they have rapidly learned that risk management is in vogue and that the cost of employing a risk manager is minimal. Many funds have anointed someone, often the CFO, a risk manager so that when investors make their due diligence visits there will be a bona fide risk manager to roll out. Unfortunately, finance is typically a control function, and these hedge fund risk cops focus on constraining risk, not deploying it efficiently. They generally do this by dogmatically defining risk limits. The limits are arbitrary and without any statistical underpinnings. This typically results in one of two outcomes:

- The limits are so wide that they have never been (and probably will never be) triggered.
- The limits are so narrow that they are not an effective warning system, and the fund manager learns to ignore them.

Hedge funds should view risk as a strategic asset rather than as something to be controlled. They should be risk aware, not risk averse. Hedge funds should develop a strategic risk management capability, which can help integrate a fundamental understanding of risk into the investment process.

Integrating Risk Management into All Hedge Fund Processes

Risk does not exist by itself; it is effectively a by-product of an investment opportunity. Risk is therefore 100 percent interdependent with other investment components. Furthermore, as previously discussed, the behavior of risk is extremely complex. It is neither linear nor additive, and the amount of it cannot be independently measured but rather can be measured only in the context of the other investments in a portfolio. Therefore, its behavior is highly interdependent with the rest of the portfolio. Consequently, this extremely complex organism can be understood and managed only on an integrated basis.

Hedge funds should develop integrated processes across the full cycle of manager identification, manager selection, portfolio construction, and monitoring. Here are some reasons why:

- Risk cannot be considered without simultaneously considering the compensating return.
- An individual position must be considered in the context of the overall portfolio.
- As discussed in detail in Chapter 14, manager selection and asset allocation in hedge funds must be simultaneously performed as part of an integrated process.
- An investor should analyze his alternative investments only in the context of his overall portfolio, including his traditional investments.
- The management process, as discussed in the balance of this chapter, must integrate qualitative and quantitative perspectives.
- Risk should be strategically integrated with research into the investment function rather than being an independent control function.

FIGURE 8.1 **Hedge Fund Return Sensitivity versus Market Correlation**

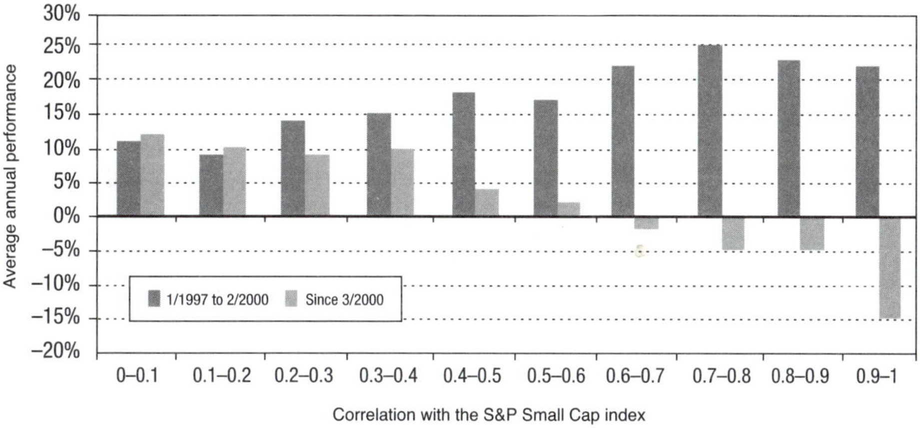

Source: HFR

Style Drift versus Nimbleness

Is manager flexibility a virtue or a vice? Is flexibility normally a symptom of style drift or a sign of nimbleness? Typically, when a fund outperforms, investors call flexibility nimbleness. When a fund underperforms, investors call flexibility style drift. The problem is that, given these definitions, one cannot differentiate between the two until after the fact, when the ultimate performance is known. Unfortunately, the cat is already out of the bag at this time.

Let's look at a specific example to better understand the issue. The average equity long/short hedge fund was up over 100 percent during the period from January 1997 to March 2000 (more than 24 percent annually!). In March 2000, most managers credited their nimbleness and skill. Their returns significantly surpassed the 17 percent annualized return of all hedge funds (the average nonequity fund returned approximately 10 percent annualized during this period). The problem is that much of this success ultimately proved to be style drift, gaining the majority of the return from exposure to the equity market while claiming to be hedge funds. These managers ultimately were not very nimble—only 8 percent of the managers who were long-biased the equity market before the burst of the bubble became short-biased after the burst.

FIGURE 8.2 **Hedge Fund Return Sensitivity versus Market Correlation**

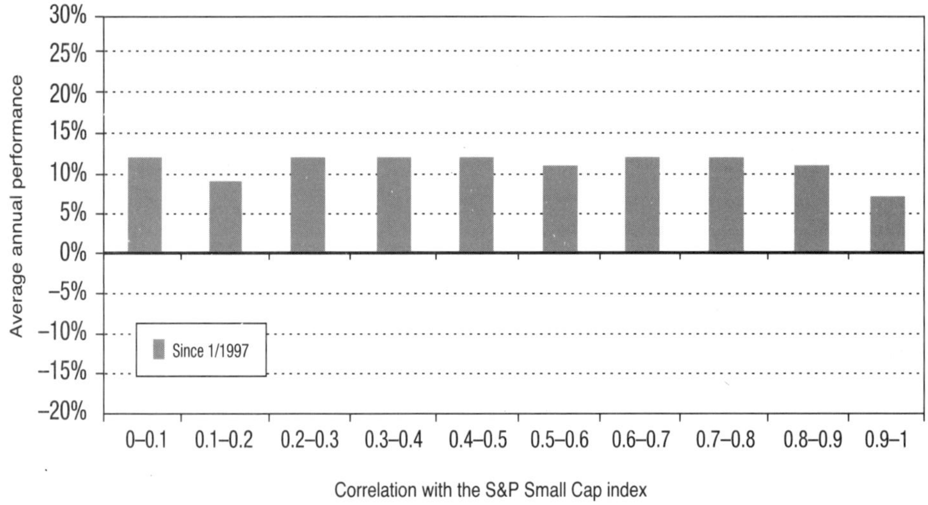

Source: HFR, Kenmar

FIGURE 8.3 **Hedge Fund Volativity versus Market Correlation**

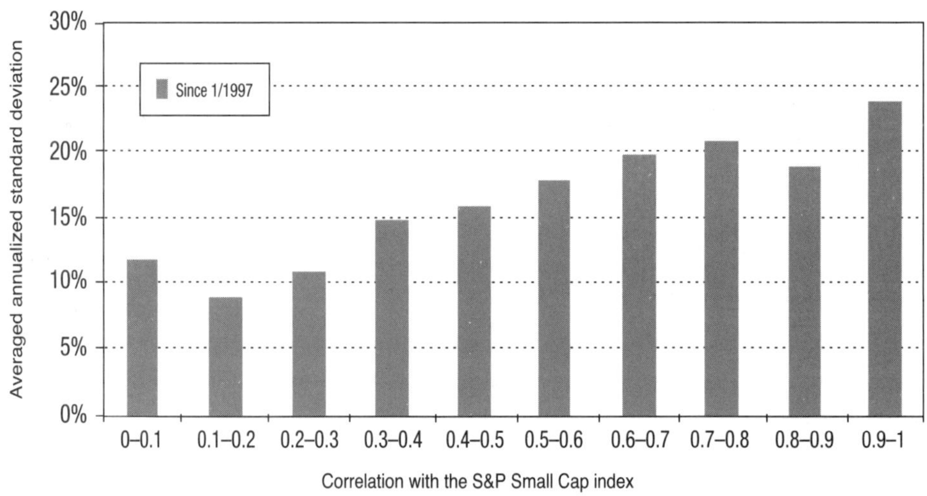

Source: HFR, Kenmar

FIGURE 8.4 **Hedge Fund Risk-Adjusted Return versus Market Exposure**

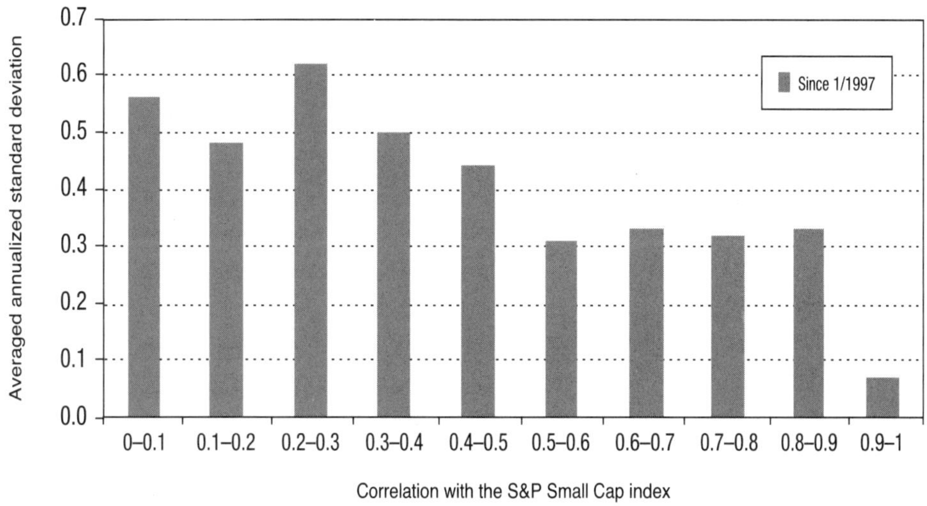

Source: HFR, Kenmar

Now consider the impact on returns over the full cycle. **Figure 8.1** segregates the 1,700 funds in the Hedge Fund Research (HFR) universe into deciles based on their correlation to the S&P Small Cap index. The funds with the lowest correlation to the market fell into the deciles on the left of the figure, and the funds with the highest correlations fell into deciles on the right side. Not surprisingly, the funds that had the greatest correlation to the equity market during the roaring market of the late 1990s had the best returns. Again, not surprisingly, these same funds performed the worst after the bubble burst. Investors who at the peak of the market selected managers with high correlation to the market by looking through the rearview mirror ultimately got punished as these managers sustained losses as the market declined.

Combining both periods, the average return over the full cycle did not vary significantly as a function of market correlation (**Figure 8.2**).

However, managers with high correlation to the market experienced significantly higher volatility as they took the roller-coaster ride along with the market (**Figure 8.3**).

Consequently, the risk-adjusted returns of those managers with high correlation to the market were significantly worse than more market-diversified funds (**Figure 8.4**).

Market timing is extremely difficult and investors must be very careful to proactively evaluate managers and not let after-the-fact returns be the differentiator between nimbleness and style drift.

Personality Risks

Although this book focuses on statistical risk management, several "personality risks" exist that are relatively unique to the world of hedge funds and are worthy of mention. As these risks generally infect the top people in a hedge fund organization, they are not presented here as a warning to the funds (if funds wanted to understand the symptoms, the disease would have been eradicated). Instead, the discussion that follows is primarily intended to caution investors to be aware. These personality risks are summarized in **Figure 8.5**.

Status Issues

Many successful people in the hedge fund world have become very wealthy. The fame and fortune have elevated them to celebrity status. People respond to this extremely differently. Some remain humble whereas many develop large egos. These managers may suffer from the following:

Hubris. Although it is OK for hedge fund managers to have big egos away from the trading desk, the markets do not treat celebrities specially. It is critical that when managers walk in the door they check their egos in the coat closet and sit down to trade with humility. He who does not recognize the ultimate force of the market will be humbled by it.

Affluenza. As noted above, many successful hedge fund managers are extremely rich. Many have achieved their success because they are naturally driven, a drive that for many may not disappear with success. For some, however, wealth extinguishes "the fire in the belly," and consequently, they lose their edge. Investors must be continually analyzing whether the manager continues to have the drive that created the initial success.

Environment Issues

Many hedge fund managers were successful proprietary traders from large financial institutions who were sitting on large trading floors with significant support infrastructure around them before they made the leap into the hedge fund world. These managers may suffer from the following:

FIGURE 8.5 **Personality Risks**

DISEASE	UNDERLYING CONDITION	SYMPTOMS	PROGNOSIS
Hubris Risk	Egocentric	Believe they are the market	Star retires No team to carry on
Affluenza Risk	Too rich to bother	No fire in the belly	Returns will decline Assets under management will dwindle
Cocoon Risk	Isolation	Disconnected from the market	"Some moths will grow into butterflies"
First Time Fund Risk	New responsibilities	Lack of focus	Bruises will go away Patient will outgrow condition

Cocoonitis. In starting hedge funds, these managers have moved to an isolated office from large trading floors with several hundreds of people shouting high-quality market information back and forth and with high visibility to deal flow. This isolation is equivalent to being in a cocoon. They have become disconnected from the natural flow of information. Although electronic communication has made information broadly available, the wires are not selective, and the amount of information that one receives electronically can be overwhelming—equivalent to drinking from a fire hose. This experience can be as risky as pushing a butterfly back into the cocoon.

First-time manager. Larger trading operations provide a great deal of support and infrastructure, right up to delivering lunch directly to the traders' desks. A successful trader is a very pampered animal. A trader who has successfully focused on what she does best is pulled from this nurturing environment and must assume the responsibility for getting the bills paid, hiring the administrative assistant, getting lunch, and so forth. These new responsibilities could divert first-time managers from the most valuable task, the one they have been superstars at—trading. Investors should determine whether there is an adequate support infrastructure so that the manager can deliver the value that she has previously proven the ability to deliver.

III

Part Three

Other Risk Processes

CHAPTER 9

Non-Market Risk Management

This book primarily focuses on market risk, risks related to the market performance of the holdings in the portfolio. These are the only risks for which the market compensates investors. In Chapter 8, the unique personality risks related to hedge funds are discussed. However, these risks manifest themselves through poor performance and, as such, should be viewed as a type of market risk. Unfortunately, there are myriad other uncompensated risks that can result in losses. These risks include:

- Fraud
- Errors
- Business interruption
- Embezzlement
- Forced liquidations
- Credit losses
- Misvaluations

In a recent research paper entitled "Understanding and Mitigating Operational Risk in Hedge Fund Investments,"[1] a proprietary database of more than 100 hedge fund failures dating back over twenty years was analyzed. The study first categorized failures based on three broad criteria:

- ***Investment risk***—market and related risks associated with the overall fund or a specific portion
- ***Business risk***—risks associated with a fund that are not directly related to market movements, such as failure to reach a base level of assets under management or a change in management of the fund
- ***Operational risk***—risks associated with and supporting the operating environment of the fund. The operating environment includes middle- and back-office functions such as trade processing, accounting, administration, valuation, and reporting

The analysis concluded that 50 percent of failures resulted from only operational risk (see **Figure 9.1**).

FIGURE 9.1 **Failed Funds by Primary Cause**

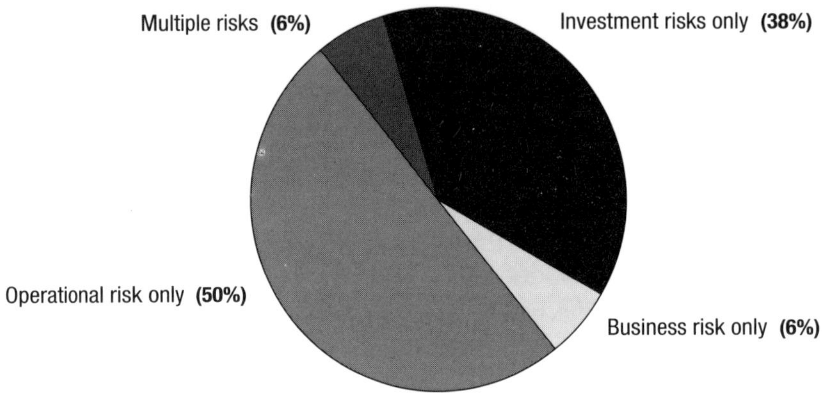

Furthermore, the total number of funds for which operational risk was a factor (versus the sole factor, as just mentioned) was 54 percent.

The study further divided the operational issues based on root cause, including the following:

- ***Misrepresentation of investments***—the act of creating or causing the generation of reports and valuations with false and misleading information.
- ***Misappropriation of funds/general fraud***—investment managers who knowingly move money out of the fund for personal use, as an outright theft, or to cover preexisting trading losses.
- ***Unauthorized trading and style breaches***—making investments outside of the stated fund strategy or changing the investment style of the fund without the approval of investors.
- ***Inadequate resources for fund strategy***—technology, processes, or personnel that are not able to properly handle operating volumes or the types of investments and activities that the fund engages in.

The 50 percent of hedge fund failures due to operational issues were divided among these root causes as shown in **Figure 9.2**.

The sobering news is that more than 70 percent of hedge fund failures due to operational issues resulted from the malicious intent of the manager operating the fund (both misrepresentation of investments and misappropriation of funds). These are the toughest risks to avoid as an investor. However, with that as

FIGURE 9.2 **Breakdown of Operational Issues by Source**

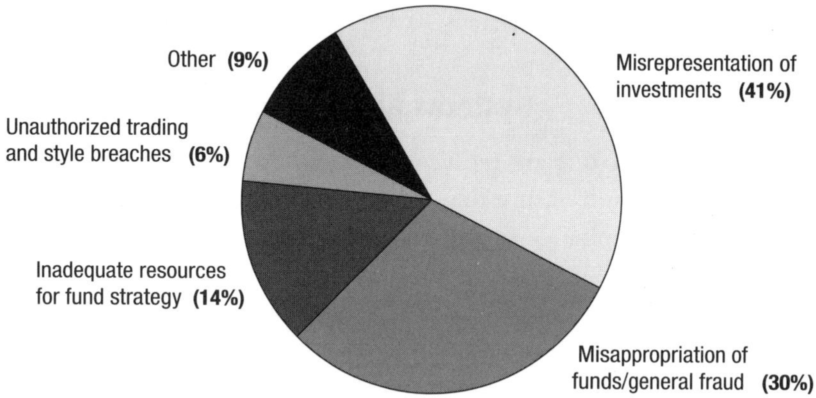

a backdrop, let's drill deeper into the topic of non-market risk management.

Major financial institutions have developed approaches to mitigate these risks. Regulators (including the Securities and Exchange Commission, National Association of Securities Dealers, and the Commodity Futures Trading Commission) have mandated the implementation of these approaches. As unregulated businesses, however, hedge funds have not been subject to these disciplines. Investors in hedge funds must be "qualified investors" (investors that the regulators have designated as have the financial means to invest in hedge funds), and as a result the philosophy is "buyer beware." Some funds have independently decided to apply some or all of the available risk-mitigating approaches. Others have opted for varying levels of "discipline" (or "bureaucracy," depending on one's viewpoint). To enable hedge funds to make clear and conscious decisions as to which approaches to implement, this chapter presents the disciplines that major financial institutions have implemented.

As has been noted, the only risks that funds are compensated for are market risks. Consequently, funds will not be compensated for non-market risks. However, Chapter 1 introduced the concept that the greater the risk, the greater the return an investor should require. Therefore, managers who assume above-average non-market risks must be able to generate above-average returns in their taking of market risk to fully compensate investors for the aggregate risk the investors are taking. For example, a fund that invests in whole loans should generate a premium risk-adjusted return (adjusted for market risk) to justify the additional fraud risk of such nonsecuritized and nonrated investments. This may suggest that larger funds that often have a larger and more formal infrastructure may have an advantage from an operational point of view.

Systems and Procedures

SEC-regulated brokers are required to maintain a comprehensive set of policies and procedures and ensure that they are followed. These SEC-regulated organizations have compliance functions, whose sole responsibility is overseeing that the regulations are being observed. Hedge funds are not controlled by the same set of rules. The vast majority of hedge funds are small organizations with informal operating procedures. Their employees often are escapees of large capital market firms who have been attracted to the informality of hedge funds.

However, a key to minimizing operational risks and achieving operational excellence is instituting disciplined systems and procedures in areas such as the following.

Integrated systems. System integration ensures the "straight through" processing of transactions without the risk of erroneous or lost information. This includes the integration of the following set of systems:

- Portfolio construction (for system-based traders)
- Trade capture (front office)
- Clearance and settlement (back office)
- Portfolio accounting
- Profit and loss
- NAV accounting
- Shareholder reporting
- General accounting

To the extent the fund has not fully integrated the complete set of systems, it is critical that it have well-defined and strong procedures to reconcile nonintegrated systems on a daily basis.

Dual entry and reconciliation. Another "check and balance" is requiring dual entry and reconciliation of input data. Although integrated systems can avoid errors after data are initially entered, input data are always susceptible to clerical errors. The only control is requiring dual entry and reconciling the multiple entries.

Disaster recovery. A hedge fund manager should have an explicit plan in the case of a disaster. This should cover both data processing and back-office operations. Adequate off-site records should be maintained to permit operations to continue in the extreme case that all records are destroyed or not accessible. Specifically, the computer system should be backed up on a daily basis with the copy being held offsite. It is helpful to document the plan on paper. This plan should be kept off-site but accessible so that it can be rapidly produced if required. A good place that may not be obvious is the trunk of a car that is driven to the office. Completing a dry run of the disaster recovery plan on a simulated basis can help identify any shortcomings of the plan.

Measurement. Large investment complexes generally have formal approaches to measuring and tracking operational performance. Many industries that have focused on operational quality have found that measuring and tracking performance contributes significantly to achieving superior performance. Relatively few of these methods have trickled down to hedge funds. However, investors should explore what measures a fund maintains, if any, and ask to see the results.

Internal review/audit. Large organizations all have internal audit functions that are responsible for reviewing the operations and procedures of every function to ensure compliance with policies and enforcement of controls. Periodic audits and reviews are taken seriously in these organizations, and the process of preparing for a review can be very therapeutic. Although most hedge funds will not have an internal staff person dedicated to this responsibility, accounting firms or other third-party compliance services are quite competent to perform this role. A hedge fund manager who is seeking to keep the costs down probably knows someone in another organization (a large investor, someone from his prime broker, his administrator, another hedge fund manager, an associate in a larger financial organization) who would be willing to come in for several hours and perform an independent review. There is no right person. Hedge funds should look for someone who will think outside the box and constructively challenge what they are doing.

Organizational Issues

We will now shift our focus from the highly tangible issues of systems and procedures to the following more abstract organizational issues:

Separation of responsibilities. In large financial organizations, a fundamental control principle is that there be separation of responsibility. This includes separating:

- Risk-taking from monitoring
- Trade entry/pricing from profit/loss responsibility
- Valuation from profit/loss responsibility

Large organizations explicitly separate responsibility between the front office and the middle and back offices. However, this is generally not feasible in many hedge funds, as the ability to do so is limited by the size of the organization. There is no simple solution for a small hedge fund. Although the degree of separation cannot be delineated as it is in larger organizations, there should, to the extent feasible, be joint responsibility to provide as much of an independent check as possible.

Joint responsibility for trading decisions. As has been noted, many hedge funds are relatively small organizations. They are often built around one central player. However, no matter how superior a track record or pedigree one manager has, it is very important that there be at least two principals participating in each trading decision. Although it is anticipated that there will be a lead portfolio manager, a robust organization will always have a second decision maker who has adequate power to be able to make the lead decision maker rethink his decisions. A one-man show is a dangerous gig.

Trade authorization. The manager should maintain, with each counterparty, a list of who within the fund is authorized to trade with that counterparty. This should be an explicit list that is religiously enforced.

Management focus. The commitment of top management to risk management and general discipline goes a long way to setting the tone. Risk management need not be formalized if is vigilantly performed on a disciplined basis. In fact, formality can lead to rote performance of risk management, a behavior that can, in fact, nurture risk, despite the appearance of control.

Alignment of interests. Although alignment of interests will not guarantee operational excellence, it significantly reduces the chance of problems. It is always easier when all parties are working toward the same objectives, and the most critical component of achieving this is creating a situation in which all parties' financial interests are aligned.

Disciplined Processes

Implementing the following disciplined cash management, financing, credit, and valuation processes will minimize the likelihood of operational problems:

Matching redemption policy with liquidity. This issue is discussed in detail in Chapter 4. The key concept is that if the redemption policy of the fund does not match the liquidity of the underlying securities, the iron law of supply and demand will ultimately prevail if there is a liquidity crunch. The fund will either be forced to liquidate in a fire sale or to halt redemptions. In the ultimate test, policies cannot control market forces.

However, increasing market pressure for enhanced redemption terms has probably increased the number of situations in which there is a mismatch between the liquidity and the redemption policy of a fund. This problem is being exacerbated by the fact that as hedge fund returns have declined, funds are sometimes reaching into less liquid securities to generate returns.

Cash management. There should be an explicit list of who within the organization is authorized to approve cash transfers. This list should include each person's stated limits. Furthermore, requiring dual signatures can be an effective control.

Financing. As discussed in Chapter 4, many of the hedge fund crises of the fall of 1998 were a result of inflexible financing arrangements. Much has been learned since then. Leverage has become something to be respected and managed. Funds have put in place long-term, revolving, and evergreen financing to provide greater flexibility. This generally comes at some cost, but the cost is small relative to the exposure of a run on the bank.

Counterparty credit risk. Counterparty credit risk is the credit exposure a fund has to the issuers of over-the-counter (OTC) instruments. As many of these arrangements are notionally funded—for example, swaps—the ultimate credit exposure can become significantly greater than the price originally paid or today's mark-to-market valuations. Therefore, the fund must be concerned about counterparty credit risk not only based on today's exposure but also based on the potential exposure the fund could have in the future. Some of the questions that should be asked include: Has the fund managed its counterparty credit risk? Has the risk been spread among a reasonable number of counterparties? Does the fund periodically set down and establish counterparty exposure targets? Is the actual allocation being monitored on a routine basis? Does the fund collect margin owed to it on a timely basis?

Valuation. Valuation is discussed in detail in Chapter 13. Suffice it to say, there is significant valuation flexibility in many hedge funds. Some funds achieve flexibility through intent and others by way of limited price discovery of illiquid securities.

Investment guidelines. As discussed in Chapter 8, the line between nimbleness and style drift is not well defined. Investors are often seeking hedge funds that can "think outside of the box." In contrast, traditional money managers typically have very specific guidelines controlling what instruments they can hold and against what benchmark they will be measured. In addition, constraints on concentrations, position size, and the like are frequently specified. Hedge funds should make a conscious decision about how disciplined they want to be in formalizing these parameters.

Although non-market risks unfortunately are very real and need to be addressed, the management of them is very different from that of market risks. Market risk management generally requires the probabilistic balancing of risk and return. It is a statistically based science. In contrast, the objective in managing non-market risk is to minimize or eliminate the risk. It is not a role of efficiently balancing these risks, but rather, a more binary role of controlling.

Although operational risk has become an important focus of risk management organizations in major capital market firms, the role of the risk management function is to statistically quantify the expected exposures by statistically combining the probability of a variety of potential events with the probable loss in the case of such an event. It is the role of the internal audit or compliance group to ensure that the procedures are in place and are followed to actually minimize the likelihood of such an event. This is often undertaken from an operational, finance, or systems/process background.

It can be argued that the skills and personality required for the balancing function and those required for the control function are significantly different and that the person evaluating the management of market risk, as discussed in Chapter 15, and the person evaluating operational, credit, and other non-market risk should be very different. In large organizations these functions generally reside in two separate groups, but in hedge funds they may have to be combined. It is important to understand the difference and explicitly make sure that each role is being appropriately performed.

Notes

[1]Published by Christopher Kundro & Stuart Feffer (Partners), The Capital Markets Company Ltd (Capco), January 2003.

CHAPTER 10

Constructing a Fund

Webster's Dictionary defines "hedge fund" as "an open-end investment company organized as a limited partnership and using high-risk *speculative* methods to obtain large profits." The dictionary separately describes "hedge" as "to enter a transaction intended to *protect* against financial loss through a complementary price movement." How can one reconcile the apparently conflicting concepts of "speculation" and "protection" in hedge funds?

The unfortunate answer is that there is no such thing as "a" hedge fund, so the concepts cannot be reconciled. If you profile the world of private investments, approximately 97 percent of funds are invested in equities, bonds, or cash equivalents (see **Figure 10.1**).

The balance is invested in what is called "alternative assets," with the lion's share of this being hedge funds. However, there is no single investment that is a "hedge fund" just as there is no single object that is "miscellaneous." From a

FIGURE 10.1 **Distribution of Assets—Private Pension Funds**

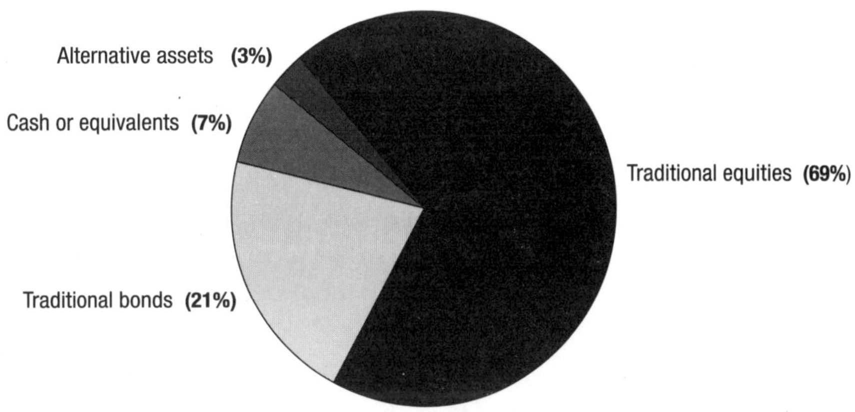

Source: Federal Reserve Statistical Release, September 2003

strategy or style viewpoint, hedge funds are the miscellaneous category of the investment world. Recognizing them as the catchall, the equivalent of the bottom of the kitchen sink, however, does not detract from the value of the many strategies that people lump under the name "hedge fund." (Think of the fine silverware and precious rings that can often be found in the drain.)

Now that we have concluded that hedge funds per se do not exist, we can explore the conflicting definitions of "hedging" above. This conflict is a direct result of the fact that hedge funds are not a homogeneous grouping. This extremely diverse set of financial strategies can range from extremely low-risk strategies that use hedging protectively to create arbitrage opportunities to extremely high-risk aggressive strategies that are highly speculative. Consider arbitrage. Again according to Noah Webster, or his disciples, arbitrage is "a simultaneous sale of a security or commodity in different markets to profit from unequal prices." This definition parallels that of hedge above, except an arbitrage results in a "profit" whereas a "hedge" results in "protection."

The implied assumption of arbitrage is that it is a hedge that has locked in or protected a profit. The term "riskless arbitrage" is sometimes used. However, this is a misnomer. Both definitions state that the hedge normally represents a sale of complementary securities in different markets. Such a sale is generally not "riskless" because the basis risk, the potential movement of one market relative to the other, has not been eliminated. For example, in the fall of 1998, mortgage-backed securities (MBS) arbitrage funds were shocked when the MBS derivatives in which they were investing disconnected from the Treasuries they were using to hedge interest rates. This basis risk resulted in both the MBS positions and the hedges generating losses.

Now let's explore how to determine whether an investment is speculative or protective. First of all, an individual security is neither speculative nor protective. What defines the level of risk is how multiple securities are put together in a portfolio. For example, selling a "naked" call is often considered one of the most risky strategies. However, selling a "covered" call, selling a call when one is long the underlying security, actually represents a form of risk reduction. Is whether a call is covered or naked an attribute of the security? No! It is an attribute of the construction. One cannot determine if a call is speculative or protective without knowing how it fits into the construction.

Similarly, a portfolio with a $10 million gross exposure consisting of a $5 million long position in 2-year Treasuries and a $5 million short position in 1-year Treasuries is significantly less speculative than a $1 million long investment in

30-year Treasuries (despite the fact that the first portfolio has financing leverage ten times that of the second). Again, risk is driven by portfolio construction and not the inherent risk of individual securities.

This chapter identifies the key sources of hedge fund value creation: construction techniques that can be applied in hedge funds that cannot easily be accomplished in traditional portfolios. It then presents how these levers are applied for a broad range of hedge fund strategies. Early in the book I mention that other risk books on hedge funds discuss each strategy as an independent silo. Even in this chapter, in which are defined the source of return of each hedge fund style, I resist the tendency to discuss hedge funds as silos. I present a comprehensive matrix of value creation levers across all strategies. Finally, I take a second trip around the block and expand on each of these value creation levers, providing examples and texture.

Value Creation Levers

Here are the key value creation levers that hedge funds can use that are generally not available to traditional, long-only managers:

Shorting. Hedge funds can short a security that they do not own. This is accomplished by borrowing the security, committing to a fixed financing fee, and selling the borrowed security in the open market. Shorts can be either speculative or hedging. For example, if you already have holdings in Citibank, a short position in Chase will significantly reduce the risk of the portfolio (the market and secondary risks will be hedged out, leaving only the idiosyncratic exposure). However, if you are long five-year Treasuries and you add a short Cisco holding, the portfolio will become significantly riskier.

Illiquid securities. Hedge funds are not required to be marked to market on a daily basis, as mutual funds are. Therefore, hedge funds can invest in significantly less liquid securities than traditional investments. This permits hedge funds to invest in such things as odd-lot asset-backed securities, mortgage derivatives, distressed debt, and private placements. Hedge funds are seeking to be appropriately, if not richly, compensated for their exposure to illiquid instruments.

Leverage. Hedge funds can take on a variety of different types of leverage. These are discussed in detail in Chapter 3. In particular, hedge funds permit investments in futures, swaps, and options, all levered instruments.

Convexity. Hedge funds are able to take exposures to risk in nonsymmetrical ways. This is achieved through the use of options (including swaptions) and

FIGURE 10.2 How Hedge Funds Apply Value Creation Levers

			SHORT	ILLIQUID	LEVERAGE	CONVEXITY	NIMBLENESS
EQUITY	Directional	Private/Restricted Equity	Small	Significant	Small	Small	Small
		Emerging Market Equity	Relevant	Small	Small	Small	Relevant
		Equity Long/Short	Significant	Small	Small	Small	Relevant
		Equity Short-Biased	Significant	Small	Small	Small	Relevant
		Market Timers	Significant	Small	Small	Small	Significant
	Volatility	Equity Volatility	Relevant	Small	Relevant	Significant	Small
	Relative Value	Equity Market Neutral	Significant	Small	Relevant	Small	Relevant
		Statistical Arbitrage	Significant	Significant	Significant	Small	Relevant
	Event	Merger Arbitrage	Significant	Small	Small	Small	Relevant
		Event-Driven	Significant	Small	Small	Small	Relevant
		Distressed Debt	Relevant	Significant	Small	Small	Relevant
		Capital Structure Arb	Significant	Relevant	Small	Small	Relevant
	Volatility	Convertible Arbitrage	Significant	Small	Small	Relevant	Significant
FIXED-INCOME		Fixed-Income Volatility	Relevant	Small	Relevant	Significant	Small
	Carry/Directional	ABS	Relevant	Significant	Significant	Small	Small
		MBS Derivatives	Relevant	Significant	Significant	Small	Small
		CDOs	Relevant	Significant	Relevant	Small	Small
		High-Yield	Relevant	Relevant	Significant	Small	Small
		Emerging Market Debt	Relevant	Small	Relevant	Small	Small
		Whole Loan	Small	Significant	Small	Small	Small
		Receivables/Factoring	Small	Significant	Small	Small	Significant
	Relative Value	Fixed-Income Rel Value	Significant	Small	Small	Small	Significant
		Credit Rel Value	Significant	Small	Small	Small	Significant
MULTI-ASSET	Macro	Macro	Significant	Small	Relevant	Relevant	Significant
	CTAs	Systematic CTAs	Significant	Small	Significant	Significant	Significant
		Discretionary CTAs	Significant	Small	Significant	Small	Significant

☐ Small factor ▒ Relevant factor ■ Significant factor

through dynamic trading strategies that create synthetic options (see Chapter 1).

Nimbleness. Hedge funds are often relatively small and consequently nimble market players. This permits them to pursue strategies that larger traditional money managers cannot pursue. It can also create a natural maximum limit to assets under management (AUM). These limits and the capacity constraints they create are major issues in the industry (see Chapter 4).

Various hedge fund strategies take advantage of different value creation levers, as shown in **Figure 10.2**.

Shorting

Most hedge fund strategies take advantage of a hedge fund's ability to short securities. The exceptions to this are long-oriented strategies such as distressed debt (generally a long-biased strategy), venture capital/restricted stocks, and long-biased volatility funds. Shorting is used to hedge other positions, to express a perspective on an overvalued asset, and to target relative misvaluations. Each application is discussed in turn.

Hedging

Of the vast majority of hedge funds that short securities, some are effectively long-oriented strategies that short securities to hedge out market exposures, including interest rate, credit, and equity exposures. Among such strategies are the following:

- Mortgage-backed securities (MBS)
- Asset-backed securities (ABS)
- Convertible arbitrage

As previously noted, even what appear to be "perfect" hedges are generally subject to basis risk. The best example is that of hedging MBS, both collateral and derivatives. Mortgage prepayment speeds are highly sensitive to ambient interest rates. MBS funds attempt to hedge out interest rates by modelling this relationship. However, the hedge is only as good as the model. Therefore, what looks like a perfect hedge can result in losses if the market behavior of the hedging instruments disconnects from that of the long position, as happened in the mortgage-backed crises of 1994 and 1998.

Overvalued Positions

Hedge funds often short individual positions that are fundamentally overvalued (as they go long positions that are fundamentally undervalued). One cannot simply assume, however, that shorting an overvalued security is the mirror image of going long an undervalued security. For example, value investors take long interests in stocks that are fundamentally quality companies going through a period of stress in the belief that the market has overreacted and that the stocks are "cheap." Value investors are generally willing to hold a position for a number of years, anticipating that the stock will be upwardly revalued when the earnings per share revert to normal levels.

Such logic does not automatically work for the mirror strategy of shorting a stock that is expensive based on long-term fundamentals. The reason is that investors in "growth" stocks, the opposite of value investors, knowingly pay a premium for long-term growth. However, proving that the company will fall short of the market's long-term expectations of growth can take dramatically longer than does demonstrating profit expansion in value stocks. Value is a strategy that will prove or disprove itself in a relatively short period of time, depending on whether the turnaround occurs. Growth is a strategy that will prove or disprove itself only over a long period of time. Growth does not have the near-term catalyst equivalent to that of improved earnings for value. Consequently, a value-oriented investor, as many hedge fund investors are, cannot simply use the mirror strategy for shorting.

Another issue to consider in long/short funds is that the strategy expressed be consistent with the fundamental market demand and supply balances. For example, an estimated 70-plus percent of new convertible issues are sold into the hedge fund industry. This raises a concern about why hedge funds value these securities more highly than do other investors. The unfavorable response is that hedge funds are demonstrating a "herd" mentality, and when sentiment changes there could be tremendous overhang and the price of these securities could drop precipitously. (As hedge funds have been consuming the majority of new convertible issues for several years the stock of these bonds is great, and a change in sentiment may not only change the demand for new issues, but it could result in much of this stock returning to the market.) This is what happened to high-yield bonds when Drexel Burnham and the Resolution Trust Corporation (RTC) attempted to liquidate large quantities of high-yield bonds over a short period of time in the late 1980s.

There are a couple of potentially favorable responses to the question of why the majority of new convertible issues are going to hedge funds:

- The traditional investors in convertible arbitrage are long-only convertible investors who do not understand the relative pricing relationship of these bonds with the stocks of the same company. Therefore, they cannot recognize or take advantage of this misvaluation.

- Convertible bonds are relatively long maturity debt, and the companies that issue them are willing to sacrifice long-term equity dilution (the result of the embedded option being in the money at maturity) for short-term reduced interest rates and consequently increased reported profits.

Similarly, there are securities that are surplus, such as WAC IOs (weighted average coupon interest only mortgage-backed derivatives) and odd-lot ABS, that traditional funds cannot purchase because they are illiquid but that hedge funds can acquire at a discount. The overall conclusion is that the portfolio manager should be aware of the supply-demand balance of various security types and think through how hedge funds can add value or be damaged in each type.

Relative Misvaluations

Many hedge funds short securities to target relative value opportunities. These funds generally target small misvaluations across securities. Relative value strategies are frequently implemented with significant leverage to amplify these relatively small misvaluations. For example, fixed-income relative value funds can target:

- ***Yield curve plays***—These can be bigger themes such as anticipated twisting (flattening or steepening) or butterflying (flexing) of the curve. They can also be micro plays such as the relative movement of the 18-year to 17-year Treasury.
- ***Basis plays***—These can be bigger themes such as the relative movement of British pound–based versus euro-based interest rates, or they can be micro plays such as the relative movement of bond futures to cash bonds.

Funds are often considered relative value when they are not. For example, merger arbitrage funds are generally considered to be relative value. However, with rare exception, these funds tend to go long the acquired company and short the acquiring company in anticipation that the deal will be completed and today's discount will ultimately be captured as gains. Such a consistent bias demonstrates that the fund is actually a fund with a directional bet on deals closing rather than a relative value fund. In a true relative value fund, the manager should logically be equally willing to bet in either direction.

Returns of relative value strategies are typically significantly lower, but they can often be justified by the significantly lower risk. For example, **Figure 10.3** shows the return and risk characteristics of equity long/short funds and equity market-neutral funds since January 1995.

FIGURE 10.3 **Returns and Risk of Equity Long/Short and Market-Neutral Funds since January 1995**

INDEX	COMPOUND ANNUAL RETURN	ANNUALIZED STANDARD DEVIATION	SHARPE RATIO
Equity Long/Short[1]	16.6%	10.1%	1.27
Equity Market-Neutral[2]	9.7%	3.4%	1.68
S&P 500	10.5%	15.1%	0.43

1. Hedge Fund Research (HFR) Equity Hedge Index
2. Hedge Fund Research (HFR) Equity Market Neutral Index

Although the compound annual return of equity long/short funds was dramatically greater than that of equity market-neutral funds, the risk-adjusted return, measured by the Sharpe ratio, was materially worse.

In other relative value strategies, a fund explicitly targets the relationship between related securities:

- Merger arbitrage (securities related through marriage)
- Capital structure arbitrage (securities related through birth)
- Option arbitrage

Illiquid Securities

Many of the hedge fund strategies are based on purchasing comparatively illiquid securities (those that would typically not be held by a traditional manager). The risks of holding illiquid instruments are discussed in detail in Chapter 4. Much of the return generation results from the market's willingness to compensate investors for accepting illiquid investments.

A number of these are long-biased strategies in relatively illiquid markets in which one is looking to generate returns through appreciation:

- Private/restricted equities
- Emerging market equity
- Distressed debt

These are all effectively equity strategies with significant price movements around key "events." However, distressed debt, which retains the "debt" label, trades most like a small-cap stock in which the vast majority of risk is idiosyncratic (this is partially because when the company is recapitalized the debt is likely to be converted to equity).

There are a variety of illiquid fixed-income instruments that generally earn high yields. A significant amount of the return from these strategies comes from "carry." Examples include the following:

- MBS derivatives (by-products of the collateralized mortgage obligation, or CMO, machine)
- Odd-lot ABS
- Whole loans
- Factoring
- Emerging market debt
- High yield

Much of the MBS derivatives (generally IOs) and the ABS (generally odd-lots) are surplus "by-products" of the core financial markets and trade at a discount to cash flows if one is willing to hold them until maturity and accept the illiquidity. For example, WAC IOs are a by-product of the CMO machine (the process of converting mortgages to CMOs selling at par) as mortgage bankers seek to get mortgages off their books.

Because of the general illiquidity of these instruments, these strategies are extremely difficult to value precisely (see Chapter 13). Consequently, these funds typically report returns that understate volatility. Although these are good strategies that offer valuable diversification, investors should not be seduced into these strategies because of their superior "reported" Sharpe ratios. Furthermore, as this chapter discusses later, utilizing risk measures that are generated based on historical simulations of current portfolios avoids these issues, as they are not subject to the same "discretion" as are those based on historical returns.

Leverage

The primary focus in constructing a fund is to manage "construction leverage." In general, hedge funds achieve an appropriate level of risk leverage, the overall risk of the portfolio, by offsetting very low construction leverage with relatively high financial leverage (the combination of borrowing leverage, option leverage, and notional funding leverage). For example, fixed-income relative arbitrage funds frequently target very micro anomalies in the yield curve or across basis. Funds magnify these micro exposures through financing leverage to achieve the appropriate risk-reward profile.

Funds must remember that although the combination of low construction leverage and high financial leverage may result in appropriate aggregate leverage, it does result in the risk of a "run on the bank" (especially with less liquid securities) if the fund sustains a significant loss or redemption. Even if the fund has adequate equity capital to cover the loss, it must be able to effectively monetize this equity when required. Therefore, funds utilizing high financial leverage must have explicit minimum cash targets and flexible financing. Funds also need an explicit escape plan, as discussed in Chapter 4.

Convexity

Unlike traditional managers, hedge fund managers actively play in options. Many hedge fund managers utilize options to mitigate or enhance risks. They reduce risk by selling covered puts or calls or by buying naked puts or calls. They increase risk by selling naked puts or calls or buying covered puts or calls. Investors should be careful to fully understand funds that are shorting naked options. The issue with these is that they generally have a return pattern that includes a significant number of relatively small gains intermingled with a small number of relatively large losses. This is a direct result of the convexity of options. However, because the frequency of small gains is significantly larger than that of large losses (the losses could be as infrequent as every four or five years), an unknowing investor could be seduced by the steady gains and may be surprised when the offsetting large loss occurs.

There are a relatively small number of managers who primarily trade volatility. As discussed, some of these are executing relative value strategies involving options. Most of these volatility funds follow a "long volatility" strategy. This is effectively "buying insurance." As with any insurance policy, it is worth buying if it avoids risks that you do not want to be exposed to; however, you should not anticipate generating a positive return in the long run with such a strategy. As with other insurance policies, on average the premium paid is greater than the expected payout.

As Chapter 1 discusses, hedge funds can create synthetic options by implementing trading strategies that are not symmetric. This introduces convexity in the returns of funds even if the funds are not directly utilizing instruments with optionality. For example, trend-following CTAs (commodity trading advisers) employ "systems" to trade that result in a high level of correlation across managers and a high level of convexity in their returns.

Nimbleness

Although nimbleness is a key component of almost all hedge fund strategies, it is particularly critical to some. This facility permits hedge fund managers to target a significantly different set of risks than those of traditional managers. You may rightfully ask, what is the barrier that keeps traditional money managers from being nimble? The answer is size. The assets under management of most institutional traditional managers are in excess of $1 billion. In contrast, significantly less than 1 percent of all hedge funds have AUM exceeding this level. In fact, the AUM of the vast majority of hedge funds are less than $50 million. This small scale permits hedge funds to nimbly move into and out of positions.

The size factor raises a significant issue: How can hedge funds sustain the very high fixed cost of an investment complex with AUM that are dramatically lower than that of their more traditional brethren? The answer is through a much richer fee structure. The average long-only equity manager earns 50 to 100 basis points of assets under management (fixed-income managers earn somewhat less). In comparison, the typical hedge fund manager earns management fees of between 1.5 percent and 2 percent and performance fees of 20 percent. Assuming an annual gross return of 10 percent (significantly lower than the long-term historical return of hedge funds) the manager will earn between 3.5 percent and 4 percent annually. This is four to seven times the fee realization of traditional managers, enabling the hedge fund manager to operate with significantly lower AUM. This is the deal that investors have cut with hedge funds.

Hedge fund strategies that require a particularly high level of nimbleness are statistical arbitrage, short-term managed futures, and market timers.

Let's use equity-based managers to further demonstrate the need for nimbleness. Even within those funds that focus on the highly liquid equity markets, there is a spectrum of styles, requiring varying levels of nimbleness. These styles involve the following:

Fundamental equity long/short. At the bottom of the ladder are the fundamental long/short funds. These managers do fundamental research on companies, go long companies they like and short companies they do not like, and generally take a position they will maintain an average of six to eighteen months.

Analytical equity long/short. On the next step up the nimbleness ladder are the analytically driven fundamental managers. These managers generally use a model (such as principal components analysis and neural networks) to look for misvaluations based on fundamental data. They typically hold positions for one to two months.

Statistical arbitrage. At the penultimate step of the ladder are the statistical arbitrage funds. These funds typically target opportunities to provide liquidity when large buyers or sellers (generally major traditional money managers) are seeking to trade. They then hold the positions for several days to earn a return as the price reverts when the major buyer or seller ceases his market activities.

Day traders. At the top of the ladder are the ephemeral day traders. They typically trade intra-day, generally exiting by the market close (day traders often trade in the futures market).

Establishing a Basis in which to View the Construction

In the traditional long-only world, all instruments are cash instruments, so you can simply view a portfolio as a "pie" that adds up to 100 percent of equity capital. Viewing portfolio constructions that include short positions, options, notional funding, and the like is significantly more complicated. Portfolio managers must often have the following multiple views of their portfolios, ranging through the following forms:

Units. These are the "natural" units in which each instrument is reported:

- Stocks are reported in shares
- Bonds are reported in face value
- Futures, options, and warrants are reported in contracts
- OTC derivatives are reported in notional value

Invested capital. For hedge funds that invest only in cash instruments (including options), the construction can simply be viewed as the value of each position (the invested capital) divided by the equity capital. However, futures and swaps are not cash funded. Funds must always put up margin with the exchange when they buy or sell futures. The invested capital required in trading futures is the exchange-established "initial margin." Swaps are traded in the OTC markets and generally have no market value at the time of issue. The invested capital related to a swap as time progresses is the mark to market value of the swap.

Cash equivalent. The cash-equivalent view of the portfolio converts all positions to their equivalent cash position size. For futures and forwards this is the notional value of the contract. For exchange-traded options this is the delta equivalent of the underlying security. For OTC derivatives (swaps, swaptions, caps, floors), this is the notional value.

Risk equivalent. This view presents the construction in risk-equivalent units. A variety of different views of risk can be useful:

- Exposure to primary market risks (beta to S&P, duration)
- Marginal standard deviation (tracking error)
- Marginal drawdown (underperformance)
- Marginal Value at Risk (relative VaR)

Balancing Risk and Return

The objective in constructing a fund is balancing risk and return. As the size of a position increases, the following risks increase:

- Concentration risk
- Correlation to the portfolio

Consequently, increased exposures to a position result in increased marginal risk. The challenge in constructing a portfolio is to balance returns with increasing risk. However, as discussed in Chapter 5, although risk (both historical volatility and correlation) tends to repeat, returns tend not to repeat. Therefore, the objective is to meld historical risk with prospective returns as a basis of constructing a "risk-efficient" portfolio. There are two ways to accomplish this:

Enhancing risk-adjusted returns. This is achieved by iteratively modifying the portfolio, always trying to enhance the risk-adjusted return of the resulting portfolio. Such modification is typically done on an incremental or "what-if" basis. It is achieved by identifying opportunities that will enhance the risk-adjusted return of the overall portfolio and increasing these positions. Remember that incremental amounts of the same position will have diminishing improvements in the overall portfolio as increasing the concentration of a position increases risk. As attractive opportunities are identified, these positions should replace holdings in positions that have an unattractive marginal risk-adjusted return profile.

Using an optimizer. An optimizer is a tool that lets you directly calculate the construction of a portfolio that maximizes the risk-adjusted returns. Although the concept is highly appealing, practical experience has shown that real-world limitations (data and position size constraints) result in this methodology ultimately being very similar to the incremental approach, but using a much more cumbersome methodology.

ONE LAST CONSIDERATION in constructing a portfolio is how the portfolio is expected to evolve over time. The next chapter, "Performance Attribution," discusses a retrospective review of how returns were generated. It is in constructing today's portfolio that a portfolio manager can control the results of tomorrow's post mortem. How much of the risk and return do you seek to achieve through idiosyncratic exposures? With respect to risk-factor sensitivities (both market and secondary) do you seek to:

- Be consistently neutral?
- Actively and opportunistically move between long and short exposures?
- Be consistently long- or short-biased?

CHAPTER 11

Performance Attribution

Although this chapter is the shortest in the book, the length is not indicative of the importance of performance attribution. Performance attribution is a critical process. It is the report card that explains to both the fund managers and to investors how the fund has earned its return. Have returns been generated by passive strategies, such as being long interest rates as rates have declined or being long tech during the Internet bubble? Or has alpha been generated by active strategies through nimble market timing, deft stock picking, or targeted pairs trading?

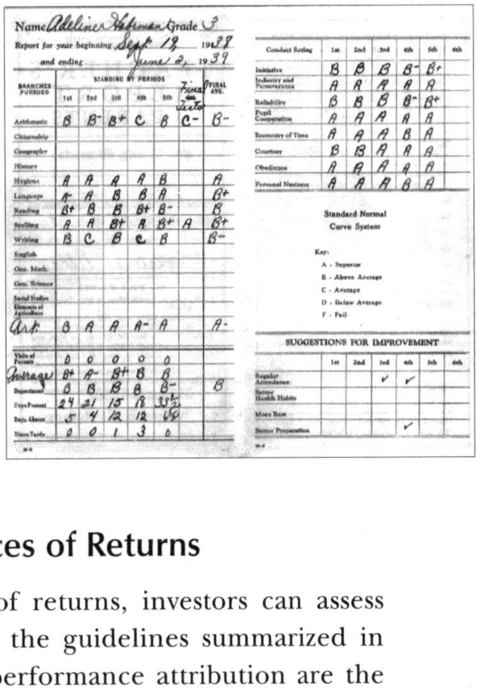

Investors should value varying sources of returns significantly differently. It can be insightful to separately perform this attribution for the long positions and short positions. The risk-factor framework is the basis of decomposing (disaggregating) returns to their underlying sources.

Assessing Primary Sources of Returns

In attributing performance to its sources of returns, investors can assess the attractiveness of the returns, based on the guidelines summarized in **Figure 11.1**. The sources to examine in a performance attribution are the following:

Market bias—a tendency or propensity toward market exposure. The first source of return is from a bias to a market exposure (such as a consistent long exposure to the S&P). Most investors already have exposure to the core markets through their traditional investments so that these are not diversifying exposures. Furthermore, investors can achieve exposure to the

FIGURE 11.1 **Attractiveness of Varying Sources of Hedge Fund Return**

SOURCE OF RETURN	BIAS	ALPHA
Market	Very Unattractive	Attractive
Secondary	Unattractive	Attractive
Idiosyncratic	N/A	Very Attractive

core markets for extremely low fees (for example, SPDRs, a type of exchange-traded fund, have fees of approximately 10 basis points). Therefore, hedge fund returns resulting from consistent market biases are considered "very unattractive."

Market alpha—active management of market exposure. The second source of return to consider in a performance attribution is from actively managing the exposure to market risks. Although a fund that maintains a consistent bias to the core markets is not attractive, a fund that can generate alpha by actively managing the market exposure—that is, actively moving between long or short market exposures to capture market opportunities—is "attractive."

Secondary bias—a tendency or propensity toward secondary risk exposures. The third source of return to consider is that resulting from a bias to secondary risks, for example, a consistent value bias in equities or a consistent bias to yield curve steepening. Although it is more difficult to gain exposure to secondary risks through traditional investments and most investors are not long-biased these exposures through their traditional investments (as with small cap or value SPDRs, for example), investors can achieve exposure to secondary risks for fees significantly lower than those of hedge funds. Therefore, hedge fund returns from consistent secondary risk factor biases are "unattractive."

Secondary alpha—active management of secondary risk exposures. The fourth source of return you need to examine in a performance attribution is that which results from actively managing the exposure to secondary risks. Although a fund that maintains a consistent bias to secondary risks is not attractive, a fund that can generate alpha by actively managing the exposure to secondary risks—that is, actively moving between long or short secondary risk exposures to capture market opportunities—is "attractive."

Idiosyncratic alpha—active management of so-called idiosyncratic exposure. The fifth source of return to consider is that resulting from idiosyncratic exposures. Idiosyncratic risks are the most desirable exposures that investors should be seeking to gain through their hedge fund investments. Idiosyncratic exposures come from stock picking, relative value funds, or statistical arbitrage. Generating alpha through idiosyncratic risk is "very attractive."

Other Factors in Performance Attribution

In addition to the principal sources of returns discussed above, investors also need to consider the following ancillary aspects of performance attribution.

Asymmetric trading. A sixth source of return is a result of an asymmetric trading strategy, as discussed in Chapter 1. Such a strategy is the cause of the option-like (convex) behavior of many hedge funds, even those that do not directly employ options.

Net cash. Funds earn interest on cash and pay interest on borrowings.

Fees. Investors should not be averse to fees. Instead investors should seek to pay fees commensurate with the value added by the manager. The performance attribution is the key input to assessing the quality of the returns the manager has generated.

IT IS INTERESTING that generating returns through exposure to market and secondary risks is not inherently attractive or unattractive. The key issue is whether the returns were achieved through a passive strategy (for example, being long-biased when the market happened to be rising) or through active strategies (alpha). Remember, however, as was noted in Chapter 8, only 8 percent of those managers who were long-biased during the tech bubble became short-biased after it burst. The broad conclusion of the related analysis was that markets are often cyclical and that investors who do not understand the source of a manager's performance are at significant risk of experiencing inferior performance when the market turns. Managers who have demonstrated biases during favorable markets will claim they will nimbly respond to sea changes in the market—however, empirical evidence suggests otherwise.

CHAPTER 12

Risk Budgeting

Risk budgeting is a management process that many large institutional investors are adopting. Much of the philosophy and discipline of risk budgeting can be extremely useful for hedge funds, although practiced on a less formal basis than by large institutions. Understanding what risk budgeting is will prepare hedge funds to communicate with large institutional clients in a language they understand.

The goal of risk budgeting is clear: To "spend" a unit of risk efficiently so as to maximize return. However, there is no clear methodology, and no accepted definition. Ask ten "experts" to define risk budgeting and you will get ten—or maybe eleven—answers. This chapter uses an analogy familiar to most people—financial budgeting in a corporation—to explain the process of risk budgeting.

Risk Budgeting Self-Assessment

Before attempting to define risk budgeting, let's begin with a simple self-assessment:

1 ***Do you asset allocate?*** Do you invest in multiple asset classes, subclasses, and styles?
2 ***Do you manage your investment program?*** Do you perform multiple investment tasks? Institute controls? Establish investment policy statements and guidelines for outside managers? Compensate staff and outside managers? Test control environments?
3 ***Do you measure your returns?*** Do you use absolute returns? Relative measures of return? Risk-adjusted measures of return?
4 ***Do you know your risks?*** Do you measure standard deviation? VaR? Tracking error? Duration? DV01, Greeks, sector credit/volatility exposures, or any of the other scores of risk measures?

Clearly, answering yes to any of the above questions means that you are trying to control risk and return. So, given the goal of "spending" risk efficiently, you are risk budgeting if you answered yes to any of the above questions.

Of course, if you didn't answer yes to at least one of those questions, you probably don't deal with investments. The more appropriate question, then, is not whether you are performing risk budgeting, but rather, are you doing it at a level that enables you to achieve your goals? All investors perform risk budgeting; what varies is the level of:

- Formalization
- Systemization
- Consistency
- Integration
- Discipline

Definition of Risk Budgeting

With that in mind, let's attempt to define risk budgeting: Risk budgeting is following an informal or formal methodology to manage an investment program. This includes the full feedback loop that many organizations follow—establishing objectives, creating strategy and tactics, measuring, analyzing, reexamining objectives, retuning strategy and tactics, and so on—applied within an investment context.

Therefore, risk budgeting is not an absolute that one either does or does not do. Rather, risk budgeting is something virtually every investor does, at some level of formality. What level of formality is appropriate? There's no right answer to that question; it's a matter of style. The level of formality must be appropriate for your organization. What is true, however, is that knowledge of formal risk budgeting permits you to make a clear and conscious decision about what is the appropriate level of formality for your organization. You can then decide which aspects of risk budgeting to formalize and which you want to continue to manage on a less formal basis.

Formal Risk Budgeting

Risk budgeting methodologies are rapidly developing and evolving. Few managers have been performing formalized risk budgeting long enough to describe it absolutely and completely. Formal financial budgeting in a large corporation, on the other hand, is a significantly more mature process supported by highly evolved systems that, by analogy, can speak to the ultimate role of risk budgeting in an investment organization.

A Management Process, Not a Back-Office Tool

Formal financial budgeting in a large corporation is not just an accountant's back-office records but also a comprehensive and disciplined management process performed throughout the organization. The process begins with the annual budget—the development of a comprehensive plan that satisfies the overall entity's financial objectives. This ensures that the whole is at least equal to the sum of the parts, rather than, without a budget, a single part benefiting at the expense of the whole. The annual budget is not simply a set of financials but an integrated operating plan including new product launches, specific client retention/development plans, plans for capital projects, and the like. Progress against the overall budget is monitored on an ongoing basis so that variances are identified and analyzed, and corrective actions are taken. If the actual overall performance begins to deviate significantly from the plan, the plan is revised with specific and actionable steps taken to respond to shortfalls. In many companies, compensation is specifically linked to performance against the plan.

Similarly, formal risk budgeting is a disciplined management process, which integrates the full set of planning, executing, measuring, and compensating processes in an investment organization. **Figure 12.1** shows the risk budgeting process flow.

The first step in financial budgeting is to establish the objectives and strategies for the overall entity. So, too, with risk budgeting. For example, a pension

FIGURE 12.1 **Risk Budgeting Process Flow**

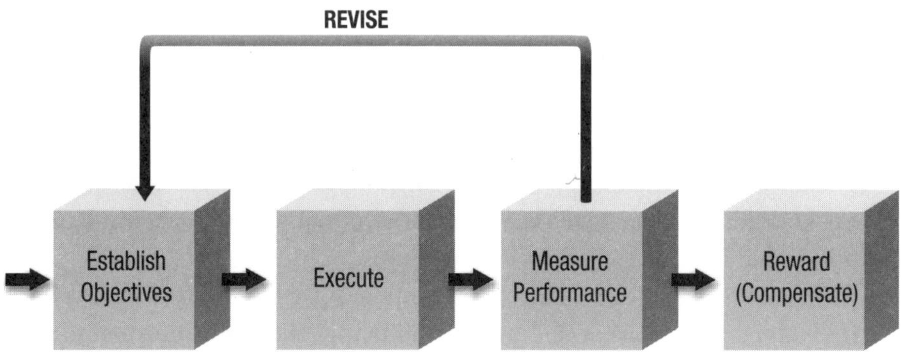

plan performs its asset-liability analysis and formulates an overarching strategy with respect to surplus growth and risk. This step includes the critical decisions of strategic asset allocation. For an investment manager, the decisions relate to the product: Relative or total return? Active or passive?

The second step in risk budgeting is to decide the tactics by which you will execute the strategy. For example, a defined benefit pension fund would decide: Which benchmarks to choose? Internal or external management? Passive or active? Core or alpha generator? Diverse managers or a smaller group of strategic relationships? Then its managers will move on to the ongoing details: How will we rebalance? Do we hedge currency exposure, and at what level? For an investment manager, the decisions are similar: How much sector over-/underweighting do I allow? What level of residual risk? Concentrated or diversified portfolio? Top-down or bottom-up?

The third step in risk budgeting is executing these strategies and tactics. This step includes the specific, day-to-day investment decisions. For a pension fund, it includes manager selection and allocation, due diligence, cash flow management, tactical allocation decisions, and so forth. For an investment manager, it includes selection, currency hedging, sector betting, security selection, risk control, cash reinvestment, and the like.

The fourth step in risk budgeting is measuring actual performance. This process combines performance measurement, accurately knowing the change in value of the portfolio, with performance attribution, knowing what caused the change in value of your portfolio. You want to perform performance attribution consistently with the way in which the organization initially analyzed risk in constructing the portfolio and in which risks were measured. For example, if an equity group is making a sector bet, it would be desirable for the sector definitions that portfolio management is using to be the same as those risk management and performance attribution are using. This consistency also enables the bets to be judged not just against the group's or sector's risk allocation but, crucially, against the overall entity's risk budget. In some cases, as we will see, this can be a distinguishing feature from traditional, asset allocation-based models that do not include formal risk budgeting.

The last step in risk budgeting is compensating based on performance against the budget. This process can range from being extremely informal to highly formalized, based on preestablished formulas or schedules. For example, within this process is compensating outside managers. They are almost always compensated based on a specifically defined schedule, the compensation increasing with a performance-based component. The concept of compensating on a basis of risk-adjusted returns is just emerging.

As a disciplined management process, financial budgeting is not an after-the-fact tattling on how a manager performed but a proactive methodology that enhances the performance of managers. Its causal modeling of the cost structures (for example, fixed/variable) supports operating management in evaluating alternate operating strategies and permits management to understand the causes of performance variance after the fact (for example, volume and spending variances). This has permitted the financial group to evolve from being the bean counters to providing advisory support as financial analysts. A parallel situation exists in risk budgeting. Implementing a comprehensive risk budgeting process aligns the goals of portfolio management and elevates the risk management function above the traditional role of risk cop to the higher, value-added position of risk strategist.

A Common Language

Financial budgeting in a large corporation represents a common language that is used across the organization. The most significant component of this is the adoption of a standard chart of accounts. This is the standard reporting structure that incorporates the profit and loss statement, the balance sheet, and the cash flow statement, and all the hierarchy of accounts within them. For example, throughout an organization, everybody uses the same account code to record the cost of auditing, making it possible to aggregate this expense and manage it uniformly.

Formal risk budgeting is similarly a shared language/framework (see **Figure 12.2**). This standardization permits all groups/staff within an organization to speak the same risk language. The most important component of this language/framework is a set of standard risk factors. This is equivalent to the chart of accounts (the specific accounts in the profit and loss statement, balance sheet, and cash flow statement) in a traditional business. The standard risk factors are a commonly accepted categorization of risks such as sectors, style factors (value/growth, momentum, capitalization), and beta for equities. Similarly, duration, yield curves, credit spreads, and prepayment functions are the common fixed-income risk factors. Volatilities and underlying relationships are the key risk factors in derivatives. (These risk categories are illustrative, and should not be considered comprehensive.) When investment management makes a bet on small-cap stocks, risk management should be able to identify the inherent risk

FIGURE 12.2 **Risk Reporting versus Traditional Chart of Accounts**

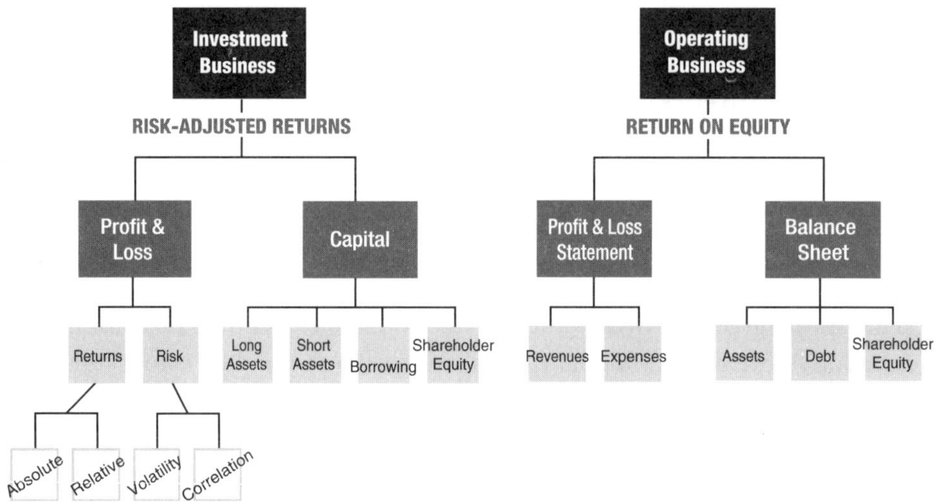

of this strategy and performance attribution should be able to report how this strategy played out. This is feasible only if all functions are calling this risk the same name and counting this risk the same way.

In fact, in financial budgeting, generally accepted accounting principles (GAAP) established standards for the top levels of the financial reporting hierarchies (twenty-five accounts in each of the P&L, balance sheet, and cash flow) to be utilized across companies. These are used in the annual reports and SEC reports (for example, the 10Q and 10K). This not only provides a shared language within a company but also makes one company's dialect similar enough to another company's that businesses can have high-level discussions across companies and outsiders, such as investors, can have a fundamental understanding of the financial well-being of the company. GAAP permits the financials of multiple companies to be compared and aggregated.

The second component of this common language is a common set of measurements. In a large corporation, employees learn the key metrics on which they will be judged. The metrics are often some measure of profitability, such as earnings before interest, taxes, depreciation, and amortization (EBITDA) and some measure of asset management such as asset turns. These measures are not always intuitive, but rather, are frequently selected because they capture financial causality and controllability. They isolate the performance for which the staff is accountable and can be consistently applied across all functions and all types of business—a good common denominator. For example, managers are typically measured on EBITDA and not operating profit because they cannot control interest, taxes, depreciation, and amortization.

Similarly, formal investment management has increasingly adopted Value at Risk (VaR) as a measure that can be consistently applied across all asset classes, geographies, and strategies, and which fully captures the risks that a portfolio manager can control. The widespread acceptance of VaR and the tying of VaR to the risk factors create a framework that consistently measures risk and links it to the sources of risk. For example, the challenge of developing a financial budget at General Electric (with global businesses including financial services, media, manufacturing, and industrial services) parallels that of developing a risk budget at CalPERS (California Public Employees' Retirement System) with global fixed income, equity, private equity, foreign currency exposure, hedge funds, and real estate investments.

A third component of this common language is a unifying framework to holistically combine all forms of financial leverage. Portfolio managers can create leverage through borrowing, long/short, selecting securities with high internal leverage—such as MBS (mortgage-backed security) inverse floaters or high beta equities—and employing optionality. There are scores of different definitions of leverage.

Managing Complex Causal Relationships

The challenge of combining nonlinear, nonadditive but interdependent activities in risk budgeting parallels that in financial budgeting. Risks increase nonlinearly as concentrations increase. This parallels the nonlinear relationships in a traditional company—for example, the relationships that demonstrate diminishing returns between revenues and an increased ad budget or the addition of a new salesperson.

There are interdependencies among multiple portfolios in an investment company that parallel the interdependencies among multiple businesses in a traditional company. For example, in a traditional business there are often intercompany sales between businesses. These must be coordinated in the development of budgets because the volume and price assumptions must be consistent. Similarly, there are correlations between portfolios in an investment business, and the diversification effect across portfolios must be fully understood to perform an efficient strategic asset allocation.

Furthermore, the components of the overall financial and risk budgets do not combine additively. In a financial budget, one can generally increase profits by extending accounts receivables (a balance sheet item), but the ultimate measure is the return on capital employed. Similarly, increasing the risk exposure of one manager who follows a strategy that is significantly diversified from the other strategies could improve the risk-return profile of the portfolio. (Hence the search for noncorrelated alpha from such sources as private equity or hedge funds.) Conversely, failing to understand the true risk factors driving the diversification effect can create significant problems. To give but one example, many investors discovered, in late 2000, that their private equity portfolios owned large quantities of technology and telecommunications public stock. This was the result of IPOs or takeovers of private companies by public companies that used stock as the currency of the acquisition. At the same time, technology and telecommunications companies represented significant portions of the traditional U.S. equity benchmarks. As a result, asset allocations based on static or historical correlations of asset classes materially underestimated the overall entity risk.

Finally, the ultimate goal in both financial and risk budgeting cannot be directly planned but is a result of many separate decisions. In a traditional business, if management has a return on equity (ROE) target, it cannot directly achieve this. It can achieve this only by sending the operating businesses back to the drawing board to revise their plans and the financial outlooks related to these plans until the aggregation of their results achieves this target. Similarly, one cannot directly establish an aggregate risk target. An optimal plan can be developed only by iteratively allocating assets and selecting the ultimate portfolio that satisfies management's overall targets. A financial budget separates the operating budget (operating profits and assets) from the capital structure budget (debt-to-equity ratio). Similarly, a risk budget separates the specific investment decisions from the portfolio leverage decisions.

A Comprehensive and Integrated Approach

Financial budgeting is a comprehensive methodology that is applied across the whole organization. The organization is divided into exhaustive and mutually exclusive units for which budgets are established. These units are structured in hierarchies, and units can be rolled up into groups, departments, functions, individual businesses, countries, and finally to the level of the corporation. Often,

FIGURE 12.3 **Formal Risk Budgeting Is Multidimensional**

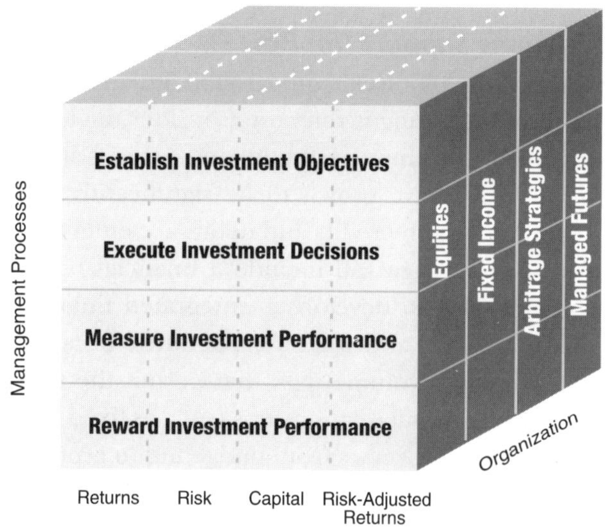

there is a reason to create multiple hierarchies so that all operations in a country can be rolled up geographically and business across countries can also be rolled up by line of business.

Similarly, formal risk budgeting is a comprehensive approach (see **Figure 12.3**). It should include all market dimensions of an investment business: all asset types, all measurements, and all geographies. It can include all internal dimensions of an investment business including all risk factors, all management processes, and all organizational units, and should include both internal and external management.

As with financial budgeting, the organization is structured into units against which these risks can be related. These organizational units will generally relate to specific asset types in an investment business (such as the MBS group or emerging market equities). However, this structure should be based on risk accountability and not asset type. For example, if the portfolio manager for European equities decides to invest in Alcoa as a more attractively valued proxy for Pechiney, the risk inherent in this decision should rest with this portfolio manager and not with a portfolio manager responsible for U.S. equities. (The key is for both portfolio managers to have a common language and common risk factors, so that senior management can aggregate the fund's total exposure to aluminum.)

Integrated Systems Support the Process

Formal risk budgeting requires sophisticated integrated systems. Again, the analogy to financial budgeting is relevant. Consider the role of a general ledger system in supporting the financial budgeting process in a large corporation. General ledger systems have grown to be significantly more than simply an accountant's tool into which credits and debits are entered. A standard, off-the-shelf general ledger package will include a financial budgeting package that permits the organization to develop an integrated financial plan. It provides extensive scenario analysis and what-if capabilities. It captures more than just financial data—including volume data that permit the system to forecast and analyze variances using causal relationships (such as fixed and variable cost structures). It supports these processes from budgeting to reporting of actual results, applying a standard chart of accounts across the full organizational structure (dividing the business into exhaustive and mutually exclusive groups). Finally, it provides a flexible and rich reporting capability (graphics, interfaces to other systems, exception reporting) that permits extensive aggregation and decomposition, reporting on actual performance compared to plan, and trending performance over time. Based on this diagnostic information, it supports the iterative process of revising and updating the budget to adjust for changes over time.

Effective formal risk budgeting requires a similarly comprehensive and integrated set of systems across the investment planning (asset allocation and portfolio construction), execution (risk management), and performance measurement (performance attribution) processes. This must be done using a standard set of risk factors that can be consistently measured, aggregated, and reported on.

How Formal Should Your Risk Management Be?

This question is equivalent to asking what is the right size of a glove. The answer is there is no one right size for everybody—it has to fit the individual. The appropriate style of risk budgeting for your organization is a function of the unique characteristics of your organization. Risk budgeting is not a one-size-fits-all solution. Indeed, it is probable that off-the-shelf, one-size-fits-all solutions may fit no one at all.

Let's return to the analogy of financial budgeting for a large corporation one last time to gain some insight into this question. Large, multinational companies utilize a highly formalized financial budgeting process. They have a disciplined calendar in which they typically begin the budget development process in late summer or early autumn for the fiscal year beginning the next January. In a large, decentralized company it is impossible to understand the aggregate result of the individual plans without a formalized approach. Large companies generally require managers to write monthly analyses of financial performance. They generally require comprehensive and formal revisions of the budget several times during the course of the year. They often have bonus pools directly linked to the organization's performance against the budget objectives.

Smaller businesses do the same things but dramatically less formally. Their plans are typically stored in the head of the owner of the business. This does not mean that they do not have plans—businesses without plans generally are not around too long. Every successful business owner has a goal for both revenues and expenses. Owners always have some sense of the drivers of profitability (such as capacity utilization, growth, and margins) and the sensitivity of the bottom line to them. The fact that these plans rest in a single head provides a comprehensive perspective of the potential aggregate results. Although smaller businesses do not have extensive management reporting, every successful smaller business owner knows how well the business is doing. Finally, smaller businesses may not have a profit-sharing plan that explicitly and formulaically links performance and compensation, but every employee understands that the better the year for the business, the better off he or she will be.

The right degree of formality in risk budgeting in an investment complex is similarly a function of the unique characteristics of the situation. On one extreme is a large plan sponsor that manages the majority of funds internally. Such an organization will frequently have a large number of relatively autonomous portfolio managers, sometimes more than fifty. These portfolios usually overlap, either because multiple managers have the same or similar mandates, or because mandates overlap (such as when the mid-cap value mandate and large-cap growth mandate overlap), or because portfolio managers select securities away from their benchmarks in an attempt to add value.

Managing a large group of autonomous managers requires an ability to understand the bets they are taking in advance and to measure their actual performance and compensate them appropriately after the fact. Furthermore, the fact that the mandates of these autonomous portfolio managers significantly overlap requires that the individual bets be aggregated to understand the overall exposure. This is particularly important to avoid a herd mentality when fads come and go. For example, by the end of 1999 some value managers had become "growth at a reasonable price" (GARP) managers and growth managers had become Internet gurus. Such simultaneous style drifts run the risk of capsizing the ship as all the passengers move to one side of the boat. In a large investment complex with many autonomous managers, it is impossible to understand the aggregate impact of the individual decisions without a formalized plan.

As with traditional businesses, smaller investment businesses can operate significantly less formally. In a situation where one or two analysts support a single portfolio manager, the portfolio manager holds a comprehensive understanding of the bets that the portfolio is taking in his or her head. The portfolio manager understands the theses of each of the analysts with respect to specific holdings and can ultimately evaluate the judgment of the analysts without a formalized measurement system. The fact that a portfolio manager can perform these tasks without a formalized system does not mean that he or she is not doing it on a disciplined basis. Just as in the case of a corporate manager looking at above- or below-budget performance, any investment management that does not understand the bets that are being taken and the ultimate results of these bets, and does not compensate staff on performance, will not be around for too long.

There is clearly a spectrum of sizes and cultures of organizations between these two examples. However, the need for more formalized risk budgeting is not only a function of the size of the organization. It is also a function of business complexity and interdependence between businesses. For example, a holding company that owns businesses without any linkages can manage these businesses independently. In contrast, a large corporation with a high level of interdependency among businesses (for example, when one business supplies another business with product or when they share customers and sell jointly) requires a highly integrated budgeting process.

This chapter set out to explore risk budgeting from two perspectives. The first perspective is the applicability of the process to hedge funds. Although I am a strong supporter of a disciplined risk budgeting process that does not necessarily translate to a formal process, I believe it nevertheless must be rigorous, integrated, and comprehensive. My experience has been that achieving this level of discipline in a large and complex organization does require formality. However, a smaller organization can achieve it on an informal basis.

The second perspective considers whether being able to speak the language of large institutional investors would assist hedge funds in marketing to and communicating with these investors. I believe that although speaking their language is not critical, as large institutions view hedge funds as "different," it is always advantageous to be bilingual.

IV

Part Four

Risk from the Investor's Viewpoint

CHAPTER 13

NAV/Return Reporting

The hedge fund industry is extraordinarily proprietary. The regulatory requirement that performance data be provided only to qualified investors (a person, company, or trust that has investments exceeding minimal levels established by the Securities and Exchange Commission for each class of investor) exacerbates the natural secretiveness of the industry. There is no other industry with as many participants (approximately 8,000 hedge funds) for which there is no organization broadly supporting the overall industry. Because of the extremely fragmented behavior of the industry and the lack of regulatory direction, the practices in the industry are very unstructured and inefficient. This chapter addresses the result of this on the reporting of net asset values (NAVs) of funds and/or returns (percentage change in NAVs). Current practices are:

- Undocumented
- Inefficient
- Incomplete
- Imprecise
- Misleading
- Masking risk
- Dressing up returns

Lack of Documentation

The Managed Funds Association (MFA) published a document titled "2003 Sound Practices for Hedge Fund Managers" in August 2003 in response to a review of hedge funds by the Securities and Exchange Commission (SEC) (see Chapter 16 for greater detail). It was intended to represent the voice of the hedge fund industry in the review process. A primary area of focus was related to valuation, as follows:

III. VALUATION POLICIES AND PROCEDURES

A Hedge Fund Manager should determine policies for the manner and frequency of computing net asset value, or "NAV," based upon GAAP (as defined below) and its management agreement with the Hedge Fund and seek to ensure valuation methods that are fair, consistent and verifiable, recognizing that investors may subscribe and redeem interests in the Hedge Fund in reliance on such values.

3.1 A Hedge Fund Manager's valuation methods should be fair, consistent and verifiable.

3.2 A Hedge Fund Manager's valuation policies and practices should incorporate the concept of "fair value."

3.3 A Hedge Fund Manager should establish pricing policies and practices that assure that NAV is marked at fair value.

3.4 A Hedge Fund Manager should choose reliable and recognized pricing sources to the extent possible.

3.5 A Hedge Fund Manager should establish practices for verifying the accuracy of prices obtained from data vendors, dealers or other sources.

3.6 A Hedge Fund Manager should establish policies for the frequency of determining a Hedge Fund's NAV both for purposes of disclosure and for internal risk monitoring purposes.

However, although the document established many proposed ground rules for the valuation of hedge funds, it did not address whether funds should make their valuation processes more transparent to investors.

In another section on the responsibilities to investors, the report suggested the funds should provide standardized performance, but again did not speak to the funds' potential responsibilities to inform investors of the process used to valued the portfolio:

II. RESPONSIBILITIES TO INVESTORS

2.3 A Hedge Fund Manager should prepare certain base-line standardized performance and other relevant information for distribution to the Hedge Fund's investors based upon relevant characteristics of the Hedge Fund.

In September 2003, the SEC published its Staff report, "Implications of the Growth of Hedge Funds, Staff Report to the United States Securities and Exchange Commission," which included the following conclusion:

> IV.C. THE COMMISSION SHOULD CONSIDER REQUIRING CERTAIN REGISTERED INVESTMENT COMPANIES TO FOLLOW BOARD ADOPTED VALUATION PROCEDURES
>
> We recommend that the Commission consider rulemaking to address our concerns about how registered investment companies, including registered FOHFs, that invest their assets in hedge funds value their portfolio holdings. As noted above, the Investment Company Act requires boards of directors to fair value in good faith any securities for which there are no readily available market quotations. Best practices would suggest that all registered investment companies adopt procedures under which they may satisfy this requirement...In making this recommendation, however, we note that the requirement under 2(a)(41) that a board of directors determine, in good faith, the fair value of securities for which there is no readily available market quotation reflects Congress's recognition that a board of directors must exercise its best judgment in valuing these types of securities. We do not recommend, therefore, that the Commission consider mandating the specific procedures that a fund must follow in valuing its assets.

As this book went to press, the industry was anticipating the majority of this report to be put into effect as of January 2005 (with the caveat that predicting regulators is even more difficult than forecasting the markets). The decision to not "mandate the specific procedures" reflects the reality that there is no single "correct" method and that there is "judgment in valuing these type of securities." The SEC staff report did not explicitly recommend that there should be more transparency to investors of the valuation process.

The problem is that there is neither a standard methodology nor a requirement to disclose the precise methodology used to value the portfolio. Beyond overt fraud (of which there have been some highly public cases) there are the "flexible" valuations. For example, one fund described its valuation practice as being "based on dealer quotes." The fund obtained a number of dealer quotes and selected the highest valuation. The fund was technically operating within the letter of its stated policy, although clearly not within a reasonable investor's understanding of the stated intent.

An investor should comprehensively understand the valuation process. How are management and performance fees calculated? When? What expenses can be charged to the fund? When? It is naïve to simply believe they will be done fairly. Even once you have pinned down the process of calculating a valuation, there is still significant flexibility in the valuation of the underlying holdings. This will be addressed later in this chapter.

Inefficiencies

Investors in hedge funds currently receive the following three flows of NAV information:

Monthly NAVs. Because purchases and redemptions occur monthly, the monthly NAV is a critical valuation. Although initial estimates are often available several days to a week after the end of the month, final numbers can take up to a month to appear. Furthermore, some funds have holdbacks pending an end-of-year audit.

Intramonth estimates. Funds generally provide weekly estimates. There is no consistency in the frequency, timing, and method of calculating these estimates. The majority are presented on a net basis, although many are reported on a gross basis. Weekly reporting as of Friday is the most common, but many report on other cycles. Furthermore, no consistency exists as to the cutoff time. Because only a single value is generally provided even when there are multiple series (because of different high-water marks based on when the shares were issued), estimates can be off significantly. For example, reporting returns based on a series for which no performance fee is being charged because it is below the high-water mark could misstate by up to 20 percent the returns of another series for which a high-water mark is calculated.

Performance histories. Several providers of hedge fund return histories, such as Hedge Fund Research (HFR) and Morgan Stanley Capital International (MSCI), distribute historical return statistics for approximately 1,700 of the estimated 8,000 hedge funds. These services provide the data on a nonselective basis—if the track record of a manager is distributed to one investor, it is available to all investors. Investors use these data to search for managers and as a basis of comparison for specific funds.

The majority of hedge funds, including most of the leading funds, do not participate in these databases. Beyond grouping funds into style buckets, these databases do not provide any causal information that explains the return behavior of the funds. The hedge fund industry has recognized that these style groupings and related indices do not meaningfully explain the behavior of specific funds. The core reason is that in the absolute return world of hedge funds, in contrast to the long-only world in which managers are evaluated on the tracking error to a benchmark, no gravitational force pulls hedge funds to behave like a style index.

Investors often devote significant effort to obtaining return data of funds in which they have invested. In particular, funds of funds require the approved month-end NAVs to calculate their own NAVs. Hedge fund database providers do not provide this on a detailed (by series) or timely enough basis to avoid the current undisciplined intramonth and month-end flows of NAV data. Intramonth estimates and end of month valuations are inefficiently distributed through e-mails, telephone calls, faxes, and the like. The inefficiency in the flow of this information is a direct result of the secrecy of the hedge fund industry and the failure of any service to provide efficient access-controlled data distribution.

Incomplete Reporting

Hedge fund return reporting is incomplete. As mentioned, the databases of hedge fund return histories include only a minority of funds; the majority of funds (particularly the most successful funds) do not participate in these databases. Therefore, investors must track down records of those managers who are unwilling to post their returns in an unsecured database. This can consume a significant amount of time. Even worse, if the investor wants to maintain an up-to-date return database, she must repeat this inefficient and frustrating process the next month, and the month after that, and so on.

Lack of Precision

Hedge fund return reporting is imprecise (although not inaccurate, because that would imply that there is a "correct" valuation). Unfortunately, this is too simplistic. For many securities, primarily less liquid over-the-counter (OTC) instruments, pricing is not transparent (the prices at which trades are executed are not publicly available) and therefore, there is no single correct valuation. Let's explore some of the issues through the following specific examples:

Private equities. Consider an extreme example, private equities. Private equities are an extreme because no price discovery is available for the majority of them. Private placements are often held at historical cost. One can theoretically proxy them based on similar publicly traded equities. However, although this is not illogical, selecting the proxy is very subjective. Furthermore, equities have so much idiosyncratic risk that utilizing a single equity as a proxy is not valid. Utilizing some index is probably the best choice, although indices are significantly less reactive to market movements and less volatile than individual stocks, so this would significantly dampen changes in valuation and consequently volatility. The issue is that the range of alternative methodologies is significant and therefore the degree of accuracy poor.

Restricted stocks. Another interesting area is valuing restricted stocks. In theory, these shares have significantly lower liquidity than general shares. Therefore, they should be valued at a discount to reflect the illiquidity penalty. However, industry practices vary widely. Some holders of such securities do not incorporate any discount versus the general share price in their valuation. Others incorporate a discount of up to 50 percent.

MBS derivatives. Mortgage-backed security (MBS) derivatives represent an excellent example of the challenge. Because of the significant complexity in valuing the prepayment risk associated with MBS derivatives, dealer valuations can vary dramatically, often by differences of between 20 percent to 40 percent (and even more). Clearly, the process is inherently an inexact science. Unfortunately, some of these variations result from differences in prepayment functions and some come from errors. Even the noblest of efforts to correctly value a fund is subject to significant judgment. For example, all managers agree that when quotes are wildly out of line one should go back to the dealer to confirm that no error was made. However, this inquiry is likely to impact the result even if it was not an error, given the inexact nature of the process. Furthermore, selecting which quotes to verify, a subjective decision, can significantly impact the overall fund valuation.

A manager running an MBS derivative fund once boasted to me of being extremely disciplined and rigorous. The manager said that the reason he is unable to calculate the NAV until almost a month after the end of a month is that dealers require that amount of time to do a detailed and careful valuation of the underlying holdings. He clearly believed he was doing a better job valuing portfolios than his competitors who invested in MBS derivatives. Several days later, another fund manager (not an MBS manager) happened to speak to me about the challenge of valuing portfolios. He suggested that by waiting several additional weeks to receive dealer quotes, managers are inadvertently incorporating the market results during the first several weeks of the next month into the delayed quotes for the previous month. If he is correct, the irony is that in an attempt to be more precise, the first manager may have introduced significant market bias. The problem is that the entire process is too imprecise to know who was right (even on an ex-post basis).

Where does this lead us? Werner Heisenberg was the founder of quantum mechanics, a Nobel laureate in physics, and one of the greatest physicists of all times. In 1927 Heisenberg published his "Uncertainty Principle." It stated: "The more precisely the position is determined, the less precisely the momentum is known in this instant, and vice versa." It is often called more descriptively the "principle of indeterminacy." You are probably asking what the relevance of this is to NAV reporting. The answer is that valuation is not a precise measurement, but rather a process of sampling market quotes in an attempt to statistically estimate a value that cannot be directly measured. This statement about the financial world is exactly the same as that which Heisenberg made about the physical world.

Administrators are technically responsible for calculating the NAV of a fund. For positions for which there is good price discovery, the administrator does do an independent valuation. Unfortunately, this is not where valuation issues typically occur. For positions for which subjectivity exists, administrators and managers jointly participate in the process. This by no means suggests that there is malevolent collusion. Quite the contrary! Unfortunately, imprecise valuations are a direct result of the fact that the process is not purely mechanical and that there is not a single correct answer. As previously discussed, the appropriate discount on restricted stock is not well defined, so industry practices can range from zero to a 50 percent discount. As long as the fund is operating within industry practices, the administrator should rationally accept the discount selected by the fund manager. However, this could lead to the illogical situation that the same administrator servicing different managers could hold similar restricted positions, but the discount for one manager may be zero, for a second 10 percent, and for a third 40 percent.

Misleading Measures

Chapter 5 discussed how measures can be very misleading. In particular, they can dramatically mask volatility, significantly distorting measures of risk-adjusted return. However, the example in that chapter of the Reg D fund (a strategy investing in private placement offerings) demonstrates that historical return series can lead to similarly misleading measures of correlation. The message to investors in this chapter is clear: Beware. Do not invest in funds with difficult-to-value holdings and anticipate that future returns will behave consistently with historical reported returns (or that reported returns reflect actual performance).

Masking Risk

Dampened returns of illiquid securities can, even worse than being misleading, actually mask risk. This can result from the fact that brokers, the source of both financing for hedge funds and of quotes to value illiquid securities, generally do not focus on their marks in normal markets. It is only in the face of a crisis, when they become concerned about the ability of the fund to repay its borrowings, that they fully concentrate on the valuation of the securities. Consequently, returns can behave as a barrier option, with extremely low volatility, until they reach a certain point and then move in a large step (almost always a loss) when they cross some natural barrier.

Dressing Up Returns

Hedge funds are increasingly seeking to cap their down months. This practice does not represent quality risk management, but rather managers' dressing up returns in an effort to understate risk. This method simply avoids large down months. However, because it does this by simply turning off the risk faucet when the sink is already overflowing, rather than proactively managing the risk in the portfolio, it does not do this efficiently.

Artificially capping the worst month at a predetermined level results in the inefficient deployment of capital (especially during the periods that investments are monetized) and additional transactional costs (the cost of closing out and subsequently reinstating the positions, both direct transaction fees and bid-offer spreads). The fundamental reason is that risk demonstrates diminishing returns, so a fund that assumes a lot of risk some of the time and zero risk other times is less risk-efficient than a fund that consistently and proactively manages its risk over time. Furthermore, a fund that automatically goes to cash at some maximum stop-loss is going to create more frequent instances when returns decline to this threshold, as it loses the opportunity to recover by earning positive returns during the balance of the month. The increased number of cases when the maximum loss occurs on average offsets the impact of a fewer number of larger losses. Although managers who cap their losses this way are rational given the way that investors generally react to large losses, investors who view this as good risk management are not rational in their reasoning.

CHAPTER 14

Constructing a Portfolio of Funds

There is a debate within investment organizations as to whether portfolio construction is an art or a science. Let's explore this through the analogy of the golden ratio. The classical Greek mathematicians Euclid and Pythagoras are credited with discovering the golden ratio. Artists throughout the ages (especially the Greeks and Renaissance artists) believed the golden rectangle, based on the golden ratio, to be the most visually appealing shape and have used it in many of the great pieces of art. For example, during the Renaissance, Leonardo da Vinci made wide use of the shape. The artistic application of mathematical theory enabled these great works of art to be created. The same is true in the construction of a portfolio of funds. Marrying

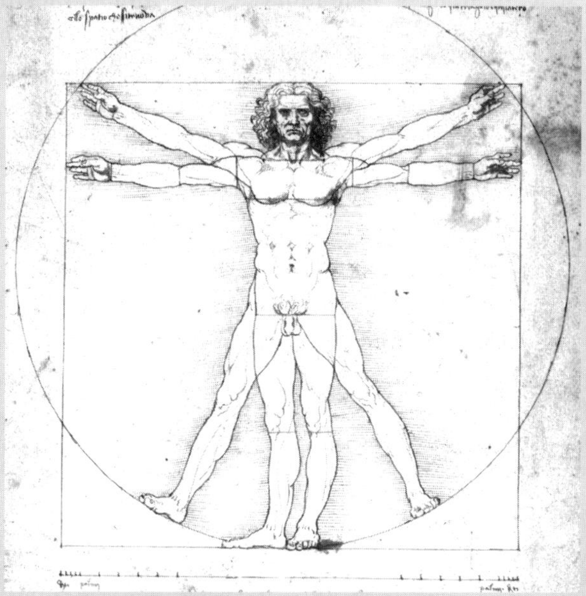

LEONARDO THE SCIENTIST

LEONARDO THE ARTIST

art and science in portfolio construction leverages the innate abilities of both sides of the human brain and enables the creation of superior portfolios of funds.

The typical investor assembles a portfolio of hedge funds by first allocating assets to styles and then "stacking" good managers for each style. Stacking funds with good historical returns does not create a risk-efficient portfolio of funds and, in fact, can lead to a "style trap."[1] For example, several of the best performing long/short equity managers over the past few years (earning better than 40 percent annually) have, not surprisingly, very strong value biases. By selecting funds based on past performance, which is akin to driving only by looking in the rearview mirror, an investor could get trapped in a single style of funds, in this case value funds, and would probably suffer severe losses over the next couple of years. Investors in portfolios of hedge funds must adopt a more integrated approach and instead construct a risk-efficient portfolio of funds.

Integrating Asset Allocation, Manager Selection, and Portfolio Construction

As discussed in Chapter 6, style mandates, benchmarks, and index tracking are concepts firmly rooted in the world of traditional investments. Because the behavior of traditional funds with common mandates is homogenous, pension

FIGURE 14.1 **Traditional versus Alternative Processes**

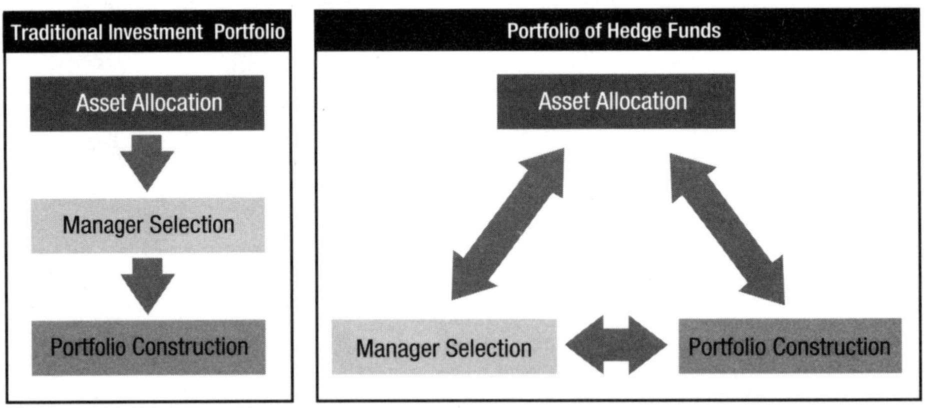

funds and endowments can follow sequential investment processes. They first can allocate to styles (such as large-cap value), and subsequently they can select specific managers within this subuniverse, knowing that the performance of these managers will closely approximate that of the respective style benchmark. Finally, a specific portfolio can be constructed based on the previous steps.

The world of hedge funds is quite different. No comparable gravitational force pulls hedge fund returns toward their respective style indices. Consequently, the returns of managers within a style classification are extremely disparate; style classifications do not represent a statistically meaningful basis by which to allocate assets, select managers, or construct portfolios. Therefore, investors constructing a portfolio of hedge funds cannot follow a sequential process of first allocating to styles and sequentially selecting managers and constructing a specific portfolio. Investors must simultaneously integrate these processes (see **Figure 14.1**).

Investors must understand how each specific manager uniquely fits into the overall portfolio construction. This does not mean all consideration of style classification should be shunned when constructing portfolios. Investors should think top-down about which strategies they would like to be in, identify specific managers within the broad style that could be candidates, and finally evaluate the fit of each manager in the overall construction. Although this is a challenging process, it is necessary given the individuality of hedge funds. In fact, investors should seek funds that pursue differentiated strategies, and, by definition, these funds will not fit neatly into slots.

Constructing a portfolio of funds is very similar to assembling a jigsaw puzzle. You identify where a puzzle piece fits by looking for two characteristics: the picture image on the piece and the pattern of interlocking shapes. Similarly, a hedge fund will fit into a portfolio because the style is appropriate and because the risk factors to which the fund is exposed fit with the other funds in the portfolio. As kids, we all learned tricks to assembling puzzles. You first sorted out the border pieces. You then grouped together pieces with pronounced colors. Finally, you searched for pieces with the right shape. You completed sections that were easy to assemble and then worked to fill in between them. Although there was no well-defined set of rules, you used "fuzzy logic" to iteratively complete the puzzle. The process of constructing a risk-efficient portfolio is very similar. There are no exact rules or specific algorithms. If there were, everybody would construct portfolios the same with equal levels of success. Instead, it is an inexact process that balances a variety of factors. The balance of this chapter enumerates these factors.

Understand Manager Risks

Understanding the current and historical risk exposures of each current and candidate manager and analyzing how a portfolio of hedge funds would behave in normal and crisis market conditions are prerequisites to constructing a risk-efficient portfolio. Furthermore, identifying and diversifying the sources of risk are more important than measuring the aggregate amount of risk.

Investors should explicitly understand the exposure of hedge fund managers to each of these types of risks, how exposures have changed over time, and how the manager has made and lost money. Trend-lining risk exposures over time lets you evaluate how the manager's strategy has evolved and is a critical control against style drift. A retrospective review of the evolution of the portfolio over time can be extremely insightful. A performance attribution (see Chapter 11) of returns will identify the value added through market, secondary, and idiosyncratic risk exposures. You should assess how actively the manager has managed market and secondary risks and whether the manager has demonstrated skill in this active management.

Finally, it is overly simplistic and misleading to assume that returns are normally distributed and that standard deviation can be used as the key to understanding risk. Hedge fund returns can often display significant fat tails, skew, short volatility behavior, and convexity. Thus, investors should identify and assess the full distribution of returns.

Understand Your Objective

Although it's a matter of common sense, this fundamental point must be stressed: Investors must define what "risk efficiency" means for them. Do you want to minimize standard deviation, VaR, semi-deviation, downside deviation, or largest drawdown? Do you want to maximize the Sharpe ratio? Do you want to limit the losses under potential stress scenarios? Or maybe you want to optimize one of these objectives under one of the other risk constraints. Once this choice is made, it's time to proceed with building the portfolio.

Adopt a Prospective Outlook

As discussed in Chapter 5, historical hedge fund returns are not statistically significant predictors of future results, although historical volatilities and correlations are meaningful indicators of prospective behavior. Therefore, the construction of a portfolio should be based on a combination of retrospective correlations and volatilities combined with a prospective return outlook. The prospective outlook should be defined based on a prospective outlook for each risk-factor exposure and a prospective outlook of the manager's ability to generate alpha. Consistently applying those prospective outlooks to all managers under consideration ensures uniformity when comparing those funds.

Focus on Marginal Risk and Return Measures

A marginal measure describes the sensitivity of the measure to a small change in the size of the holding. The primary reason to focus on marginal risk-adjusted returns in constructing a portfolio is that an optimal portfolio is one in which the marginal risk-adjusted returns of all holdings are equal. In a portfolio in which this is not the case, you can improve the portfolio by increasing the weight of holdings with higher marginal risk-adjusted returns and commensurately reducing the weight of holdings with lower marginal risk-adjusted returns. The portfolio can continue to be improved incrementally until all positions have the same marginal risk-adjusted returns. An additional reason for quantifying risk on a marginal basis is that risk is additive on a marginal basis (see Chapter 6).

Construct the Portfolio Incrementally

Risk is inherently nonadditive in nature, so neither volatility nor correlation behave additively. Consequently, the risk of a fund cannot be independently measured, but must be measured and analyzed in the context of the entire portfolio. By extension, the risks assumed by a single fund must be measured and analyzed in the context of the entire portfolio of hedge funds.

Therefore, portfolios are generally constructed on an incremental basis. This lets the investor compare the relationship of a candidate fund with those already in the portfolio. Consequently, portfolio construction becomes a process of iteratively analyzing the impact of a candidate fund on the funds that are already in the portfolio.

Minimize Exposure to the Underlying Market

Although hedge funds advertise themselves as being insensitive to market performance, they have proven to be significantly more correlated than most investors realize. Assuming a preexisting exposure to traditional long-only equity investments, investors should actively manage the exposure of their alternative investment managers to the equity market. They should demand significantly higher returns from those funds that have a higher correlation to markets to which they already have exposure. Chapter 2 discussed a risk-return measure, called the BAVAR ratio (beta and volatility adjusted return; see the Appendix), which is a derivative of the Sharpe ratio that adjusts for correlation in addition to volatility. The BAVAR ratio permits you to rationally analyze whether the additional return provided by a hedge fund that is more correlated to the market justifies its lower diversification.

Manage Secondary Risk Exposures

Investors should understand the correlated exposure to secondary risks they are taking. For example, the crisis in the fall of 1998 (Long-Term Capital Management) resulted from a correlated exposure to illiquidity. The average fund of funds experienced a decline of 13 percent during this crisis, despite the fact that the average fund declined only 11 percent. Diversification had not worked. The portfolio of funds should be managed to avoid those risks that the investor chooses not to take, while targeting systemic risks that he explicitly seeks. (See Chapter 2 for an example of the value and small-cap bias of equity hedge funds.)

Maximize Idiosyncratic Risks

Hedge funds should explicitly target idiosyncratic, or security-specific, risk. Traditional risk-factor–based systems assume that the specific risk of one security is normally distributed and independent of the specific risks of other securities. This oversimplification failed miserably in the tech bubble, as telecommunications and Internet stocks had not been identified as sharing unique risk factors; portfolio managers significantly underestimated the risk of portfolios with concentrated exposures to these industries.

Idiosyncratic risk can be divided into "correlated" and "independent" idiosyncratic risk. Many hedge funds explicitly target relationships between securities through relative value, pairs trading, or arbitrage strategies. Consequently, analyzing risks in hedge funds requires an explicit understanding of the correlation of the idiosyncratic risk across individual holdings. Correlated idiosyncratic risk recognizes the significantly greater risk of such portfolios whose security-specific risks are correlated.

Limit Offsetting Exposures

Investors should analyze and quantify the risk efficiency of managers within their construction. For example, they do not typically want one manager to be long value while another manager is long growth. Usually, this results in both the risk and the related return being hedged out. This does not mean investors should never have two managers with opposite exposure to specific risks. But investors should evaluate the overall exposures of these managers and be sure that their idiosyncratic strategies—through superior stock selection, for example—are unique and significant enough relative to their overall risk exposure. This then compensates the investor for the inefficiency of their offsetting structural exposures.

Diversify the Portfolio

The obvious challenge is to achieve the right level of diversification. As discussed in Chapter 2, overdiversification will diversify away the valuable idiosyncratic risk investors explicitly target. The strongest evidence that overdiversification diversifies away idiosyncratic risk is that the Hedge Fund Research (HFR) Composite Index (representing a highly diversified portfolio of 1,700 funds) has a 0.86 correlation to the S&P Small Cap Index, whereas the average correlation of the individual hedge funds to the S&P Small Cap Index is 0.38. On the other hand, a portfolio of funds must have adequate diversification to reduce fund-specific risk. Were hedge funds not capacity-constrained, an appropriately diversified portfolio of funds would probably have 20 to 30 underlying funds. Given the realistic constraints of capacity, a well-diversified portfolio of funds might require additional underlying funds. However, many of the highly diversified funds of funds that contain up to 100 underlying funds begin to look like an equity index fund.

Plan for the Worst

Even when an investor constructs a portfolio that is consistent with his or her required risk-reward profile, having been mindful of the pitfalls that can be encountered, the process isn't over. Most hedge fund disasters have occurred during relatively short market crisis periods, and it's at just such times that correlation increases. Stress testing is essential in order to understand how a portfolio would perform in extreme market conditions. By subjecting all underlying funds to the same battery of historical crisis scenarios and hypothetical stress tests, investors should be able to understand how a portfolio of funds will perform under such situations. In treacherous markets, investors who haven't spent significant time and effort investigating their portfolio of funds' performance under extreme market moves could find themselves sunk, whereas their stress-testing competitors manage to stay afloat.

Consider Using Optimizers

Because portfolio construction tends to be an incremental process, optimizers can play a role in constructing a portfolio. Optimizers are mathematical algorithms that maximize (or minimize) an objective function within a set of constraints. You would logically optimize a portfolio construction by maximizing the risk-adjusted return (minus related transaction costs) within the constraints of position size. You can insert additional constraints such as limiting volatility, drawdown, and so on. Optimizers can help you think outside the box by giving you a "clean sheet" analysis—an analysis unconstrained by previous thinking.

The practical failure of optimizers is that they tend to be drawn to extreme solutions (for example, putting 80 percent of the assets in a couple of funds that have superior expectations). One generally ends up adding constraints to limit the weight of these investments. Relatively soon, it is the subjective weight constraints that are driving the results rather than the optimization. Although optimizers do provide "shadow prices" that represent feedback to human decision makers about what is driving the "black box" decision, it is generally difficult to integrate the results of optimizers and human decision makers. Experience has shown that beyond calculating an unconstrained solution as "food for thought," optimizers are general not extremely valuable.

Notes

[1]A strategy whose returns have historically been cyclical and that has recently enjoyed a period of outperformance will ultimately be followed by a period of underperformance.

CHAPTER 15

Risk Due Diligence

An important part of the manager selection process is the risk due diligence. It is through this process that a potential investor assesses whether a fund both understands and controls its risk.

The primary focus of a risk due diligence should be on market risk, the most significant risk to which an investor is exposed. The first step is to interview the portfolio manager to see if she fundamentally understands her risk. Portfolio managers should be able to:

THE RISK SLEUTH

Articulate the overall strategy. Ask: How is technical and fundamental research translated into a decision to enter a trade? What risks are you targeting? What risks are you hedging out? How active a strategy is it? What is the average holding period?

Explain how portfolios are constructed. Ask: How frequently do you trade? How are trades assembled into a portfolio? Are you seeking a large number of micro trades or a small number of more significant trades? What do you think about the trade-off between idiosyncratic exposure and liquidity?

Define the supporting trading strategy. Ask: How do you size positions? How do you enter into a position? When do you exit a position? What rules do you use to expand/reduce a position?

When exploring a portfolio manager's understanding of the risks he is taking, you should consider how the manager articulates his approach. For example, before introducing the Risk Fundamentals Solution to him, I had a detailed discussion with a portfolio manager in which Kenmar was invested about the risk exposures he believed he was taking. He held more than 300 equity and equity option positions, most of them in small- to medium-cap stocks. Although the portfolio manager was not able to describe his process in the language of risk, he described himself as a "stock picker," and whatever style or sector bets he had were transitory and resulted from his stock selection. After implementing the system, I found that the portfolio manager was on track. The majority of the risk in the fund was idiosyncratic. In any construction (at any point in time) there were style and sector bets, but they were quite actively managed and were relatively short-lived. Although the system did confirm his overall approach, it also identified that the fund had achieved its idiosyncratic focus by investing in less liquid small-cap stocks, resulting in less overall liquidity in the portfolio than other equity long/short funds. Having identified this and being provided a way to routinely measure it, the fund was able to maintain its overall idiosyncratic focus, which was extremely attractive, while improving its liquidity. Furthermore, the exercise served to expand the manager's lexicon, as the fund cleverly introduced the concepts of idiosyncratic exposure and active management of market and secondary risk exposures into its marketing message.

Analyzing Previous Portfolios

An analysis of a candidate fund's prior constructions over a period of time can be extremely valuable. Although I do not recommend that you dogmatically require back constructions, most managers should be willing to supply stale constructions after you have demonstrated a high level of interest and commitment during the due diligence process. I recommend that you do not request back constructions if you do not have the tools with which to analyze them, as receiving data and not doing anything with them actually creates greater liability than not receiving the data (it is all but impossible to glean anything from a list of positions that someone else has constructed in the absence of an appropriate analytical system). Assuming you can obtain back constructions, I recommend that you process these constructions through a risk-factor–based analysis system. Such an effort would identify:

- How the managers earned their return
- Whether return was primarily generated through market, secondary, or idiosyncratic risk exposures
- Whether return was generated through active or biased management
- How performance and the long and the short side compared
- How the performance (both the return and risk) compared to that of its peers

- How the portfolio changed over time
- How the manager has chosen between idiosyncratic exposure and liquidity

Were the hedge fund industry to adopt a standard set of risk factors, it would dramatically simplify this process—to the point that it would become a simple and routine part of any due diligence. If you are unable to analyze previous constructions (either because the manager was unwilling to share back constructions or because you do not have the capability to analyze them), you should attempt to gain through the interviewing process some of the insights that might have been gained through a rigorous analysis.

Having comprehensively assessed the portfolio manager's understanding of the risk inherent in the portfolio, the next area to explore is the fund's use of independent, statistical risk management. You should take some extra comfort with funds that wear "belts and suspenders" (i.e., both elements of risk management are present):

- A portfolio manager who truly "gets" risk
- An organization that has an independent risk management oversight function

Only a small fraction of hedge funds can rightfully claim both. Given the choice of only one, my strong preference is for a portfolio manager who has a comprehensive and fundamental understanding of the risks he is taking. Independent, statistical risk management is a good check that nothing has slipped through the ranks of your front line portfolio manager(s), but is definitely not an acceptable alternative to a portfolio manager who does not fundamentally and comprehensively understand the risks he is taking.

Your review of market risk should cover all of the key components. As has been already suggested, analyzing previous portfolios is the most rigorous approach, but if that is not feasible, the due diligence process should touch on all of the following:

- ***Volatility***—Explore how the fund might behave under both normal and crisis market conditions.
- ***Diversification***—Explore the degree of diversification within the fund, between the fund and other funds, and between the fund and the primary markets.
- ***Leverage***—Explore each of the component sources of leverage and the total risk leverage of the fund.
- ***Liquidity***—Explore the liquidity of the fund. Explore what security has been created through flexible financing or a cash buffer.

If the candidate fund is currently utilizing a formal risk management system, an investor should seek to understand the system and how it is being applied. You should ask to review sample reports, especially stress tests. You should inquire as to who gets the reports, how the analyses are reviewed, and what responses are typical.

Determining Transparency and Risk Culture

The next step is to determine what transparency the fund provides to its investors. Transparency is discussed in detail in Chapter 16. Again, I anticipate that Risk Fundamentals, presented in detail in Chapter 18, will significantly enhance transparency throughout the industry. However, until funds in which you invest adopt a standard solution, you should understand what information the fund does supply and develop a plan to take advantage of whatever transparency is provided. We have already recognized the limitations of receiving data in vastly varying formats from different funds. However, given the current practices of the industry, you should monitor whatever information is made available.

Another key objective of a risk due diligence is to understand the risk culture of the organization. First, is there a designated risk manager? If yes, what are her skills and orientation? Managing market risk requires skills in the following disciplines:

- ***Statistics***—The risk manager must perform complex statistical analyses providing quantitative input to the decision process.
- ***Systems***—The risk manager must maintain and operate risk and other analytic systems.
- ***Financial engineering***—The risk manager must understand financial models and the causal relationships between markets and hedge fund performance.
- ***Trading***—Risk managers in large financial institutions almost always have had trading experience at some time during their careers. This permits them to fully understand the process they are trying to control/influence.
- ***Judgment of people***—Risk management is a consultative process. A good risk manager must have good judgment of people and know when to intervene.
- ***Risk strategy***—Risk managers must be able to view risk as a strategic resource and guide its deployment.

- ***Portfolio theory***—Risk managers must be able to combine the knowledge of risk and the construction of a risk-efficient portfolio, be able to construct a portfolio that is primarily composed of idiosyncratic risk, and actively manage market and secondary risks.

An investor should also explore the processes related to risk management: Is risk explicitly discussed in the investment/research meeting? Is there a separate risk meeting? If the answer to either of these questions is yes, how often? Who participates? It is important to understand how risk is managed within the organization and the degree of focus on risk.

Many hedge funds have responded to the market pressure for enhanced risk management by naming an individual in the firm as risk manager. This is most often the chief financial officer (CFO). However, risk is an amorphous resource that, even for those people who understand it, is difficult to manage. Managing market risk is a "fuzzy" process that requires rationally balancing risk and return. Managing market risk in a "control" manner can be damaging. I have seen numerous funds attempt to control risk by establishing firm stop-loss limits. However, naïve limits made without sound statistical underpinnings can be more risky than not having any limits at all. Many funds boast of firm stop-loss limits, but many of these limits are in fact so relaxed that they will never be triggered. Consequently, they do not represent a threshold that forces the portfolio manager to rethink her thesis—the ultimate goal of a stop-loss limit. Many other funds have limits that prove to be too sensitive, tripping the alarm too frequently with the result that the fund ignores the alarm—remember the tragic childhood story of the boy who cried wolf?

Although the primary focus of a risk due diligence should be market risk, a vigilant investor should investigate the myriad other risks. Risks other than market risks do not generate a return and, consequently, the goal is to eliminate or at least minimize them. As discussed in Chapter 9, even though the market does not compensate for non-market risks, any investor who invests in funds that have such exposures should seek to be appropriately compensated. Therefore, investors should demand a higher risk-adjusted return (adjusted for market risks) when they invest in funds with other risks. For example, consider the previously discussed valuation issues and consequent risk when funds invest in illiquid instruments (funds that typically report superior Sharpe ratios). An investor should invest in such a fund only if it delivers such superior results.

Unlike market risk that should be balanced or optimized, other risks should be mitigated through an uncompromising commitment to operational excellence. Although it is virtually impossible to uncover fraud in the due diligence process, you can learn a lot about the mind-set of the organization and be in a significantly better position to make a general assessment of its operational quality. I will not in this chapter enumerate all the topics related to non-market risk that should be explored because they are discussed at length in Chapter 9. The message to investors is that you should care about these potential other risks and spend time exploring them as part of the risk due diligence process.

There is a specific non-market risk discussed in Chapter 9 that the investor should explicitly evaluate as part of the risk due diligence process: the potential mismatch of the redemption policy of a fund and the liquidity of the underlying holdings. As previously discussed, hedge funds are increasingly responding to the demands of investors by offering shorter redemption/notice periods. The problem is, if the liquidity of the underlying holdings does not enable this, investors may find that the manager cannot satisfy the redemption policy without incurring losses in liquidating. Almost every hedge fund has a clause in its private placement memorandum (PPM) that permits it to halt redemptions if the fund will be adversely impacted. This is the fund's safety valve. Investors should explicitly explore whether the redemption policy is supportable in a liquidity event, in the case of either market liquidity drying up or large redemptions. As such events often come after a period of poor returns, you should consider the potential compound impact of concurrent losses followed by high redemptions. Remember, the majority of redemptions take place when a fund is having problems, not when things are going swimmingly.

As part of the risk due diligence, you should find out how large the largest investor is and whether that investor has any special relationship with the fund (seed investors can often have either more restrictive or less restrictive requirements). You should ask whether the fund has signed any "side letters" with other investors with respect to liquidity (and with respect to any other commitment such as to future capacity). You should also understand all of the components of liquidity discussed in Chapter 4 (such as cash reserves, financial leverage, financing arrangements, actual fund size versus capacity, and cash generation). There is no way you can guarantee that the fund will not have a run on the bank, but there is a lot you can do to determine how likely such a crisis might be.

In contrast to the balancing skills required to manage market risk, control skills are required to mitigate other risks. Investors should explore who is responsible for managing these risks and assess whether they have been adequately managed. The skills required to manage market and other risks are significantly different, and, consequently, investors should look skeptically upon a single person serving both roles.

Risk due diligence is not something that an investor does once and completes. Risk due diligence is an ongoing process for the full life of the investment—the colloquialism is “from cradle to grave,” but the practice actually begins at conception (before the investment is born). Although quality transparency can significantly facilitate the process, enabling the investor to focus on exploring strategy rather than putting together data, this exploration must be one of ongoing vigilance. These risk issues should be covered as part of the periodic conversations that every investor should hold with his managers. These conversations should occur at least quarterly. Furthermore, a more comprehensive review should be part of an annual site visit, which is strongly recommended.

CHAPTER 16

Transparency

Webster's Dictionary provides multiple definitions of "transparency." The first is: "Having the property of transmitting light through its substance so that bodies situated beyond or behind can be distinctly seen."

Applying this to portfolio disclosure would suggest that each position, the "bodies" of a portfolio, should be explicitly disclosed, or "distinctly seen."

Another definition of transparency is: "Having the quality of being easily understood, manifest, obvious." Transparency, then, according to this second definition, shows the important figures while filtering out the subtle details. The increased transparency that Federal Reserve chairman Alan Greenspan has been calling for in the hedge fund industry is clearly the latter definition.

Two terms are often used in discussions of hedge fund transparency: *position disclosure* and *risk transparency*. Position disclosure is the practice of providing raw data by reporting detailed positions. Risk transparency is the practice of providing processed risk information *without* revealing position data.

Changing Investor Requirements

Until recently, the hedge fund industry was focused on high-net-worth investors (private money). Over the past couple of years the focus has shifted to the institutional market. The institutionalization of the hedge fund market has dramatically raised the due diligence hurdle and created a demand for institutional-quality hedge funds. A strong consensus exists that there is a shortage of hedge

FIGURE 16.1 **Investment and Pensions Europe Survey (May 2001): Why Pension Funds Did Not Invest in Hedge Funds**

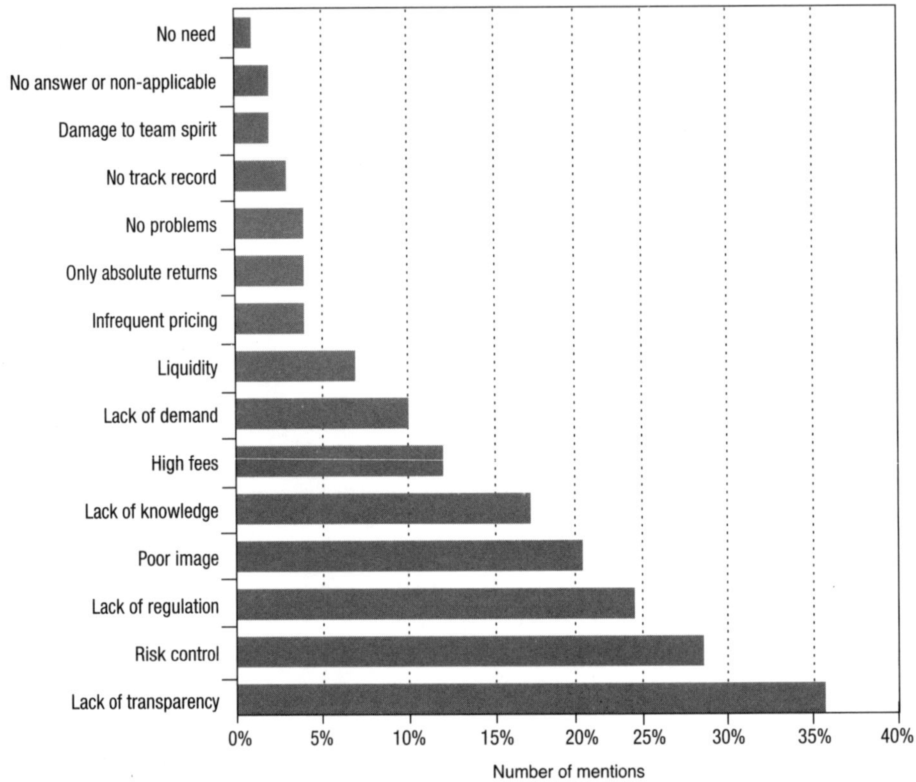

fund capacity. In fact, more than 8,000 hedge funds are in existence today, with the majority having less than $50 million in assets. There is no shortage of hedge funds. There is a shortage of institutional-quality hedge funds, hedge funds with the depth and discipline to satisfy sophisticated institutional investors.

Institutional investors' concerns about risk management and transparency are demonstrated by the responses of pensions funds in a survey performed by Investment and Pensions Europe. When asked why they do not invest in hedge funds (see **Figure 16.1**), the most frequent response was "lack of transparency," and the second most frequent response was the related issue of "risk control."

However, a survey (*Hedge Fund Risk Transparency,* January 31, 2002) per-

FIGURE 16.2 **AIMA Survey—Transparency (January 2002)**

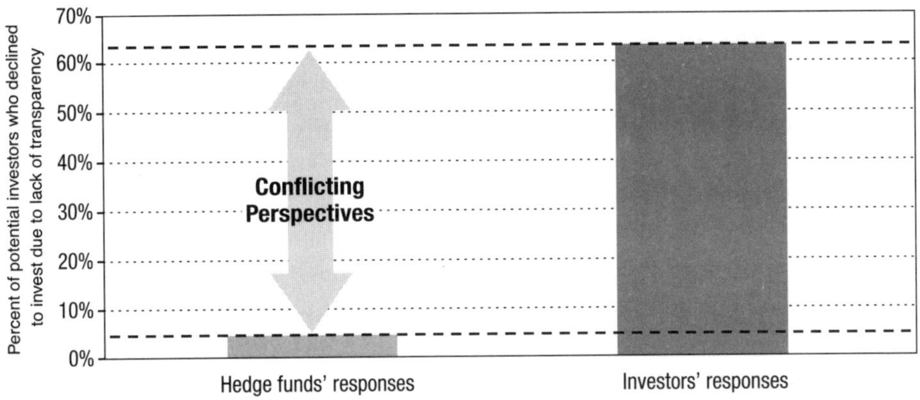

formed by Capital Market Risk Advisors (CMRA) for the Alternative Investment Management Association (AIMA) identified a large difference of opinion between investors and hedge funds as to whether potential investors decline to invest because of lack of transparency (see **Figure 16.2**).

Institutional investors, including funds of funds, are the primary driver of improved risk management in hedge funds, not the funds' internal demands. Hedge funds are intimately knowledgeable about their investment strategy and their holdings. They are fully aware of style drift, generally as a very active participant in pursuit of performance. It is the investor, who has generally been required to settle for a "trust me," who is increasingly demanding to know more. The hedge fund investor has been riding in the back seat, blindfolded, careening down a mountain, praying that the driver is sober. The ultimate customer for hedge fund risk management and transparency is the investor, not the hedge fund manager.

Sophisticated institutional investors have five broad requirements. They want to:

- Fully understand their risk exposures
- Be able to compare risks across portfolios
- Be able to aggregate risks across portfolios
- Construct risk-efficient portfolios of portfolios
- Guard against style drift, concentrations, and other unexpected and often unrewarded risks.

Furthermore, institutional investors have recognized that diversifying risk is significantly more rewarding than concentrating risk. Most investors already have significant directional equity and interest rate exposure. They are looking for investment strategies that will provide diversification from these naturally long positions. Investors require analytical tools that will permit them to understand the diversification provided by individual funds, and even more important, to aggregate multiple funds and measure whether they are diversifying or concentrating.

Institutional investors are frustrated by hedge funds' limited transparency and their own consequent inability to reasonably apply long-established portfolio theory to the portfolio of funds. Risk is an extremely complex, stochastic, nonadditive, nonlinear function, which is hard enough to understand for a single simple instrument but extremely complex to understand for portfolios of multiple instruments. Then add strategies with binary (noncontinuous) outcomes such as merger arbitrage and other event-driven strategies and strategies for which market-based valuations are extremely difficult such as private equity and real estate, and properly managing risk "by the seat of the pants" appears impossible. Finally, cap it all off by combining multiple separate portfolios into a fund of funds format, and you may want to throw in the towel. But should you?

The Political Environment

In April 1999, in the aftermath of the Long-Term Capital Management (LTCM) crisis, the President's Working Group (PWG) on Financial Markets (comprising the Secretary of the U.S. Department of the Treasury and the respective chairs of the Board of Governors of the Federal Reserve System, the Securities and Exchange Commission, and the Commodity Futures Trading Commission), published its report entitled "Hedge Funds, Leverage and the Lessons of Long-Term Capital Management." This report recommended that a number of measures be implemented by financial institutions, regulators, and hedge funds to enhance risk management practices. The report recommended that:

> A group of hedge funds should draft and publish a set of sound practices for their risk management and internal controls. Such a study should discuss market risk measurement and management, identification of concentrations, stress testing, collateral management, valuation of positions and collateral, segregation of duties and internal controls, and the assessment of capital needs from the perspective of hedge funds.

> In addition, the study should consider how individual hedge funds could assess their performance against the sound practices for investors and counterparties.

Although lacking specificity, the PWG report suggested that hedge funds should "disclose additional, and more up-to-date, information to the public":

> ***Disclosure and Reporting***
> Improving transparency through enhanced disclosure to the public should help market participants make better, more informed judgments about market integrity and the creditworthiness of borrowers and counterparties. Currently, the scope and timeliness of information made available about the financial activities of hedge funds are limited. Hedge funds should be required to disclose additional, and more up-to-date, information to the public.

In February 2000, a group comprising some of the largest independent hedge fund managers published "Sound Practices for Hedge Fund Managers" in response to the PWG report. In the section "Issues Relating to the Potential Impact of Public Disclosure on Market Integrity," the report concluded:

> The dialogue with Hedge Fund Managers, counterparties and regulators should assess the goals to be achieved by public disclosure. To the extent that public disclosure is to assist creditors and investors in making informed decisions about the credit they extend or the investments they make, the benefits of the recommendations for improved risk management and internal controls by Hedge Fund Managers and for the expanded disclosure to counterparties and investors should be considered. Issues related to the potential relationship between market integrity and public disclosure should be addressed by broad classes of market participants so that a better understanding of the benefits and cost can be achieved.
>
> Because of the broad recognition (including recognition in the PWG Report) that disclosure of Hedge Funds' proprietary information on strategies or positions should not be required, any approach to public disclosure should consider what information can be collected, aggregated and disseminated without exposing sensitive strategies and positions.

In September 2000 a bill titled "Hedge Funds Disclosure Act" was introduced into the House of Representatives. It was "to require unregulated hedge funds to submit regular reports to the Board of Governors of the Federal Reserve System, to make such reports available to the public to the extent prescribed by the

Board, and for other purposes." The bill called for "the meaningful and comprehensive measures of market risk (such as value-at-risk or stress test results) as of the end of a calendar quarter." The bill did not progress through the House.

In July 2001 the Investor Risk Committee (IRC) of the International Association of Financial Engineers (IAFE) published a report titled "Hedge Fund Disclosure for Institutional Investors." The report first reaffirmed the committee's conclusion of its October 2000 report that position disclosure should not be required:

> IRC Members agreed that full position disclosure by Managers does not always allow them to achieve their monitoring objectives, and may compromise a hedge fund's ability to execute its investment strategy.
>
> Despite the fact that many Investors receive full position disclosure for many of their investments, the members of the IRC who have participated in the meetings to date were in agreement that full position disclosure by Managers is not the solution. Managers expressed significant concerns over the harm that full position disclosure could cause for many common hedge fund strategies (for example macro and risk arbitrage). Investors agreed they did not wish to force disclosure that would be adverse to the Manager, and therefore to their investment. In addition, many Investors expressed concern over the operational difficulties associated with processing such vast quantities of diverse data.

The report identified the solution for transparency as "summary risk, return and position information":

> IRC Members agreed that the reporting of summary risk, return and position information can be sufficient as an alternative to full position disclosure. Content covers information about the risk, return and positions on an actual as well as on a stress-tested basis. Regarding content, the IRC was in agreement that:
>
> VaR can be useful information but should be calculated using an industry-standard definition.
>
> Aggregate measures of a fund's exposure to different types of asset classes can be useful.
>
> Aggregate measures of a fund's exposure to different geographic regions can be useful.
>
> Net asset value (NAV) and stress measures of NAV appropriate to the strategy can be useful.

> Cash as a percent of equity can be useful.
>
> Correlation to an appropriate benchmark can be useful.
>
> Delta, gamma and other measures of optionality, as appropriate, can be useful.
>
> Key spread relationships, as appropriate, can be useful.

The report recommended providing summary risk measures including stress tests, VaR, asset concentrations, geographic concentrations, cash, correlations, measures of optionality, and measures of spread relationships.

Although the IRC of the IAFE has continued to meet over the several years since this report was issued to discuss the issue of hedge fund risk transparency, no specific and actionable results have emerged.

In June 2002, the SEC began a fact-finding mission aimed at reviewing the operations and practices of hedge funds. As part of this initiative the SEC hosted a roundtable discussion (held May 14 and 15, 2003). The Commission was seeking information as it assesses the regulatory framework applicable to hedge funds and their investment advisers. The Roundtable covered a number of topics, including: (1) the structure, operation, and compliance activities of hedge funds; (2) marketing issues; (3) investor protection issues; (4) the current regulatory scheme; and (5) whether additional regulation is warranted. Although this was the first regulatory review of hedge funds since the PWG in early 1999, its explicitly stated focus did not include transparency. However, transparency is so intimately intertwined with the stated issues under consideration, it became an area of focus at the roundtable discussion.

In August 2003, the Managed Funds Association (MFA) published "2003 Sound Practices for Hedge Fund Managers." This report was submitted to the SEC as part of the review and was presented as representative of the thinking of the hedge fund community. The document did not address risk transparency, although it explicitly recommended that hedge funds establish a risk monitoring function:

> ***Structure of Risk Monitoring Function***
>
> 1.6 A Hedge Fund Manager should establish a Risk Monitoring Function, either internally or in reliance upon external resource. The Risk Monitoring Function should review objective risk data and prepare analysis of a Hedge Fund's performance and current risk position, the sources of risk and resulting exposures to changes in market conditions.

The fact that the document did not speak to disclosure is a significant statement in itself. The message is that the industry does not seek a regulated solution to transparency.

In September 2003, the SEC published "Implications of the Growth of Hedge Funds, Staff Report to the United States Securities and Exchange Commission." In Chapter IV, titled "Operations of Hedge Funds," the report made the following comments about transparency (this is in the descriptive rather than the prescriptive part of the report):

> ***3. Transparency***
> Hedge fund advisers may provide investors with a list of hedge fund securities positions and holdings (position transparency) or information about the risks associated with the hedge fund's market positions (risk transparency). This information may be provided in full or in part and on a current or delayed basis.

About risk management, the report said:

> ***I. Risk Management***
> Hedge fund advisers are expected to achieve performance returns for investors by using strategies that are designed to assume or eliminate calculated risks consistent with the hedge fund's investment objective. The observation that some hedge funds are riskier than others reflects the wide latitude hedge funds have to operate their funds and the potential that exists for some hedge funds to suffer significant losses. An effective risk management system, therefore, is important to a hedge fund's operations.

In Chapter VIII, "Recommendations," the report stated:

> A. The Commission Should Consider Requiring Hedge Fund Advisers to Register as Investment Advisers under the Advisers Act, Taking into Account Whether the Benefits Outweigh the Burdens of Registration

However, the recommendations proceeded to state:

> Registration would not place any restrictions on hedge fund advisers' ability to trade securities, use leverage, sell securities short or enter into derivatives transactions. Nor would registration under the Act require the disclosure of any proprietary trading strategy. In addition, registration would not result in hedge funds and hedge fund advisers being subject to any additional portfolio disclosure requirements.

In summary, there have been a series of initiatives prior to the recent SEC review of hedge funds addressing the disclosure and transparency of hedge funds. They have uniformly recommended against the required disclosure of positions. Furthermore, they have consistently recommended that summary levels of risk information be provided, although none have been specific as to how this should be accomplished. All of the initiatives have left open the core question of how. The recent SEC review of hedge funds recognized transparency and risk management as key responsibilities of hedge funds, but in the recommendations, having focused on the highly controversial issue of hedge fund registration, it explicitly stated that registration would not require additional disclosure.

The Pros and Cons of Position Disclosure

The major advantage of hedge fund position disclosure is that it provides the raw data to perform whatever analyses one might conceivably want to perform. I view this as an inefficient and ineffective approach to providing transparency; however, it clearly would fully satisfy all the potential requirements of any investor who was inclined to incur the significant expense of processing these data into meaningful risk information. Reporting the information in its most granular form affords the greatest flexibility to an investor willing to work with the data.

There are three major disadvantages of hedge fund position disclosure:

- Revealing positions can adversely impact the performance of the fund, especially for short positions.
- A significant amount of "processing" is required to convert these position data into meaningful risk information.
- From a legal perspective, it is worse for an institutional investor to have received position data and to have not analyzed them than to not have received position data at all.

Current Practices

Current transparency practices vary significantly. Before discussing these practices, it is important to first discuss the structure of the industry. As noted, there are an estimated 8,000 hedge funds. Several dozen of these are extremely large and sophisticated funds (such as Caxton, Citadel, Tudor, and Soros). They each manage in excess of $1 billion. These funds employ hundreds of people and operate as if they were the proprietary trading operations of an investment bank.

They have scores of traders who are all tied together through a sophisticated, proprietary systems infrastructure, including integrated risk management systems. They have a separate risk management group of significant size. Although these funds have the strongest internal capability, they have generally provided very limited transparency. This is justified by their size and the fact that providing greater details could adversely impact their performance. Furthermore, they are extremely successful and are closed to new investment, so they have the market clout to embrace such a policy.

However, as also was noted, the vast majority of hedge funds have less than $50 million under management. They employ a handful of people and rely on third-party systems, generally those of their administrator or prime broker. As previously discussed, many of these funds have recognized that risk management has become a visible issue and have assigned one of the team the additional responsibility of being the designated risk manager. Some of these funds provide some form of transparency, although each in its own format (the issue that the next chapter will address).

A small number of institutional investors (including some funds of funds) make position data a prerequisite to their investing. However, this significantly limits the universe of managers who will accept these terms. Furthermore, because a fund's willingness to provide position disclosure (estimated to be less than 50 percent of hedge funds) is often related to the success of the fund, this is believed to result in "adverse selection" (weaker funds are generally believed to be more willing to provide position disclosure). Other institutional investors obtain position data only for those funds that will provide them. These investors have generally been able to obtain position data from somewhat less than 50 percent of their underlying funds.

Furthermore, although large institutional investors have greater clout in obtaining position details, the trends suggest their clout is declining. As the hedge fund industry institutionalizes, funds are becoming less willing to execute "side letters." Prospective investors are increasingly asking about what side letters exist with other investors and are seeking to achieve the same terms. Funds are increasingly seeking to treat all investors equally. Consequently, funds are looking for a solution to transparency that can be uniformly applied to all investors.

V

Part Five

The Solution

CHAPTER 17

Industry Standard Solution

NOW THE WHOLE EARTH had one language and few words. And as men migrated from the east, they found a plain in the land of Shinar and settled there. And they said to one another, "Come, let us make bricks, and burn them thoroughly." And they had brick for stone, and bitumen for mortar. Then they said, "Come, let us build ourselves a city, and a tower with its top in the heavens, and let us make a name for ourselves, lest we be scattered abroad upon the face of the whole earth." And the LORD came down to see the city and the tower, which the sons of men had built. And the LORD said, "Behold, they are one people, and they have all one language; and this is only the beginning of what they will do; and nothing that they propose to do will now be impossible for them. Come, let us go down, and there confuse their language, that they may not understand one another's speech." So the LORD scattered them abroad from there over the face of all the earth, and they left off building the city. Therefore its name was called Babel, because there the LORD confused the language of all the earth; and from there the LORD scattered them abroad over the face of all the earth. (Genesis 11:1-9)

The genesis of hedge funds parallels the biblical story of the tower of Babel. In the beginning, a small number of investment banks all spoke the same language. However, the best and the brightest were scattered, and each adopted its own reporting language. This has "confused" them, and they cannot "understand one another's speech."

FIGURE 17.1 **Benefits of Company Financial Fundamentals and Risk Fundamentals**

		COMPANY FINANCIAL FUNDAMENTALS	RISK FUNDAMENTALS
Understandable	A standard reporting structure represents a shared lexicon.	Operating profit, shareholders equity, short-term debt, etc. will have the same definition across companies.	Leverage, volatility, liquidity will have the same definition across investments.
Comparable	A standard reporting structure makes the results of one entity comparable to those of others.	The leverage of one company can be directly compared to that of another.	The leverage of one investment can be directly compared to that of another.
Aggregatable	A standard reporting structure permits results of multiple entities to be aggregated.	The pro forma of a merger can be developed by combining the financial fundamentals of the individual companies.	The risks of a portfolio of investments can be analyzed by combining the risk fundamentals of the investments.
Benchmarkable	A standard reporting structure enables comparative benchmarking.	The financial fundamentals of a specific company can be compared to benchmarks of related companies.	The risk fundamentals of a specific investment can be compared to benchmarks of similar investments.
Trendable	A standard reporting structure permits trends to be rapidly identified.	Changes in performance can be identified by tracking financial fundamentals over time.	"Style drift" can be immediately identified (rather than by waiting for it to evidence itself in trailing returns).
Decomposable	A standard reporting structure permits performance to be decomposed to its root causes.	ROE can be decomposed into operating margins, asset turnover, financial leverage, etc.	Risk can be decomposed to sensitivities to specific risk factors (e.g., market, style, industries, stock specific).
Attributable	A standard reporting structure explains historical performance.	EPS growth can be attributed to revenue growth, margin expansion, changes in financial leverage, etc.	Returns can be attributed to market exposures, other systematic exposures, security selection, etc.
Camouflagable	A standard reporting structure avoids disclosing sensitive or proprietary details.	Financial fundamentals will not disclose sensitive specifics such as pricing, suppliers, customers, etc.	Risk fundamentals will not disclose sensitive specifics such as holdings, financing rates, etc.

The biggest challenge is for investors who must speak to many hedge funds and attempt to create a consistent picture across managers in which they have invested. Investors want to be able to compare and aggregate risk across all the funds in which they are invested.

The big question is how this fragmented industry that cherishes privacy can speak to investors in a common language. Analogies to other industries can offer some ideas.

Reporting Standards—A Common Language

Returning to an analogy from the Introduction, what makes company financial fundamentals so valuable to equity analysts? The answer is that they are presented based on a consistent reporting framework—that is, by applying generally accepted accounting principles, or GAAP. The application of a standard framework makes the statistics comparable across companies. This enables company-to-company comparisons. For example, it is extremely insightful to compare the return on sales or asset turnovers of competitors in the same industry if the fundamental information is calculated similarly. **Figure 17.1** presents the full set of benefits provided by a standard set of company financial fundamentals.

Achieving maximum value through risk fundamentals similarly requires the adoption of an industry standard set of fundamental risk measures. Figure 17.1 also presents the benefits realized by a standard set of risk fundamentals. Now let us explore what these essential risk characteristics are. The risk fundamentals of an investment in fact closely parallel the financial fundamentals of a company (see **Figure 17.2**).

The Case for Standardization

The challenge is to establish standardized risk fundamentals. Let's examine how standardized reporting has been achieved elsewhere. In many situations, the standardization can be achieved simply by introducing a reporting framework that individual reporting entities can consistently apply. Governments, industry groups, and international accords have established many such reporting standards. For example, the accounting industry has developed GAAP.

In other instances, applying the framework is significantly more complex than simply requiring a standard reporting framework. In these cases, standardization has often been enabled through third-party application of the standard.

FIGURE 17.2 **Company Financial Fundamentals versus Risk Fundamentals**

	COMPANY FINANCIAL FUNDAMENTALS	RISK FUNDAMENTALS
Leverage	Net debt-to-equity ratio	Gross long to equity; VaR to equity
Concentration	Revenues, operating profit, assets by sector reporting	Concentration by geography, market cap, industry
Liquidity	Working capital turnover; current ratio	Days to liquidate
Return Behavior	Return on sales; return on equity	Sharpe ratio; largest drawdown
Sources of Performance	Pareto decomposition	Risk-factor decomposition

For example, credit-rating services operate between the issuers of debt and investors and apply a consistent rating process and reporting discipline. College admission testing represents another example of fundamentals. These tests are complex to develop and expensive to administer. Testing services operate between colleges and students.

Third-party administration of standards generally evolves when economies of scale make the economics compelling. For example, a single review by a credit-rating service will satisfy the requirements of hundreds of investors. Similarly, the cost of each college individually developing and administering its proprietary entrance exam to each candidate would dramatically exceed the $28.50 charged by the Educational Testing Service for the SAT or the $26 fee for the ACT. Furthermore, instead of a standard exam being given once and the scores being sent to multiple colleges, multiple exams would be required. In both of these examples, the scale economies are so large that comprehensive credit reviews and college admission testing would not be universally performed were it not for third-party application. Therefore, a key component of the broad acceptance of third-party application of standardized fundamentals is the driving down of price through scale economies and routinization to an "industry utility" price.

Similarly, the effort of performing quality analyses of the risk of investments is too expensive to be separately performed by each fund for each investor. Furthermore, managers are unwilling to commit the time and effort required to report risk in the structure of each and every investor, just as companies are unwilling to support separate credit reviews by each and every potential investor.

The calculation of risk statistics is equally as complex. Therefore, a third-party solution is compelling. However, achieving broad application of an industry standard solution will require that risk statistics be made available at an "industry utility" price, as compared to the $75,000–plus annual fee typical for traditional third-party risk management systems.

The value of an industry standard set of risk factors was strongly indicated by a survey of institutional investors (Hedge Fund Risk Transparency, January 31, 2002) performed by Capital Market Risk Advisors, Inc. (CMRA) for the Alternative Investment Management Association (AIMA). Approximately two-thirds of institutional investors interviewed believed that an industry standard set of risk factors would be either "valuable" or "extremely valuable."

CHAPTER 18

The Risk Fundamentals® Solution

Chapter 16 discusses the compelling need for improved risk transparency in the hedge fund industry. Chapter 17 concludes that only a standard reporting framework, universally applied across the industry, would permit investors to compare and aggregate their risks. This chapter presents a solution, being provided by Kenmar, a global investment management and fund of hedge funds firm. Recognizing the critical need for such a solution, Kenmar plans to provide a basic service intended to function as an "industry utility," to be made available through prime brokers and fund administrators.

This chapter will first present an overview of this Risk Fundamentals solution. The balance of the chapter will then apply the system to concrete examples of the concepts that have been discussed throughout this book. The intent is to demonstrate how a system can provide consistent risk transparency without disclosing sensitive or proprietary data. To this end, specific sample data are presented and discussed as to how risk information should be interpreted and applied.

As much of the value of the solution is derived from the consistent, universal application of an industry standard and from the integration of the many capabilities (risk management, transparency, constructing a portfolio of funds, performance attribution), this chapter presents the "end-game" vision. Note that the core functionality and asset class coverage currently available will be expanded over time.

Overview of the Service

The hedge fund service comprises three key components:

1. NAV/return reporting
2. The Risk Fundamentals system
3. The Risk Fundamentals statistics

Much of the value of this comprehensive service stems from the integration of its three components. Its focus is on hedge funds, because this is where the need for standardized risk management and transparency is the greatest.

However, Risk Fundamentals has been designed to support both traditional and alternative investments. The plan is eventually to extend the service to traditional investments so that an investor can incorporate all of his or her investments in a unified reporting process.

The service has been designed to provide the reporting standardization required to permit comparability in risk reporting based on an open and flexible distributed approach. Following are the key components of this approach:

- Distributed solution
- Standardization with flexibility
- Risk budgeting support
- Effective risk communication

NAV/Return Reporting

An NAV/return reporting service is the cornerstone of the hedge fund offering. Available via the Bloomberg Professional service, it streamlines the information flows within the industry, making them significantly more efficient and valuable. Here are some of its features:

- Bloomberg's database is daily, in contrast to existing hedge fund data services that are monthly. Bloomberg can capture interim NAVs as frequently as they are reported. This serves in effect as "real time" reporting, by which is meant the most current information that each fund has provided. Although the service can accept NAVs for any date (and can accommodate daily NAVs if funds were so inclined), funds are encouraged to consistently provide weekly estimates as of the close of trading on Friday.
- Bloomberg's ability to query the database and retrieve the most recent estimate (independent of whether it is provided daily, weekly on Monday, weekly on Friday, bi-monthly, etc.) provides a logical way to access irregularly reported data.
- The service permits managers to identify NAVs as either gross estimates, net estimates, preliminary NAVs, revised NAVs, or final NAVs and will retain which type of NAV the value represents.
- Bloomberg's NAV reporting service permits individual hedge funds to control (by Bloomberg ID) which investors can access NAVs and returns.
- The service reports NAVs by manager/fund/share class/series. This ensures that investors track their specific returns. Access is controlled at the share class level so that investors holding a particular share class will not be privy to data on other classes.
- Finally, if investors enter into Bloomberg their portfolio of hedge funds (and

ultimately traditional investments), Bloomberg provides "real time" reporting of the consolidated value of the portfolio.

The Risk Fundamentals System

The Risk Fundamentals system functions as a powerful vehicle for risk management/transparency. For those users who so desire, a risk budgeting framework, a process that has been adopted by many leading institutional investors, has been integrated across the system. The basic risk report providing all of the fundamental risk measures is to be made available through prime brokers and fund administrators. The system has been modularly designed for distributed operation. Here are the system's features:

Risk Fundamentals Risk Factors. A set of hedge fund–oriented risk factors are identified that include, for example, equity risk factors broken down into seven style factors (such as value versus growth, large versus small cap, and so on) for each country and twenty-four GICS[1] (Global Industry Classification Standard)–based industry risk factors. In contrast to traditional risk factors that assume that idiosyncratic risk is normally distributed and independent across securities, Risk Fundamentals' Risk Factors measure the actual distribution of returns and actual correlation across securities. Although the traditional approaches work adequately for long-only portfolios, they dramatically misinterpret the risk of hedge funds with long/short strategies explicitly targeting relative valuations. The risks of hedge funds are communicated as sensitivities to risk factors, obviating the need for position disclosure. Because sensitivities are additive, the risk of a portfolio of hedge funds can be analyzed by consolidating the risk exposures of all of the underlying funds.

Risk Fundamentals Fund Subsystem. A sophisticated risk management application is made available to managers that provides measures of liquidity, concentrations, and risk-factor sensitivities. The application creates a long-term historical simulation to analyze the performance of the portfolio in normal markets and applies a battery of stress tests to analyze the behavior of the portfolio in crisis environments. Furthermore, the application permits risk to be "sliced and diced" by position, risk factor, geographic market, and so on and decomposes risk to market, secondary, and idiosyncratic sources. The application uses the historical simulation to calculate a full set of hedge fund statistics including volatility (standard deviation, semi-deviations), drawdowns, risk-adjusted return measures (such as Sharpe and Sortino ratios), correlations, and the like. The application comes with a set of standard assumptions, permitting consistent cross-fund comparisons, but also permits users to analyze custom assumptions. The application can support what-if analyses of alternative constructions and provides measures of marginal risks and marginal risk-adjusted returns and an optimizer to support the construction of the portfolio.

Risk Fundamentals Transparency Subsystem. This system operates as a hub-and-spoke distribution of risk profiles from managers to investors. Access to hedge fund profiles is controlled by user ID. Profiles of funds expressed as so-called risk fundamentals, including sensitivities to risk factors, are automatically sent electronically from the Risk Fundamentals Fund Subsystem. Consolidated profiles of portfolios of funds, including summary statistics on each underlying fund, are sent electronically to the appropriate Risk Fundamentals Investor Subsystem.

Risk Fundamentals Investor Subsystem. This sophisticated risk management system provides investors with the same rich functionality to analyze their portfolios of hedge funds as is provided to hedge funds by the Risk Fundamentals Fund Subsystem. This can include extensive what-if analysis capabilities, measures of marginal risk and marginal risk-adjusted return, and a very sophisticated portfolio optimizer. For funds of funds, the application can provide an aggregate risk profile based on standard risk statistics that the manager can then offer to his investors that is fully compatible with the risk profile provided by the underlying hedge funds.

Risk Fundamentals Performance Attribution Subsystem. A related service analyzes the performance of prior portfolios and uses risk factors to attribute returns to: exposure to the market (such as beta to the equity market), exposure to styles (such as value versus growth or large- versus small-cap stocks), value added in sector or industry betting, active management of the structural risk exposures, and security selection (such as stock picking). The analysis of historical performance is available to both managers and investors.

The Risk Fundamentals Statistics

The Risk Fundamentals statistics generated by the Risk Fundamentals system provide a wealth of causal information. I use the term "causal" because, unlike hedge fund style indices, these data truly explain the return behavior of hedge funds. For example, a convertible arbitrage fund can be long or short interest rates, credit spreads, yield curve relationships, volatility, and equities. The returns of a convertible arbitrage fund are driven by the risk exposures of each specific fund and the returns of these risk exposures and not by the fact that they are all called "convertible arbitrage." Both sensitivities to each of these risk exposures and percentile rankings of the specific fund's exposure to each risk are provided. Existing hedge fund reporting services are unable to provide any of this causal information.

Just as company fundamentals permit an equity analyst to understand the financial health of a company, risk fundamentals provide an investor with an understanding of a fund's risk. The Risk Fundamentals statistics (in particular the risk factor sensitivities) represent an elegant solution to risk transparency for the hedge fund industry. First, I would argue that synthesized risk statistics are, in fact, more valuable than holdings detail. Furthermore, without requiring disclosure of specific holdings, Risk Fundamentals statistics provide:

- A fundamental understanding of the risk exposures of a fund
- The ability for an investor to manage its structural risk exposures across funds
- A framework to track and protect against style drift
- A methodology to permit investors to construct a "risk efficient" portfolio of funds
- Transparency that truly explains the inherent risk of a fund
- Consistent measures of leverage, convexity, and diversification
- An integrated framework to construct portfolios, measure risk, and attribute actual performance (risk budgeting)
- The ability to integrate traditional (long-only) and alternative (hedge fund) investments in a portfolio
- The ability to compare and aggregate across funds
- A consistent framework to "bucket" concentrations
- The ability to decompose risk to its underlying sources

The Risk Fundamentals statistics are utilized across funds to generate the following:

- Standard indices that communicate the norms
- Percentile rankings of specific funds

These tools permit an investor to explore how a specific fund compares to the norms. An example of an index that might be generated is a time series of the average leverage of all equity long/short managers. This permits investors to compare the leverage of a manager in whose fund they are invested to a norm.

Moreover, the index analyzes how the norms change over time. For example, as the volatility of equity markets has increased, many managers have delevered their funds, to the extent that many hold a significant percent of capital as cash.

Although this may be an acceptable interim situation as a fund decides where to deploy its capital, it is an extremely inefficient ongoing form of risk management. In 2004, cash was earning less than the 1.5 percent management fee typical of most equity hedge funds, guaranteeing a loss from capital deployed in cash. The percentile rank function could be used to report the percentile ranking of the leverage of a specific fund relative to the equity long/short universe.

In addition, the investor can create a universe by screening all funds that satisfy specific risk criteria. For example, the investor could select all equity long/short hedge funds that are in the top quartile of leverage. The user can select to save either the resulting universe or the screening criteria to be applied later (this would permit the user to routinely screen the top quartile of leverage—the constituency of which will change over time). More complex screens can combine multiple criteria. For example, an investor could identify all convertible arbitrage funds with a leverage of between 2 and 4, that are fully hedged with respect to interest rates and equities, but which are in or above the 75th percentile in credit exposure.

Some of the other Risk Fundamentals features that are available include:

- Liquidity measures (percent of holdings able to be liquidated within a specified period of time)
- Concentrations (industry, maturity, market capitalization)
- Risk-factor sensitivities
- Impact of a battery of standard stress tests

Other Risk Fundamentals statistics decompose the overall risk of the most current construction into market, style, industry, correlated idiosyncratic, and independent idiosyncratic risks. Still other statistics attribute historical fund returns to systematic exposures to risk factors, manager skill in managing risk factor exposures, and manager idiosyncratic skill (such as stock picking).

Finally, Risk Fundamentals statistics are provided in the language of hedge funds. This includes volatility statistics such as annualized standard deviation or tracking error, characterizations of potential losses such as largest drawdown, and measures of risk-adjusted return such as Sharpe and information ratios. Risk Fundamentals combines actual fund returns and risk measures calculated based on a historical simulation of the current construction (the rational for this is discussed later in this chapter under "Risk-return statistics"). In calculating norms for all hedge funds, by strategy or by style, an appropriate adjustment factor is used to compensate for funds whose histories vary in length.

Distributed Solution

Risk Fundamentals has been designed as a distributed solution. As noted earlier, it was designed around the ubiquitous Bloomberg terminal and uses a risk reporting framework that is additive, permitting risk profiles of multiple funds to be combined without drawing all the underlying positions into a centralized system.

The hedge fund industry has a proprietary and individualistic culture. As discussed in Chapter 16, numerous groups that have opined on transparency have consistently argued against requiring the disclosure of position-level data, although they have supported increased standardized reporting of summary risk data. No such standard has emerged. However, the distributed Risk Fundamentals system permits funds to independently but consistently map their portfolios to a risk profile that does not disclose confidential position-level information while providing a comprehensive set of fundamental risk information.

Risk Fundamentals creates a standard template of fundamental risk statistics—the key measures that characterize the risk of the portfolio construction. These fundamental risk measures have been defined so that they are comparable, and even more important, additive, across funds. These include:

- Concentrations
- Risk-factor sensitivities
- Stress test behavior
- Liquidity
- Leverage

Risk Fundamentals represents a hierarchical solution. A portfolio (or fund) in Risk Fundamentals is a generic structure that can include any combination of securities or other portfolios. This is enabled by the fact that the summary risk profile of a portfolio includes sensitivities to the same risk factors, and aggregations to the same groupings (such as GICS level 2 and credit ratings), that individual securities are mapped to. Therefore, the risk profiles of portfolios can be reloaded with the same exposures as an individual security. Applying Risk Fundamentals to a fund of funds creates the same risk profile of the fund of funds as applying Risk Fundamentals to an individual hedge fund would create. Furthermore, a user can include securities in the portfolio analysis of a portfolio of funds to support the analysis of potential hedging strategies. For example, if a user wants to consider hedging the beta to the market using SPDRs or futures, Risk Fundamentals supports this analysis. Furthermore, if a user wants to consider managing risk in potential extreme events, Risk Fundamentals analyzes the potential impact of hedging with options on equity indices.

Finally, the system has been designed to electronically communicate the risk profiles. Risk Fundamentals maintains a centralized database of risk profiles. Investors can connect to this central database and get a complete portfolio of their holdings, including a consolidated picture of their portfolio of funds and the summary information on each of the underlying funds. Access to this data is tightly controlled, with individual hedge funds being able to designate which users should have access to their fund's information.

Standardization with Flexibility

Although a significant amount of the value of Risk Fundamentals is based on the utilization of "standardized" fundamental risk measures, the system has been designed for flexibility. Here are some of the flexible features:

Standard/custom assumptions. Achieving comparability across funds requires the application of a standard set of assumptions, for example, the percentage of market turnover willing to capture (discussed later in this chapter). Ten percent has been established as the standard, based on the fact that long-term traditional managers typically are willing to capture 20 percent of equity turnover, and nimble hedge funds targeting smaller misvaluations should logically be willing to capture less. The point is that the assumed level is arbitrary and there is no single "correct" level. However, if one is to compare liquidity across managers it is critical that the same assumption has been applied.

Risk Fundamentals provides each individual user with the ability to customize her assumptions, and the system simultaneously maintains a set of standard assumptions and a second set of custom assumptions. For example, a specific user can select 20 percent as the percent of market turnover she is willing to capture, and the system can perform the liquidity analysis based on this assumption. The user can simply toggle back and forth between the standard and custom set.

Absolute and relative measures. Risk Fundamentals has been designed for both traditional and alternative investments. As such, it supports both absolute and relative measures of risk and return, as shown in **Figure 18.1**.

The fact that Risk Fundamentals handles all investments holistically permits investors with portfolios including both traditional and alternative investments to analyze their consolidated portfolio. A significant amount of the value of alternative investments is their synergistic behavior with traditional investments. Being able to explicitly track this synergy and manage the complete portfolio is extremely valuable.

FIGURE 18.1 Risk Fundamentals Absolute and Relative Measures

MEASURE	ABSOLUTE	RELATIVE
Volatility	Standard Deviation	Tracking Error
Return	Absolute Return	Relative Return
Risk-Adjusted Return	Sharpe Ratio	Information Ratio
Value at Risk	VaR	Relative VaR
Marginal Measures	Marginal Risk	Marginal Relative Risk

Modular setup. Risk Fundamentals includes five modules:

- Risk-return statistics
- Concentrations
- Risk factors
- Liquidity
- Portfolio management

Each module includes a detail worksheet (with position-level detail), a summary sheet (with portfolio-level summary information), and a graphic sheet (that presents the summary data graphically).

Measures of marginal risk. As discussed in Chapter 3, risk is multidimensional and requires many different measures. These include measures of volatility such as the standard deviation, measures of decline such as drawdown, and measures that capture the distribution of returns such as VaR. Risk Fundamentals permits the user to select the measure of marginal risk. The default measure is standard deviation, which characterizes the full distribution with a single value (although it does not capture fat tails and skew).

Advanced Excel "table" functionality. In addition to the standardized profiles included in the summary sheets, the concentration and risk-factor modules include flexible tools to slice and dice the details. The detail sheets permit the user to filter the data to flexibly search, select, and aggregate the tables. The analysis sheets provide extremely powerful "pivot table" functionality of the detail data, permitting the user to flexibly aggregate the detail. These capabilities have all been implemented using standard Microsoft Excel functionality, providing a breadth of functionality with which many users will already be familiar.

Investor package. Rather than being dogmatic with respect to transparency, Risk Fundamentals is flexible. The system can control the level of detail provided in the summary risk profile. For example, although the system by default captures concentrations by country, the user can choose to capture them only by geographic region. Similarly, although the system by default captures industry concentrations at the twenty-four-industry GICS level 2, the user can choose to capture them only at the ten-sector GICS level 1. The user can also select to show:

- No position names
- Long-only position names
- Long and short position names

These names are displayed when viewing the largest long and short positions and the longest to liquidate long and short positions. The objective is to capture a minimum set of data that permits multiple funds to be compared and aggregated while enabling funds that want to share more information to do so in a structured way.

Risk Budgeting Support

Risk Fundamentals is based on an integrated risk budgeting framework. As presented in Chapter 12, risk budgeting is a process whose objective is to spend "units of risk" as efficiently as possible. In contrast, traditional processes of asset allocation/portfolio management generally are based on allocating "units of capital."

Allocating capital is particularly inappropriate in hedge funds with long/short strategies displaying significant convexity and utilizing notional funding. In these strategies, the relationship between capital and risk can vary dramatically. Being able to construct a portfolio based on risk is extremely valuable. For example, many investors who allocate capital to managers create portfolios in which the vast majority of risk rests in a small minority of funds. An investor who allocates 50 percent to directional funds and 50 percent to relative-value funds may find that a few high-volatility directional funds (such as emerging market or biotech funds) dominate the risk profile. But allocating to funds based on risk, explicitly integrating the diversification benefit of each fund into the process, results in a significantly more balanced and risk-efficient portfolio. This framework permits the investor to efficiently incorporate high-risk/high-return funds into his portfolio, but appropriately size the investments to maximize the impact on risk-adjusted returns without adding unwanted volatility.

However, although providing multiple views of the portfolio based on risk, Risk Fundamentals also presents the traditional view of the portfolio based on invested capital. The system handles the challenge of notional funding by presenting the portfolio based on both invested capital and cash equivalent bases.

Another key component of risk budgeting is that a single risk framework be applied on an integrated basis across the portfolio management, risk management, and performance attribution processes. Consequently, the basis on which the portfolio is constructed is the same as that used to measure the risk in the portfolio and is subsequently applied in a post mortem to understand how returns were actually generated.

Effective Risk Communication

As discussed in Chapter 7, risk is inherently difficult to communicate. A key is presenting risk on a relative basis. Risk Fundamentals provides for each risk measure:

- ***Summary statistics*** of the risk measure for previous months' constructions
- ***Peer comparables*** for the risk measure for all hedge funds, the strategy, and the style
- ***Historical values*** of the risk measure for previous months' constructions

Figure 18.2 is an example of the full set of information provided for each risk fundamental (the examples in the balance of this chapter display selected sections, although the system consistently provides the complete profile).

The summary and history sections provide a comparison of the risk measure of the current construction to that of previous months' constructions. The history section presents the comparable value for each previous months' constructions (averaging the values of each statistic across all constructions during the month if multiple constructions have been processed) for which data are available. This permits the user to analyze the trends in the risks of the portfolio—in other words, to perform a style drift analysis. Based on this history, the summary statistic section presents the minimum, average, and maximum of the comparable values for all previous months' constructions. If the current value is below the minimum or above the maximum of the comparable value for previous months' constructions, the current value is shaded in red (shown as black). If the current value is below the 20th percentile or above the 80th percentile of the comparable value for previous months' constructions, the current value is shaded in yellow (shown as gray).

In Figure 18.2, the maximum days to liquidate all long holdings (to 0 percent) was 66 days in February 2004's construction. The minimum days to liquidate all long holdings was 29 days in the constructions of March and April 2003. The average of the days to liquidate all long holdings of all of the previous constructions that have been processed is 40 days. In comparison, the current

FIGURE 18.2 **Risk Fundamentals Standard Information**

Current Construction		Summary—Previous Months' Constructions			Peer Comparison					
DAYS TO LIQUIDATE VARIOUS PERCENTAGES OF HOLDINGS					COMPOSITE		EQUITY		LONG/SHORT US	
% REMAINING	MAR-04	MIN	AVG	MAX	AVG.	% RANK	AVG.	% RANK	AVG.	% RANK
Long Positions 10%	10	5	9	16	1	84%	3	73%	6	68%
5%	16	10	17	30	3	87%	6	74%	12	65%
1%	30	20	27	40	5	88%	9	86%	21	70%
0%	67	29	40	66	8	97%	16	93%	31	89%
Short Positions 10%	2	1	2	2	1	68%	1	67%	1	59%
5%	2	2	3	5	1	63%	1	64%	2	55%
1%	5	3	5	7	2	83%	2	69%	3	67%
0%	11	7	10	14	3	85%	5	75%	7	61%

days to liquidate all long holdings is 67 days, which is shaded in red (shown as black) because it is greater than the historical maximum.

The peer comparison section provides, as a basis of comparison, the average and the percentile rank of that fund relative to those of each of the following peer universes:

- All funds
- Funds with the same strategies (in this example "Equity")
- Funds with the same styles (in this example "Long/Short US"). The percentile ranking is shaded in red (shown as black) if the rank is in the top or bottom 5 percentile. The percentile ranking is shaded in yellow (shown as gray) if the rank is in the top or bottom 20th percentile.

In Figure 18.2, the average days to liquidate long holdings to 10 percent of current holdings for all hedge funds is 1 day, and the hedge fund being analyzed is in the 84th percentile of all funds based on this statistic. The average days to liquidate long holdings to 10 percent of current holdings for a peer universe of all equity funds is 3 days and the fund being analyzed is in the 73rd percentile of all funds in this sub-universe. The average days to liquidate long holdings to 10 percent of current holdings for a peer universe of all long/short US funds is 6 days and the fund being analyzed is in the 68th percentile of all funds in this sub-universe.

History—
Previous Months' Constructions

	FEB-04	JAN-04	DEC-03	NOV-03	OCT-03	SEP-03	AUG-03	JUL-03	JUN-03	MAY-03	APR-03	MAR-03
	7	7	10	16	13	7	7	10	10	7	7	5
	16	30	20	16	25	16	13	16	16	13	13	10
	40	40	25	30	30	25	20	25	20	25	20	25
	66	61	41	41	45	33	33	33	33	34	29	29
	2	2	1	1	1	2	1	2	2	2	2	1
	3	3	2	2	2	2	2	2	2	3	5	5
	5	5	5	3	5	3	5	5	5	7	7	7
	9	14	12	7	7	7	10	11	8	12	11	12

Whereas comparative risk measures are based on the current portfolio construction of each fund, comparative return and risk-adjusted return statistics incorporate the historical actual returns of each hedge fund. Varying length return histories represent a significant challenge in achieving comparability of such measures across funds. Risk Fundamentals has solved the challenge of variable-length return histories by calculating appropriate adjustment factors. This is discussed in detail later in this chapter in the "Risk-return analyses" section.

Interpreting Risk Management Reporting

The balance of this chapter provides concrete examples of how the concepts presented throughout this book can be applied to the management of risk in hedge funds. It is also presented as a model of effective and high-quality transparency (without disclosing proprietary data). Examples related to each of the following topics will be presented:

1. Concentrations
2. Leverage
3. Liquidity
4. Risk Factors
5. Historical Simulation

FIGURE 18.3 Position Detail

	COMPANY NAME	POSITION TYPE	MARKET/ COUNTRY	COMPANY COUNTRY	COMPANY REGION
AAPL US	Apple Computer Inc	Equity	US	US	North America
AMCC US	Applied Micro Circuits Corp	Equity	US	US	North America
ADP US	Automatic Data Processing	Equity	US	US	North America
BMC US	BMC Software Inc	Equity	US	US	North America
CEN US	Ceridian Corp	Equity	US	US	North America
CSC US	Computer Sciences Corp	Equity	US	US	North America
DELL US	Dell Inc	Equity	US	US	North America
EMC US	EMC Corp/Massachusetts	Equity	US	US	North America
FISV US	Fiserv Inc	Equity	US	US	North America
IDTI US	Integrated Device Technology Inc	Equity	US	US	North America
ISIL US	Intersil Corp	Equity	US	US	North America
LRCX US	Lam Research Corp	Equity	US	US	North America
MCDTA US	McData Corp	Equity	US	US	North America
MSFT US	Microsoft Corp	Equity	US	US	North America
NOVL US	Novell Inc	Equity	US	US	North America
ORCL US	Oracle Corp	Equity	US	US	North America
QLGC US	QLogic Corp	Equity	US	US	North America
SEBL US	Siebel Systems Inc	Equity	US	US	North America
SNPS US	Synopsys Inc	Equity	US	US	North America
WIND US	Wind River Systems Inc	Equity	US	US	North America

6 Stress Tests
7 Convexity
8 Risk-Return Analyses
9 Constructing a Fund
10 Constructing a Portfolio of Funds
11 Performance Attribution

Quality risk information facilitates good decision-making, but much work is required of investors to take full advantage of the resource. Quality information represents a starting gate, to ensure a fair start—it's not a finishing line.

GENERAL INDUSTRY CLASSIFICATION SYSTEM				MARKET CAP	LONG/	%
GICS LEVEL 1	GICS LEVEL 2	GICS LEVEL 3	GICS LEVEL 4	GROUP	SHORT	NET VAL
InfoTech	TechHardEquip	ComptrsPeriph	ComptrHardware	$5-10	Short	–1.1%
InfoTech	Semiconductor	SemiconEquip3	Semiconductors	$1–2	Long	2.7%
InfoTech	SoftwareServ	ItConsultSvc	DataProcOutServices	$10+	Short	–0.1%
InfoTech	SoftwareServ	Software	SystemsSoftware	$2–5	Long	1.9%
InfoTech	SoftwareServ	ItConsultSvc	DataProcOutServices	$2–5	Long	1.9%
InfoTech	SoftwareServ	ItConsultSvc	DataProcOutServices	$5-10	Long	3.7%
InfoTech	TechHardEquip	ComptrsPeriph	ComptrHardware	$10+	Short	–2.5%
InfoTech	TechHardEquip	ComptrsPeriph	ComptrStoragePeriph	$10+	Long	1.6%
InfoTech	SoftwareServ	ItConsultSvc	DataProcOutServices	$5–10	Short	–0.7%
InfoTech	Semiconductor	SemiconEquip3	Semiconductors	$1–2	Long	1.7%
InfoTech	Semiconductor	SemiconEquip3	Semiconductors	$2–5	Long	3.5%
InfoTech	Semiconductor	SemiconEquip3	SemiconEquip4	$2–5	Short	–0.1%
InfoTech	TechHardEquip	CommnEquip	TelecomEquip	$1–2	Short	–2.1%
InfoTech	SoftwareServ	Software	SystemsSoftware	$10+	Long	4.1%
InfoTech	SoftwareServ	Software	SystemsSoftware	$2–5	Short	–3.1%
InfoTech	SoftwareServ	Software	SystemsSoftware	$10+	Short	–0.1%
InfoTech	Semiconductor	SemiconEquip3	Semiconductors	$2–5	Long	3.3%
InfoTech	SoftwareServ	Software	ApplicationSoftware	$5–10	Short	–1.3%
InfoTech	SoftwareServ	Software	ApplicationSoftware	$5–10	Long	1.9%
InfoTech	SoftwareServ	Software	SystemsSoftware	$.5–1	Long	4.5%

Concentrations

Chapter 6 concludes that slicing and dicing positions is not an effective way to understand the risks in hedge funds. However, even as a committed devotee of representing hedge fund risk as sensitivities to risk factors, I have a natural instinct to "bucket" holdings by various classification schemes, if only to confirm that risk exposures in a long/short portfolio do not flow with asset exposures. It provides comfort on the nature of the underlying holdings and, even if it does not explain the underlying risk at any one time, it is a good way of monitoring for style drift. Consequently, Risk Fundamentals provides summary information on concentrations of positions across multiple dimensions:

- Asset class
- Position type
- Equity and fixed income by market
- Equity and corporate debt by country of company
- Equity and corporate debt by GICS
- Equity by market cap
- Fixed income by maturity
- Debt by credit rating
- Commodity group exposure

Risk Fundamentals categorizes each holding based on these various dimensions, as shown in **Figure 18.3**. Risk Fundamentals permits the fund to slice and dice these holdings, supporting both filtering of the list of holdings and pivot table analytics. The position detail is presented to the fund, whereas typically only the concentration summaries will be included in the investor package (Risk Fundamentals' solution to transparency).

Along each of these dimensions, Risk Fundamentals calculates the concentrations for each category, separately bucketing long and short exposures. Both gross and net exposures are presented. Comparable net exposure aggregations are provided for previous months' constructions. Averages and percentile rankings for multiple peer groups are also displayed. Risk Fundamentals presents concentrations based on cash equivalent exposures.

Risk Fundamentals first displays the concentrations of the largest long and short positions. As discussed earlier, the goal is to provide a minimum standard transparency while enabling managers to disclose as much detail as they feel comfortable doing. In this spirit, **Figure 18.4** shows the concentration of the largest long and short positions of a technology sector fund. In this example, the fund chose to display the specific long positions while displaying only proxy data for the short holdings (country, GICS group, and position size). The fund could have opted to display the details for both the long and short holdings, or to mask the specifics of both the long and short positions (displaying only the proxy data). The concept is that the fund can select the level of transparency with which it feels comfortable. In Figure 18.4, "WIND US" is the largest long position at 4.5 percent of equity capital; and the largest short position, the specific name of which is masked, is 3.1 percent of equity capital.

Risk Fundamentals displays for both the long and the short holdings the concentrations of the largest holding, the largest five holdings, and the largest ten holdings. In **Figure 18.5**, the concentrations of the largest long holding of the same tech fund,

FIGURE 18.4 **Concentration Summary**

Largest Long Holdings

	POSITION	COMPANY NAME	SIZE	INDUSTRY
1	WIND US	Wind River Systems Inc	4.5%	SoftwareServ
2	MSFT US	Microsoft Corp	4.1%	SoftwareServ
3	CSC US	Computer Sciences Corp	3.7%	SoftwareServ
4	ISIL US	Intersil Corp	3.5%	Semiconductor
5	QLGC US	QLogic Corp	3.3%	Semiconductor
6	AMCC US	Applied Micro Circuits Corp	2.7%	Semiconductor
7	BMC US	BMC Software Inc	1.9%	SoftwareServ
8	CEN US	Ceridian Corp	1.9%	SoftwareServ
9	SNPS US	Synopsys Inc	1.9%	SoftwareServ
10	IDTI US	Integrated Device Technology Inc	1.7%	Semiconductor

Largest Short Holdings

	POSITION	COMPANY NAME	SIZE	INDUSTRY
1	Short 1	US	3.1%	SoftwareServ
2	Short 2	US	2.5%	Semiconductor
3	Short 3	US	2.5%	TechHardEquip
4	Short 4	US	2.1%	TechHardEquip
5	Short 5	US	1.3%	SoftwareServ
6	Short 6	US	1.1%	TechHardEquip
7	Short 7	US	0.7%	SoftwareServ
8	Short 8	US	0.1%	SoftwareServ
9	Short 9	US	0.1%	Semiconductor
10	Short 10	US	0.1%	SoftwareServ

representing 4.5 percent of equity capital, is larger than that of the largest position of all previous constructions, the previous maximum being 4.4 percent. Therefore the current value is highlighted in red (shown as black in the exhibit).

Risk Fundamentals next displays concentrations by asset class, as shown in **Figure 18.6**. This example profiles the diverse asset class exposures of a global macro fund and reveals that the fund is more exposed to commodities (49 percent net long) than the average of its peer universe. The average net exposure to commodities of

FIGURE 18.5 **Concentration of Largest Holdings**

		NET	MIN	AVERAGE	MAX
Long Positions	Largest	4.5%	3.5%	3.8%	4.4%
	Top 5	18.9%	13.4%	14.5%	20.3%
	Top 10	29.1%	20.2%	26.9%	32.4%
Short Positions	Largest	3.1%	2.9%	3.3%	3.5%
	Top 5	11.5%	10.4%	11.6%	12.8%
	Top 10	13.6%	13.2%	14.8%	16.7%

FIGURE 18.6 **Concentrations by Asset Class**

		COMPOSITE		OPPORTUNISTIC		GLOBAL MACRO	
	NET	AVG.	% RANK	AVG.	% RANK	AVG.	% RANK
Total	**58%**	**31%**	**68%**	**26%**	**82%**	**33%**	**77%**
Equity	8%	32%	23%	21%	32%	16%	43%
Fixed Income	–12%	–7%	43%	–6%	41%	–5%	37%
Commodity	49%	1%	98%	4%	92%	14%	87%
Currency	12%	5%	63%	7%	56%	8%	53%

the universe of global macro funds is 14 percent. The fund being analyzed is in the 87 percentile of exposure to commodities of all global macro funds.

Risk Fundamentals also displays concentrations by position type, as shown in **Figure 18.7**. This analysis aggregates position types to instrument types (cash, futures, options, OTC derivatives). This figure shows a convertible arbitrage fund. It clearly identifies the basis risk (corporate versus sovereign debt and swaps) of such a strategy.

Risk Fundamentals profiles concentrations by markets: fixed-income by currency and equities by country of exchange. The fixed-income concentrations by currency aggregates fixed-income instruments (debt, financial futures, financial options, and OTC derivatives) by the currency in which they are issued. For example, the yen-denominated debt issued by a German subsidiary of IBM is captured as Japanese. **Figure 18.8** shows that an emerging market fund's fixed-income exposure to Russia (52 percent) is significantly greater than the average exposure of peer emerging market debt funds (12 percent). Based on this

FIGURE 18.7 **Concentrations by Position Type**

	LONG	SHORT	GROSS	NET
Total	**227.6%**	**–311.6%**	**539.2%**	**–84.0%**
Equity		**–97.2%**	**97.2%**	**–97.2%**
Equity		–97.2%	97.2%	–97.2%
ETF				
Debt	**212.3%**	**–73.9%**	**286.2%**	**138.4%**
Sovereign		–73.9%	73.9%	–73.9%
Corporate				
Convertible	212.3%		212.3%	212.3%
ABS				
Muni				
Currency				
Futures	**15.3%**	**–5.7%**	**21.0%**	**9.6%**
Equity Fut				
Finan Fut				
Cmdty Fut				
Crncy Fut	15.3%	–5.7%	21.0%	9.6%
Options				
Equity Opt				
Finan Opt				
Cmdty Opt				
Crncy Opt				
OTC Derivatives		**–134.8%**	**134.8%**	**–134.8%**
IRS		–87.4%	87.4%	–87.4%
CDS		–47.4%	47.4%	–47.4%
FI Options				
Real Estate				
Funds				
Hedge Funds				
Mutual Funds				

statistic, the fund is ranked in the 97th percentile of all emerging market debt funds. Risk Fundamentals separately presents equity concentrations (including equities, ETFs, equity futures, and equity options) by country of exchange.

FIGURE 18.8 **Fixed-Income Concentrations by Currency**

	LONG	SHORT	GROSS	NET
Total	**191%**	**–90%**	**281%**	**101%**
North America		**–47%**	**47%**	**–47%**
US		–47%	47%	**–47%**
Latin America	**71%**		**71%**	**71%**
Argentina	19%		19%	19%
Brazil	24%		24%	24%
Chile	28%		28%	28%
East Europe	**65%**	**–9%**	**74%**	**56%**
Czech	5%		5%	5%
Hungary		–9%	9%	–9%
Poland	8%		8%	8%
Russia	52%		52%	52%
Other Asia	**32%**	**–34%**	**66%**	**–2%**
China		–25%	25%	–25%
Hong Kong	14%		14%	14%
Philippines	4%	–9%	13%	–5%
South Korea	12%		12%	12%
Taiwan	2%		2%	2%
Africa/Middle East	**23%**		**23%**	**23%**
Turkey	23%		23%	23%

Risk Fundamentals profiles the distribution of both equity and corporate debt exposures by country of company (the country is based on the location of the headquarters of the company independent of the location of the exchange). **Figure 18.9** highlights how an emerging market equity fund's exposure to Latin America is captured despite the fact that the majority of the exposure is gained through ADRs traded on U.S. exchanges. In this example, the net exposure to Brazil is 21.7 percent, versus net exposures to Brazil in all of the previous months' constructions ranging from 4.2 percent to 19.0 percent and averaging 11.0 percent. Risk Fundamentals similarly aggregates corporate debt based on the country of the parent company of the issuing entity. In this aggregation, the yen-denominated debt issued by a German subsidiary of IBM is captured as U.S.

COMPOSITE		EMERGING MARKET		EM DEBT	
AVG.	% RANK	AVG.	% RANK	AVG.	% RANK
16%	**63%**	**48%**	**64%**	**52%**	**67%**
12%	**9%**	**–2%**	**14%**	**–5%**	**12%**
12%	7%	–2%	14%	–5%	12%
1%	**92%**	**12%**	**83%**	**10%**	**77%**
0%	91%	4%	79%	4%	67%
1%	94%	5%	87%	2%	73%
0%	97%	3%	84%	4%	81%
1%	**94%**	**14%**	**82%**	**25%**	**81%**
0%	87%	2%	55%	4%	53%
0%	12%	3%	15%	5%	37%
0%	88%	2%	57%	4%	62%
1%	99%	7%	98%	12%	97%
1%	**42%**	**20%**	**25%**	**14%**	**25%**
0%	8%	2%	7%	–2%	11%
1%	87%	4%	63%	3%	68%
0%	21%	3%	39%	4%	6%
0%	83%	6%	56%	5%	56%
0%	56%	5%	46%	4%	47%
0%	**97%**	**4%**	**59%**	**8%**	**62%**
0%	99%	4%	63%	5%	67%

Standard and Poor's (S&P) and Morgan Stanley Capital International (MSCI) have jointly defined the Global Industry Classification Standard (GICS). This four-level hierarchy groups equities into:

- 10 sectors
- 24 industry groups
- 62 industries
- 132 subindustries

Risk Fundamentals maps over 200,000 equities and significantly more corporate debt issues globally to this four-level structure. For both equities and corporate debt, summaries for each of the twenty-four industry groups, aggregated to ten sectors, are provided in the risk profile (ETFs are included when they can be associ-

FIGURE 18.9 **Equity Concentrations by Country of Company**

	LONG	SHORT	GROSS	NET	MIN	AVG	MAX
Total	**69.5%**	**–33.3%**	**102.8%**	**36.1%**	**–6.3%**	**21.4%**	**42.3%**
Latin America	**41.4%**	**–21.1%**	**62.5%**	**20.3%**	**–3.6%**	**13.4%**	**24.1%**
Argentina	5.4%	–7.2%	12.6%	–1.8%	–3.5%	1.2%	6.7%
Brazil	27.3%	–5.6%	32.9%	21.7%	4.2%	11.0%	19.0%
Chile	3.0%		3.0%	3.0%		2.4%	5.1%
Mexico	5.7%	–8.3%	14.0%	–2.6%	–4.3%	–1.2%	2.3%
East Europe	**9.5%**	**–3.5%**	**13.0%**	**6.0%**	**3.2%**	**6.4%**	**9.1%**
Czech	6.3%	–1.4%	7.7%	4.9%		2.4%	5.4%
Hungary	3.2%		3.2%	3.2%	0.5%	2.8%	4.9%
Russia		–2.1%	2.1%	–2.1%	–5.2%	–2.3%	–0.5%
Other Asia	**14.0%**	**–8.7%**	**22.7%**	**5.2%**	**–18.4%**	**4.5%**	**12.3%**
China	0.7%	–0.2%	0.9%	0.5%	–3.7%	1.4%	4.7%
Hong Kong	3.1%	–2.1%	5.2%	1.0%	–6.2%	–1.5%	2.3%
South Korea		–6.3%	6.3%	–6.3%	–8.2%	–5.2%	–3.5%
Taiwan	10.2%		10.2%	10.2%	–0.3%	4.5%	8.4%
Africa/Middle East	**4.6%**		**4.6%**	**4.6%**	**–2.3%**	**2.1%**	**6.2%**
South Africa	4.6%		4.6%	4.6%	–2.3%	2.1%	6.2%

ated with a specific sector, such as a semiconductor ETF). **Figure 18.10** shows the GICS summary of the corporate debt for a capital structure arbitrage fund. The example shows that the fund is significantly more exposed to PharmaBiotech 11.9 percent net exposure than it had previously been (ranged from –9.7 percent to 11.3 percent). Risk Fundamentals provides a similar profile of the equity summary by GICS, presenting, in a consistent framework, the complementary side of the debt-equity trades of this capital structure arbitrage fund.

As discussed in Chapter 2, hedge funds' bias to be long illiquid instruments and short more liquid instruments generally results in a small-cap bias in equity funds. Although the risk in any such bias is explicitly measured by the large-cap risk factor, it is useful to segment both long and short positions by market cap to profile the distribution of the holdings of a statistical arbitrage fund as shown in **Figure 18.11** (shares for companies with multiple share classes are combined for determining the market capitalization grouping; equity options are grouped based on the market capitalization of the underlying equity; ETFs are excluded). This figure

FIGURE 18.10 **Corporate Debt Concentrations by GICS Grouping**[2]

	LONGS	SHORTS	GROSS	NET	MIN	AVG	MAX
Total	**81.4%**	**–51.1%**	**132.5%**	**30.3%**	**–51.5%**	**23.6%**	**69.2%**
Energy	**3.4%**	**–0.4%**	**3.8%**	**3.1%**	**–2.3%**	**2.0%**	**5.7%**
Energy	3.4%	–0.4%	3.8%	3.1%	–2.3%	2.0%	5.7%
Materials	**2.9%**	**–1.8%**	**4.8%**	**1.1%**	**–1.8%**	**2.2%**	**7.6%**
Materials	2.9%	–1.8%	4.8%	1.1%	–1.8%	2.2%	7.6%
Industrials	**7.8%**	**–2.2%**	**10.0%**	**5.6%**	**–5.2%**	**2.5%**	**9.9%**
CapitalGoods	4.8%	–1.3%	6.2%	3.5%	–2.0%	2.6%	9.5%
CommlSvcSuppl	1.4%	–0.7%	2.1%	0.7%	–3.3%	–0.1%	1.6%
Transportation	1.6%	–0.2%	1.7%	1.4%	–1.2%	0.0%	1.5%
ConsumDiscr	**6.5%**	**–6.8%**	**13.2%**	**–0.3%**	**–15.7%**	**0.4%**	**10.9%**
AutoCompon	0.6%		0.6%	0.6%	–6.0%	–1.2%	1.3%
ConsDurApparel	1.4%	–1.4%	2.8%	–0.1%	–5.3%	0.0%	4.6%
HotelsRestLeis	0.8%	–0.3%	1.1%	0.5%	–1.3%	0.3%	1.7%
Media	2.5%	–1.3%	3.8%	1.2%	–2.7%	1.9%	6.9%
Retailing	1.2%	–3.8%	5.0%	–2.6%	–4.6%	–0.7%	4.8%
ConsumStap	**3.9%**	**–0.2%**	**4.1%**	**3.6%**	**–2.1%**	**2.1%**	**4.7%**
FoodDrugRetl	0.5%		0.5%	0.5%	–1.2%	–0.1%	1.5%
FoodBevTobac	2.9%	–0.2%	3.2%	2.7%	–0.6%	2.3%	4.9%
HousePersProd	0.5%		0.5%	0.5%	–2.2%	–0.1%	0.9%
HealthCare	**25.0%**	**–4.7%**	**29.6%**	**20.3%**	**–14.4%**	**7.5%**	**20.6%**
HCareEquipSvc	12.3%	–3.9%	16.2%	8.4%	–6.4%	2.5%	9.5%
PharmaBiotech	12.7%	–0.8%	13.5%	11.9%	–9.7%	5.0%	11.3%
Financials	**6.6%**	**–11.8%**	**18.5%**	**–5.2%**	**–10.9%**	**–0.1%**	**8.0%**
Banks	3.0%	–5.0%	8.0%	–2.0%	–3.7%	0.5%	3.5%
DiversFinanc	1.1%	–6.8%	8.0%	–5.7%	–6.9%	–1.9%	2.1%
Insurance	2.5%		2.5%	2.5%	–3.2%	1.3%	4.8%
RealEstate						0.4%	0.8%
InfoTech	**22.3%**	**–23.1%**	**45.3%**	**–0.8%**	**–8.8%**	**5.8%**	**24.1%**
Semiconductor	4.5%	–11.8%	16.2%	–7.3%	–11.2%	–2.4%	7.9%
SoftwareServ	11.1%	–7.9%	19.0%	3.1%	–1.6%	6.5%	14.2%
TechHardEquip	6.7%	–3.3%	10.1%	3.4%	–4.3%	1.7%	6.8%
TelecomSvc	**1.2%**	**–0.1%**	**1.3%**	**1.1%**	**0.0%**	**1.1%**	**3.5%**
TelecomSvc	1.2%	–0.1%	1.3%	1.1%	0.0%	1.1%	3.5%
Utilities	**1.8%**		**1.8%**	**1.8%**	**–0.7%**	**0.2%**	**2.8%**
Utilities	1.8%		1.8%	1.8%	–0.7%	0.2%	2.8%

FIGURE 18.11 **Equity Concentrations by Market Cap—% of Equity**

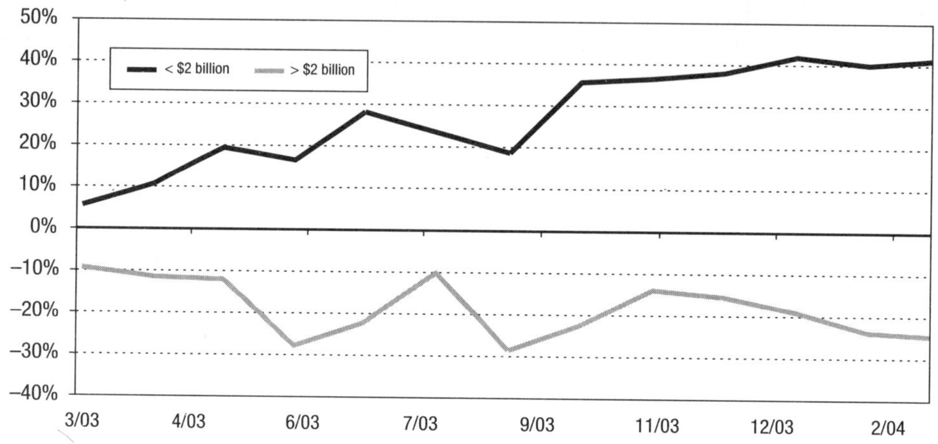

FIGURE 18.12 **Fixed-Income Concentrations by Maturity**

	LONG	SHORT	GROSS	NET
Total	**1419%**	**–539%**	**1958%**	**880%**
≤ 5 Yrs	**1395%**	**–416%**	**1811%**	**979%**
0–1 Yr	952%	–75%	1027%	877%
1–2 Yr	420%	–120%	540%	300%
2–5 Yr	23%	–221%	244%	–198%
> 5 Yrs	**24%**	**–123%**	**147%**	**–99%**
5–10 Yr		–123%	123%	–123%
10+ Yr	24%		24%	24%

demonstrates that the statistical arbitrage fund being analyzed is consistently small-cap biased, being long small-cap stocks and short large-cap stocks. Furthermore, the graph shows that the bias has been broadly increasing over time.

Figure 18.12 shows how Risk Fundamentals profiles fixed income by maturity of a long/short credit fund. This example displays the "barbell" strategy of a fixed-income relative value fund.

Furthermore, Risk Fundamentals aggregates debt into eight S&P rating groups (for debt not rated by S&P but rated by Moody or Fitch, the rating of the other agency is converted to an equivalent S&P rating).

In **Figure 18.13**, the concentration summary by credit rating of a distressed debt fund clearly displays that the exposure to "non-performing" debt has increased over the last year.

Risk Fundamentals displays concentrations in physical commodities by commodity group. **Figure 18.14** shows how a trend-following CTA has a heavy bet on livestock (19.2 percent net exposure) relative to that of its peer universe of trend- following CTAs which has averaged 1.4 percent. The fund is in the 97th percentile based on exposure to livestock of all trend-following CTAs.

Leverage

Chapter 3 presents a multilevel leverage framework and discusses each form of leverage in depth. Risk Fundamentals applies this framework to isolate the different types of leverage. The inherent risk of the instruments in the portfolio, or ***instrument risk***, is reduced through diversification, or ***construction leverage***, resulting in the ***unlevered risk***. ***Financing leverage*** either increases or decreases the unlevered risk to generate the ***levered risk***. The specifics of this structure are presented top down as follows:

Levered risk—The levered risk is the combination of the financing leverage multiplied by the unlevered risk.

- ***Financing leverage***—The financing leverage is the sum of the borrowing leverage plus the notional leverage.
  - ***Borrowing leverage***—The borrowing leverage is the difference between the invested capital as a percent of equity capital minus 1.
  - ***Notional leverage***—The notional leverage is the sum of the option, future, and swap leverages.
    - *Option leverage*—The option leverage is the difference between the delta equivalent value of the underlying security minus the market value of the option (option premium) as a percent of equity capital.
    - *Futures leverage*—The futures leverage is the difference between the notional value of the futures minus the initial margin as a percent of equity capital.
    - *Swap leverage*—The swap leverage is the difference between the notional value of the swap minus the market value of the swap as a percent of equity capital.

Unlevered risk—The portfolio leverage is the product of the instrument risk multiplied by the construction leverage.

Construction leverage—The construction leverage of the portfolio construction is calculated as the ratio of the unlevered risk (the risk of the portfolio given the actual diversification/hedging) divided by the instrument risk (the risk were there to be no diversification/hedging benefit). It represents one minus the diversification benefit, the percent reduction in risk resulting from diversification/hedging.

Instrument risk—Risk Fundamentals calculates what the risk of the portfolio construction would have been if there had been no diversification or hedging benefit. The aggregate risk represented by exposure to risk factors was calculated by applying the gross exposure (thereby assuming no netting or hedging benefit) to both the market and secondary risks. The idiosyncratic risk is calculated as the sum and of the standard deviations of the idiosyncratic returns of each holding, thereby assuming no diversification benefit. Finally, the risks from exposure to risk factors and the idiosyncratic risks are combined assuming statistical independence (the variance of the sum is equal to the sum of the variances).

Risk Fundamentals applies this paradigm to analyze the leverage of hedge funds. **Figure 18.15** is an example of the leverage of a merger arbitrage fund that uses options to express its view. This analysis shows that, based on the bor-

FIGURE 18.13 **Debt Concentrations by Credit Rating**

	LONG	SHORT	GROSS	NET	FEB-04	JAN-04	DEC-03
Total	**150%**	**–69%**	**219%**	**81%**	**75%**	**66%**	**80%**
Investment Grade		**–42%**	**42%**	**–42%**	**–45%**	**–43%**	**–40%**
AAA							
AA							
BBB		–42%	42%	–42%	–45%	–43%	–40%
Non–Investment	**150%**	**–27%**	**177%**	**123%**	**120%**	**109%**	**120%**
BB	23%	–27%	50%	–4%	–1%	–8%	–2%
B	26%		26%	26%	25%	27%	27%
CCC	42%		42%	42%	39%	37%	41%
Non–Performing	59%		59%	59%	57%	53%	54%
Not Rated							

rowing leverage, the fund is 99 percent invested (–1 percent borrowing leverage). However, the option leverage of 20 percent represents a historical high. The resulting financial leverage of 119 percent approximates that of the average of the previous portfolio constructions (127 percent) and is well below the historical maximum of 153 percent.

In **Figure 18.16**, the 230 percent borrowing leverage of a fixed-income relative value fund is significantly below the 1230 percent average of the fixed income relative value peer universe. For this statistic, the fund is in the 18th percentile rank of peer funds. However, the fund has compensated by gaining notional leverage through the use of futures and options and, in fact, the financial leverage of 3742 percent for the portfolio is approximately equal to the comparable statistic for the peer universe of fixed income relative value funds.

Liquidity

Risk Fundamentals provides liquidity analyses projecting the time to liquidate each position and aggregating the results to the portfolio level. Different methodologies are used for the following different asset classes:

- ***Equities***—The days to liquidate equity holdings is calculated based on:
  - —Position size (number of shares long or short)
  - —Average daily turnover (Risk Fundamentals permits the user to select between 5-day, 10-day, 30-day, 3-month, or 6-month averages)

NOV-03	OCT-03	SEP-03	AUG-03	JUL-03	JUN-03	MAY-03	APR-03	MAR-03
83%	**89%**	**85%**	**79%**	**75%**	**74%**	**80%**	**80%**	**80%**
–43%	**–39%**	**–42%**	**–43%**	**–47%**	**–46%**	**–44%**	**–40%**	**–42%**
–43%	–39%	–42%	–43%	–47%	–46%	–44%	–40%	–42%
126%	**128%**	**127%**	**122%**	**122%**	**120%**	**124%**	**120%**	**122%**
3%	5%	–1%	–6%	–2%	–4%	–2%	–1%	1%
28%	27%	31%	29%	30%	32%	31%	29%	31%
42%	43%	46%	47%	48%	48%	48%	50%	52%
53%	53%	51%	52%	46%	44%	47%	42%	38%

FIGURE 18.14 **Concentrations by Commodity Group**

	LONGS	SHORTS	GROSS	NET	COMPOSITE AVG.	COMPOSITE % RANK	CTAS AVG.	CTAS % RANK	TREND FOLLOWERS AVG.	TREND FOLLOWERS % RANK
Total	**69.2%**	**–19.8%**	**89.0%**	**49.4%**	**2.0%**	**94%**	**32.9%**	**67%**	**33.7%**	**62%**
Energies	13.8%	–5.3%	19.1%	8.5%	0.7%	79%	10.3%	39%	12.4%	42%
Base Metals	22.4%		22.4%	22.4%	0.4%	96%	8.9%	89%	7.5%	86%
Precious Metals	10.4%	–4.2%	14.6%	6.2%	0.5%	89%	6.5%	48%	8.2%	47%
Agricultural	3.4%	–10.3%	13.7%	–6.9%	0.3%	21%	4.9%	15%	4.2%	14%
Livestock	19.2%		19.2%	19.2%	0.1%	99%	2.3%	98%	1.4%	97%

FIGURE 18.15 **Leverage Analysis of a Merger Arbitrage Fund**

	MAR-04	MIN	AVERAGE	MAX
Levered Risk	**8.6%**	**7.4%**	**10.2%**	**11.6%**
Financing Leverage	**119%**	**107%**	**127%**	**153%**
Equity	100%	100%	100%	100%
Borrowing Leverage	–1%	–2%	28%	47%
Notional Leverage	20%	3%	5%	11%
Option Leverage	20%	3%	5%	11%
Future Leverage				
OTC Derivative Leverage				
Unlevered Risk	**7.2%**	**5.7%**	**6.4%**	**7.8%**
Construction Leverage	31%	19%	27%	34%
Instrument Risk	**23.2%**	**19.2%**	**24.7%**	**28.4%**

—Percent of market turnover willing to capture (the default is 10 percent)
—Constraints of restricted stocks

- ***Exchange futures/options***—The days to liquidate holdings of exchange-traded futures and options is calculated based on:
  —Position size (number of contracts long or short)
  —Average daily turnover of all futures or similar option contracts (call or put) related to the underlying security (Risk Fundamentals permits the user to select between 5-day, 10-day, 30-day, 3-month, or 6-month averages)
  —Percent of market turnover willing to capture (the default is 10 percent)

FIGURE 18.16 **Leverage Analysis of a Fixed-Income Relative Value Fund**

	MAR-04	COMPOSITE AVG.	COMPOSITE % RANK	FIXED INCOME AVG.	FIXED INCOME % RANK	FIXED INC REL VALUE AVG.	FIXED INC REL VALUE % RANK
Levered Risk	**9.2%**	**7.6%**	**56%**	**12.8%**	**44%**	**10.6%**	**47%**
Financing Leverage	**3742%**	**429%**	**89%**	**1327%**	**79%**	**3684%**	**65%**
Equity	100%	100%		100%		100%	
Borrowing Leverage	230%	23%	75%	430%	34%	1230%	18%
Notional Leverage	3412%	306%	89%	797%	76%	2354%	67%
Option Leverage		34%	47%	37%	44%	70%	49%
Future Leverage	472%	140%	78%	320%	57%	150%	78%
OTC Derivative Leverage	2940%	132%	96%	440%	82%	2134%	62%
Unlevered Risk	**0.2%**	**1.8%**	**21%**	**1.0%**	**26%**	**0.3%**	**37%**
Construction Leverage	35%	41%	42%	31%	55%	19%	64%
Instrument Risk	**0.7%**	**4.3%**	**17%**	**3.1%**	**23%**	**1.5%**	**27%**

- ***OTC instruments***—The days to liquidate holdings of OTC instruments is calculated based on the trailing average bid-offer spread of each specific instrument and relationships that Risk Fundamentals will develop between instrument turnover and bid-offer spreads. These relationships will be developed for each type of OTC instrument (such as corporate bonds, muni bonds, and credit default swaps).

The concept behind the percent of market turnover willing to capture is that if one either buys or sells a significant percent of the market turnover, the trading activity will impact the market price. Large equity money managers typically use 20 percent as their guideline. However, these are long-term investors with extremely large positions who would be willing to accept a relatively small impact. I believe that nimble hedge funds that are seeking to exploit extremely small misvaluations should seek to capture only a maximum of 10 percent of equity market turnover. Again, the objective is consistency in measurement, so that if all funds apply the same methodology and assumptions, the results will be comparable and aggregatable.

Risk Fundamentals projects the time to liquidate each individual position, separating the long positions from the short positions. **Figure 18.17** presents only the long positions of an equity market-neutral fund, but a similar time-phased analysis of the liquidation of short positions is also provided. In this

FIGURE 18.17 **Long Position Liquidity**

	AVG DAILY TURNOVER	SHARES IN CONSTRUCTION	DAYS TO LIQUIDATE LONGS	SHORTS		< 0.1	< 0.2
Portfolio			**48.30**	**17.72**	**100.00%**	**73.70%**	**62.52%**
TFSM US	3,081,428	62,400	0.20		0.07%	0.04%	0.00%
CEN US	387,269	91,100	2.35		6.24%	5.97%	5.71%
CSC US	1,421,373	88,500	0.62		11.96%	10.04%	8.12%
BAC 5/04 P80	10,420	−85		0.08			
CAI US	Integrated Device Tech		0.58		0.76%	0.63%	0.50%
IDTI US 5/04 P17	450	225	0.45		5.63%	4.39%	3.16%
CERS US	305,207	132,800	4.35		0.76%	0.74%	0.72%
SCH US	5,198,547	85,000	0.16		0.68%	0.25%	0.00%
WIND US	544,765	2,654,329	48.20		0.82%	0.82%	0.81%
SNPS US	2,349,056	56,300	0.24		6.13%	3.58%	1.02%
TQNT US	2,134,168	−342,600		1.61			

figure, the portfolio holds 2,654,329 shares of the stock WIND and the average daily turnover of the stock is 544,765. Therefore, assuming that the fund is willing to capture 10 percent of the average daily turnover the position would take 48.20 days (2,654,329/54,476) to fully liquidate. WIND represents 0.82 percent of the current construction's aggregate long (cash equivalent) asset value. By the end of ten days, the value of this holding is projected to decline to 0.65 percent of the current aggregate long assets. By the end of ten days, the value of all of the long holdings of the portfolio could be liquidated to 9.64 percent of their current asset value.

Whereas the details by position are provided to the fund, summary results are provided as part of the investor package. For example, **Figure 18.18** shows the portfolio-level summary results for the equity market-neutral fund presented in Figure 18.17. The time to liquidate 100 percent of the holdings for both the long (50 days) and the short (20 days) positions are shaded in red (shown as black). The time to liquidate 95 percent of the holdings for both the long (20 days) and the short (2 days) positions are shaded in yellow (shown as gray).

DAYS TO LIQUIDATE LONG HOLDINGS										
< 0.5	< 1	< 2	< 5	< 7	< 10	< 13	< 20	< 30	< 40	< 50
47.72%	**32.49%**	**21.76%**	**14.12%**	**11.95%**	**9.64%**	**7.40%**	**2.97%**	**0.67%**	**0.14%**	**0.00%**
4.91%	3.59%	0.93%	0.00%							
2.36%	0.00%									
0.11%	0.00%									
0.00%										
0.67%	0.59%	0.41%	0.00%							
0.81%	0.80%	0.78%	0.73%	0.70%	0.65%	0.60%	0.48%	0.31%	0.14%	0.00%
0.00%										

However, the risk of a portfolio will often not decline linearly with the liquidation of assets. Often the riskier holdings are less liquid, and, consequently, the risk of either the long or short holdings might not decline nearly as rapidly as do the assets. Furthermore, if the portfolio is long less liquid assets and short relatively more liquid assets, the rapid liquidation of the short positions can actually increase the risk of the remaining portfolio as natural hedges are decoupled. Consequently, an analysis that can be even more interesting than the time to liquidate analysis is a projection of evolution of the risk of the portfolio as it might progress through a rapid liquidation, as is also shown in Figure 18.18. Note that by the end of the first day, while the long assets would have declined to 32.49 percent and the short assets to 7.50 percent of their respective current levels, the risk would have declined to only 42.18 percent of the portfolio construction's current risk as the short hedge would be liquidated more rapidly than the long holdings.

Notice that the risk of the long positions starts at 128.82 percent, not 100 percent. In this analysis, the total current risk of the portfolio (both the long and short holdings) is calibrated to be 100 percent, with the risk of the long holdings typically being greater than 100 percent offset by negative risk

FIGURE 18.18 **Days to Liquidate Analysis**

	ASSETS		RISK		
DAYS	LONGS	SHORTS	LONGS	SHORTS	TOTAL
0.0	**100.00%**	**100.00%**	**128.82%**	**–28.82%**	**100.00%**
0.1	73.70%	27.45%	100.46%	–7.13%	93.33%
0.2	62.52%	19.78%	85.93%	–3.57%	82.36%
0.5	47.72%	10.56%	64.81%	–0.57%	64.24%
1	32.49%	7.50%	42.65%	–0.47%	42.18%
2	21.76%	4.72%	27.37%	–0.40%	26.97%
5	14.12%	0.90%	16.10%	–0.27%	15.83%
7	11.95%	0.76%	12.74%	–0.25%	12.49%
10	9.64%	0.54%	9.80%	–0.19%	9.61%
13	7.40%	0.33%	7.19%	–0.12%	7.07%
20	2.97%	0.00%	3.02%	0.00%	3.02%
30	0.67%		0.36%		0.36%
40	0.14%		0.01%		0.01%
50	0.00%		0.00%		0.00%
75					
100					

associated with the short positions (the short positions typically hedge the long positions).

Risk Fundamentals presents various key measures of portfolio liquidity. For the same equity market neutral fund, **Figure 18.19** shows how long it takes to liquidate both long and short holdings to 10 percent, 5 percent, 1 percent, and 0 percent of current values. Presenting the data graphically provides a clear picture of the current level of liquidity relative to historical norms and the trend in liquidity over time. Figure 18.19 shows that the time required to fully liquidate the fund has recently increased, although this has resulted from the time to liquidate the last 1 percent increasing and not from an across the board shift in liquidity.

If the fund desires, Risk Fundamentals can provide specifics on both the long and short holdings that would take the greatest time to liquidate as part of the investor package. The fund can select to display the specific holdings requiring the longest time to liquidate for:

FIGURE 18.19 **Days to Liquidate Long Positions**

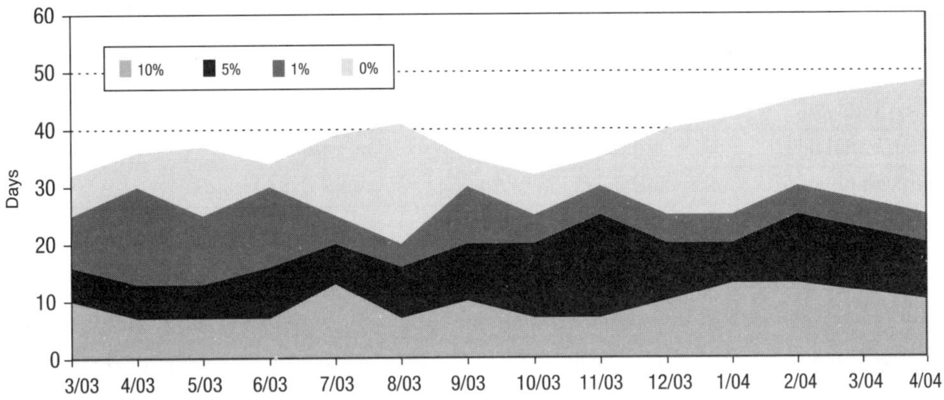

- Neither the long nor short holdings
- Only the long holdings
- All of the holdings

Risk Factors

Although risk factors form a framework that permits the sources of risk to be explained, remember that, as with any such framework, it is an abstraction. Risk Fundamentals' equity risk factors have a 56 percent explanatory power for all U.S. stocks on a market cap–weighted basis and a 43 percent explanatory power on an absolute basis (the explanatory power is typically greater for large-cap stocks). One can always increase the explanatory power by adding additional risk factors. However, the objective is to explain the primary risks in a manageable number of factors. In comparison, BARRA, the leading risk management system for the traditional buy-side, claims a 43 percent explanatory power with more than double the number of risk factors while focusing exclusively on the large-cap universe.

Furthermore, it is worth stating that the identification of risk factors is somewhat of an art, although their explanatory power and statistical significance can be statistically tested. An example of the art form, as practiced by the system's designers, was deciding to group poultry under livestock rather than under agriculture despite the fact that neither provided statistically significant explanatory

FIGURE 18.20 Equity Style Risk Factors

RISK FACTOR	DESCRIPTION
Value	Weighted combination of price-to-earnings, price-to-book, and dividend yield
Large Cap	Company market capitalization
Earnings Growth	EPS growth trailing six years
Earnings Variability	Standard deviation of trailing six years earnings
Return Volatility	Standard deviation of trailing two months daily returns
Illiquidity	Debt-to-equity ratio for the company
Leverage	Ratio of shares outstanding to monthly turnover

information. An even more esoteric decision involved whether to group silk into livestock or agricultural. After an in-depth statistical analysis followed by heated debate, the system's designers decided to group silk as a agricultural commodity, despite the fact that silk worms could easily have been considered livestock. The bottom line is that risk factors are an imprecise abstraction that do not perfectly cover the full universe of risks. However, despite their weaknesses, their ability to provide structure in the analysis of something that is as amorphous as risk is extremely valuable.

Here is a description of how the risk factors related to each of the primary market risks have been developed:

Equity. Equity risk factors are expressed as return series. Equities are modeled for each country (based on exchange) as:

- Beta
- Volatility—"equity vol"
- Style—There are seven equity style risk factors shown in **Figure 18.20**.
- Industry—Each of the twenty-four GICS level 2 industry groupings has an industry risk factor as shown in **Figure 18.21**.

The beta of each country is modeled as a sensitivity to the S&P 500 (explicitly recognizing the correlation across markets) and the residual or orthogonalized return of the local market.

The idiosyncratic risk of equities is calculated as the residual between the actual returns and the modeled returns. The modeled returns are calculated by multiplying the actual weekly returns of each risk factor by the position's sensitivity to that risk factor.

FIGURE 18.21 **Equity Industry Risk Factors**

AutoCompon	FoodDrugRetl	RealEstate
Banks	HcareEquipSvc	Retailing
CapitalGoods	HotelsRestLeis	Semiconductor
CommlSvcSuppl	HousePersProd	SoftwareServ
ConsDurApparel	Insurance	TechHardEquip
DiversFinanc	Materials	TelecomSvc
Energy	Media	Transportation
FoodBevTobac	PharmaBiotech	Utilities

Interest rates. Interest rate risk factors are expressed as a series of yields. Interest rate risks are separately modeled for each currency:

- Parallel shift—"curve shift"
- Interest rate volatility—"interest vol"
- Relative movement of short-term rates—"curve twist"
- Relative movement of long-term rates—"curve butterfly"

The history of the "curve shift" is defined as the synchronous movement of the curve based on the movement of the five-year point of the government curve. The "curve twist" is defined as the relative movement (above that explained by the curve shift) of the yield at the one-year point. The "curve butterfly" is defined as the relative movement (above that explained by the combination of the curve shift and curve twist) of the yield at the 30-year point (20-year for currencies that do not have a 30-year history).

The curve shift of each currency is modeled as a sensitivity to the U.S. curve shift (explicitly recognizing the correlation across markets) and the residual or orthogonalized yield of the local market.

Credit. Credit risk factors are expressed as a series of spreads. Credit risks are separately modeled for each currency:

- Parallel shift of spreads—"spread shift"
- Credit volatility—"credit vol"
- Twisting of spreads around the five-year point—"spread twist"
- Butterflying of spreads around the five-year point—"spread butterfly"
- Relative movement of high-quality credit spreads—"high-grade spreads"
- Relative movement of low-quality credit spreads—"junk spreads"

The history of the "spread shift" is defined as the synchronous movement of spreads of the industrial A2 (or the nearest approximation for currencies for which the industrial A2 is not available) to the government curve based on the movement of the five-year point. The "spread twist" is defined as the relative spread (above that explained by the spread shift) of the industrial A2 to the government at the one-year point. The "spread butterfly" is defined as the relative spread (above that explained by the combination of the spread shift and spread twist) of the industrial A2 to the government at the 30-year point (20 year for currencies that do not have a 30-year history). The "high-grade spread" is defined as the relative change of the industrial AA spread to the industrial A2 spread. The "junk spread" is defined as the relative change of the industrial B spread to the industrial A2 spread.

The spread shift of each currency is modeled as a sensitivity to the U.S. spread shift (explicitly recognizing the correlation across markets and the residual or orthogonalized yield of the local market).

Commodity. Physical commodity risk factors are expressed as return series. Physical commodities utilize a three-level risk-factor structure. The Goldman Sachs Commodity Index (GSCI) defines the primary market risk related to physical commodities. The relative returns of the following Goldman Sachs subindices (commodity group) are the second level of explanation:

- Goldman Sachs Energy Commodity Index (GSEN)
- Goldman Sachs Precious Metals Commodity Index (GSPM)
- Goldman Sachs Industrial Metals Commodity Index (GSIN)
- Goldman Sachs Agricultural Commodity Index (GSSA)
- Goldman Sachs Livestock Commodity Index (GSLV)

Finally, individual commodities are the third level of explanation. The idiosyncratic returns of commodities are based on the relative performance of specific contracts (months forward), specific exchanges, specific bases (Brent versus West Texas crude), and specific grades (LME high-grade aluminum versus aluminum alloy). As physical commodities are global industries, the commodity risk factors are similarly global. In addition, there is a commodity volatility risk factor as shown in **Figure 18.22**.

Currency. Currency risk factors are expressed as return series. Currencies utilize a two-level risk-factor structure. The U.S. Dollar Index (DXY) defines the primary market risk related to currencies. The return of each currency relative to this index represents the currency secondary risks. There are no currency idiosyncratic risks. In addition, there is a currency volatility risk factor.

FIGURE 18.22 **Commodity Risk Factors**

COMMODITY GROUP	COMMODITY				
Energies	Oil	Natural Gas	Gasoline	Heating Oil	Distillates
	Kerosene	Coal			
Precious Metals	Gold	Silver	Platinum	Palladium	
Base Metals	Copper	Aluminum	Nickel	Zinc	Tin
Agricultural	Corn	Wheat	Barley	Oats	Rice
	Cocoa	Coffee	Sugar	Soybean	Orange Juice
	Canola	Cotton	Crude Palm	Flax	Dairy
	Potatoes	Rubber	Silk	Rapeseed	Red Beans
	Sunflower				
Livestock	Cattle	Hogs	Chicken	Wool	

A portfolio derives currency exposure through two sources. The first is in direct currency holdings, either spot or forward positions. The second is from holding non-dollar denominated noncurrency holdings.

Real estate. Real estate risk factors are expressed as return series. The general movement of U.S. real estate is based on the data calculated by the National Council of Real Estate Investment Fiduciaries (NCREIF). NCREIF data are quarterly. The system synthesizes monthly real estate risk factors by utilizing the quarterly reporting results and replicating the volatility and correlation for the other months within the quarter. The overall index (unlevered) is used as the primary market real estate risk. The natural correlation with fixed income is recognized. The relative returns of the following groupings define the secondary risks:

- Region (East, West, Midwest, South)
- Property type (Apartment, Hotel, Industrial, Office, Retail)

Each holding can be mapped to a specific return stream. Risk Fundamentals utilizes regression analysis to isolate the sensitivity of the specific return stream to the overall real estate market, the region, and the property type. The idiosyncratic risk is based on the residuals of these analyses.

Event. The two primary event-oriented strategies are merger arbitrage and distressed debt. Each is handled through strategy-specific models. Merger arbitrage utilizes Bloomberg's "merger and acquisition" (MA) function. The histories of the performances of the acquiring and target companies are utilized as the ongoing risk of the position. The event risk is calculated based on the empirical probability of deals being closed during the last year and the relative performance of the stock of the target company since the announcement of the deal (with the assumption that this amount will be given back were the deal to terminate).

Risk Fundamentals explicitly analyzes the idiosyncratic behavior of each position and that of the portfolio. The system isolates 52 trailing weeks of idiosyncratic returns of each position as the residual after the returns explained by the risk factors. This is done by multiplying each position's risk-factor sensitivity by the actual weekly performance of that risk factor. The portfolio's 52-week idiosyncratic returns are calculated as the risk-weighted return of each of the underlying position's idiosyncratic returns. The serial correlation of idiosyncratic returns is based on the relationship between the standard deviation of 52 weeks of idiosyncratic returns and the standard deviation of 13 periods of four weeks of idiosyncratic returns.

Risk Fundamentals then separates the portfolio idiosyncratic return into "correlated" and "independent" idiosyncratic return. This is accomplished by, for each position, creating a hypothetical portfolio of all positions excluding that position and performing a statistical analysis (linear regression) to determine how much of the behavior of the idiosyncratic returns of that position is related to that of all other positions (removing each position from the hypothetical portfolio avoids measuring the impact of that position on itself). These correlations are then used to determine the correlated idiosyncratic risk of the portfolio. Finally, the statistical analysis (again linear regression) is used

FIGURE 18.23 **Risk-Factor Detail**

	COMPANY	MARKET	RISK FACTOR CATEGORY	RISK FACTOR TYPE	RISK FACTOR
GE US	General Electric Co	US	Equity	Market	Beta
GE US	General Electric Co	US	Equity	Style	LargeCap
GE US	General Electric Co	US	Equity	Style	Value
GE US	General Electric Co	US	Equity	Style	EPSGrowth
GE US	General Electric Co	US	Equity	Style	Illiquidity
GE US	General Electric Co	US	Equity	Style	Leverage
GE US	General Electric Co	US	Equity	Industry	CapitalGoods
GE US	General Electric Co	US	Equity	Correlated	All
GE US	General Electric Co	US	Equity	Independent	All

to determine the specific sensitivity of each position to the correlated idiosyncratic risk. Although this does not explain the root source of the correlated behavior, it fully recognizes the existence of this behavior. The 52-week independent idiosyncratic return is calculated as the weekly difference between the total portfolio idiosyncratic risk and the portfolio correlated idiosyncratic risk. Finally, the independent idiosyncratic return is attributed to each position based on the volatility of each position.

Recognizing the degree to which idiosyncratic risk is correlated is critical to fully understanding diversification. For example, during the Internet bubble, existing risk-factor–based systems used by traditional managers did not recognize the extreme risk inherent in a concentrated portfolio of Internet stocks. Established risk factors did not identify the correlated but unique behavior of Internet stocks, classifying the high volatility as security-specific behavior. These systems assume (they did then and they still do) that a stock's security-specific behavior is independent of that of all other stocks (an assumption made for computational efficiency). However, this simplification ultimately dramatically underestimated the risk. Although the Risk Fundamentals' approach would not have identified the correlated behavior of Internet stocks as the cause of this behavior, it would have fully recognized the correlated risk inherent in such a portfolio.

Risk Fundamentals determines the risk of each risk-factor exposure for each position based on the marginal risk sensitivity. As previously discussed, this provides a risk framework that is additive and for which all of the exposures of all of

POSITION SIZE	SENSITIVITY	NET EXPOSURE	GROSS EXPOSURE	CONTRIBUTON	MARGINAL STD DEV
0.12%	1.289	0.002	0.002	–0.01%	0.10%
0.12%	0.976	0.001	0.001	0.01%	–0.02%
0.12%	0.246	0.000	0.000	0.00%	0.00%
0.12%	–0.812	–0.001	0.001	0.00%	0.00%
0.12%	–1.214	–0.001	0.001	0.00%	0.01%
0.12%	1.722	0.002	0.002	0.00%	0.00%
0.12%	1.391	0.002	0.002	–0.01%	–0.01%
0.12%	–0.025	0.000	0.000	0.00%	0.00%
0.12%	0.203	0.000	0.000	0.00%	0.00%

the positions total to 100 percent. Risk Fundamentals permits the user to select from the following multiple measures of risk:

- Standard deviation or tracking error
- Drawdown or underperformance
- Absolute or relative VaR (user-selected confidence limit)

The default selection is the standard deviation.

Risk Fundamentals provides the details of each position's risk-factor exposures. For a US equity long/short fund, **Figure 18.23** shows that GE has a "Beta" of 1.289 and a sensitivity to the equity "LargeCap" risk factor of 0.976. The risk factor detail displays the marginal standard deviation of each position for each risk factor. This are bucketed and aggregated in different ways by other functions.

Risk Fundamentals aggregates to the portfolio level the exposures of all positions to each risk factor. For the same fund, **Figure 18.24** shows the gross exposure to value is 0.443 and the net exposure is –0.142. Consequently, only 32 percent (see "Efficiency" column) of the risk resulting from exposure to the value risk factor is ultimately not hedged out. Notice that "Beta" (the third risk factor on Figure 18.24) represents 39.7 percent of the marginal standard deviation but 84.9 percent of the marginal drawdown.

Risk Fundamentals decomposes risk of a portfolio to its sources. **Figure 18.25** identifies that the majority of risk (65 percent) in the current construction of the same U.S. equity long/short fund results from the exposure to equity risk factors. The 35 percent of risk of the current construction is idiosyncratic, at the lower end of the historical range (between 29 percent and 91 percent).

Risk Fundamentals presents the history of risk-factor exposures of the U.S. equity long/short fund, as shown in **Figure 18.26**. This analysis provides the information to determine that the significant equity market exposure of the current construction is a result of the fund actively managed the beta exposure of the fund across the previous months' constructions rather than passively maintaining a long bias to the equity market (note how the exposure moves from positive to negative on a month to month basis).

Historical Simulation

Risk Fundamentals combines the current portfolio construction, recent sensitivities to risk factors, and long-term histories of risk factors to create a historical simulation that is sensitive to current markets while incorporating long-term market behavior to provide a fundamental outlook. The sensitivities of different asset groups are calculated differently:

FIGURE 18.24 **Risk-Factor Summary**

RISK FACTOR TYPE	RISK FACTOR	GROSS EXPOSURE	EFFICIENCY	NET EXPOSURE	CONTRIBUTION	MARGINAL STD DEV	MARGINAL DRAWDOWN	MARGINAL 95% VAR
Idiosyncratic	Correlated	0.289	71%	0.206	–2.53%	24.1%	15.0%	–7.3%
Idiosyncratic	Independent	0.997	100%	0.997	–2.18%	10.7%	11.4%	25.9%
Market	Beta	1.370	43%	0.590	–5.59%	39.7%	84.9%	29.4%
Style	LargeCap	1.430	58%	–0.830	–4.55%	12.5%	–15.8%	38.8%
Style	Value	0.443	32%	–0.142	–0.03%	0.9%	21.4%	–7.5%
Style	Volatility	0.601	46%	0.275	–1.12%	11.0%	–12.6%	19.1%
Style	EPSGrowth	0.308	41%	0.126	–0.02%	0.3%	1.8%	–2.9%
Style	EPSVariability	0.319	50%	0.159	–0.08%	1.0%	3.0%	4.4%
Style	Illiquidity	0.280	43%	–0.121	–0.19%	0.4%	0.9%	2.3%
Style	Leverage	0.372	20%	0.073	0.07%	0.0%	–0.3%	–0.5%
Industry	Energy	0.029	100%	0.029	–0.08%	0.8%	1.2%	1.0%
Industry	Materials	0.031	8%	–0.003	0.00%	0.0%	0.0%	0.1%
Industry	CapitalGoods	0.036	1%	0.000	0.00%	0.0%	0.0%	0.0%
Industry	CommlSvcSuppl	0.006	36%	–0.002	0.00%	0.0%	0.3%	0.0%
Industry	Transportation	0.002	100%	0.002	–0.01%	0.0%	–0.1%	–0.2%
Industry	AutoCompon	0.002	100%	0.002	–0.01%	0.0%	0.1%	–0.1%
Industry	ConsDurApparel	0.018	63%	0.011	–0.08%	–0.1%	–1.7%	–0.7%
Industry	HotelsRestLeis	0.005	100%	0.005	–0.05%	0.0%	–0.3%	0.1%
Industry	Media	0.011	100%	0.011	–0.03%	0.0%	0.4%	–0.6%
Industry	Retailing	0.012	22%	0.003	–0.01%	0.0%	–0.1%	–0.1%
Industry	FoodDrugRetl							
Industry	FoodBevTobac	0.000	100%	0.000	0.00%	0.0%	0.0%	0.0%
Industry	HousePersProd							
Industry	HCareEquipSvc	0.062	51%	0.032	0.23%	–0.4%	–5.7%	1.2%
Industry	PharmaBiotech	0.130	82%	0.106	0.17%	–0.5%	–3.6%	–2.4%
Industry	Banks	0.017	100%	0.017	0.08%	–0.2%	–0.7%	–0.1%
Industry	DiversFinanc	0.024	8%	–0.002	0.00%	0.0%	0.0%	–0.1%
Industry	Insurance	0.041	75%	0.030	0.21%	–0.6%	0.0%	–2.3%
Industry	RealEstate							
Industry	SoftwareServ	0.081	58%	0.046	0.11%	–0.5%	–1.1%	–0.1%
Industry	TechHardEquip	0.039	15%	0.006	0.00%	0.0%	0.3%	0.2%
Industry	Semiconductor	0.102	50%	0.052	–0.57%	0.8%	0.4%	2.9%
Industry	TelecomSvc	0.007	100%	0.007	0.06%	0.0%	1.0%	–0.6%
Industry	Utilities							

- Equity sensitivities are based on regression analyses using one year of daily returns.
- Fixed-income sensitivities are based on the Bloomberg Fair Value (BFV) models and, when these are not available, regression analyses using one year of weekly return data.
- Commodity sensitivities are based on regression analyses using one year of weekly returns.

FIGURE 18.25 **Risk-Factor Decomposition**

			MAR-04	MIN	AVERAGE	MAX
Equity			65%	9%	35%	71%
Market		Beta	40%	0%	20%	50%
Factor	**Total**		25%	2%	15%	27%
	Style	LargeCap	12%	0%	6%	19%
		Value	1%	0%	1%	2%
		Other Style	13%	0%	4%	10%
	Industry		–1%	–1%	4%	16%
	Volatility	Equity Vol				
Idiosyncratic			35%	29%	65%	91%
Independent			11%	11%	26%	51%
Correlated			24%	17%	39%	70%

FIGURE 18.26 **Risk-Factor Exposures**

				MAR-04	FEB-04	JAN-04	DEC-03	NOV-03
US	Equity	Market	Beta	0.590	0.570	0.435	–0.252	0.031
US	Equity	Style	LargeCap	–0.830	–0.919	–0.896	–0.132	–0.327
US	Equity	Style	Value	–0.142	–0.103	0.020	0.139	0.089
US	Equity	Industry	CapitalGoods	0.000	0.003	0.013	0.020	0.028
US	Equity	Industry	CommlSvcSuppl	–0.002	–0.005	0.006	–0.013	–0.011
US	Equity	Industry	Transportation	0.002	0.003	0.003	–0.006	–0.006
US	Equity	Industry	AutoCompon	0.002	0.014	0.014	–0.005	–0.002

- Real estate investments are proxied by the appropriate NCREIF return history.

These sensitivities are applied to ten-plus years of risk-factor histories to generate a long-term monthly historical simulation that captures the actual volatilities and correlations. This historical simulation is used to analyze risks in "normal" markets. It is also the basis for calculating the marginal risk-adjusted return measures that are used to support the construction of a risk-efficient portfolio.

Recent idiosyncratic behavior (weekly over the last year) is integrated into the long-term (monthly ten-plus years) historical simulation to provide a comprehensive picture of risk. Risk Fundamentals synthesizes monthly idiosyncratic returns by applying the serial correlation factor of the idiosyncratic returns to the fifty-two weeks of correlated and independent idiosyncratic returns. These returns are repeated to create a history of comparable length to the risk-factor–based historical simulation.

The ability to create a long-term historical simulation represents an extremely significant advantage over using actual historical returns to measure risk. The section "Risk measures based on actual fund returns," presented in Chapter 5, identified four major problems with utilizing historical returns. Utilizing a historical simulation avoids all four of these problems:

Short history. A long-term historical simulation can be developed independent of how long the fund has existed.

Valuation flexibility. There is a significant amount of discretion/subjectivity in valuing any but the most liquid instruments. As discussed in Chapter 13, this

OCT-03	SEP-03	AUG-03	JUL-03	JUN-03	MAY-03	APR-03	MAR-03
0.078	0.445	0.545	–0.257	–0.486	–0.134	0.077	–0.042
–0.337	–0.465	–0.552	–0.248	–0.087	–0.145	0.178	0.290
0.038	–0.016	–0.069	0.116	0.047	0.057	0.010	–0.007
0.028	0.088	0.030	–0.017	–0.031	–0.014	0.031	0.007
–0.016	–0.014	–0.009	–0.018	–0.033	–0.025	–0.002	–0.003
–0.003	0.009	–0.010	0.002		0.000	0.031	0.038
–0.004	–0.002	0.002	–0.015	–0.027	–0.011	–0.007	–0.002

can result in a significant understatement of the risk of a fund, as measured based on reported returns. A historical simulation consistently applies third-party market data, totally avoiding this issue.

Changing portfolio. The historical simulation is based on the current construction and does not intermingle an evolving construction with market performance over time.

Limited data. Relationships can be developed (such as equity risk factor sensitivities) bottom up rather than limiting the analysis to monthly top-down actual return data, providing a dramatically richer data environment in which to operate.

Stress Tests

Stress tests permit the user to analyze how the portfolio might perform in "crisis" market conditions.

Each position is subjected to the following four standard stress scenarios for each primary market factor and both equity and interest rate volatility:

- A ***significant negative*** move (two standard deviation event) in the primary market risk factor(s) of the position
- A ***significant positive*** move (two standard deviation event) in the primary market risk factor(s) of the position
- An ***extreme negative*** move (four standard deviation event) in the primary market risk factor(s) of the position
- An ***extreme positive*** move (four standard deviation event) in the primary market risk factor(s) of the position

The result of the market move incorporates all of the natural convexity of the position (such as options and fixed income). For positions with sensitivities to multiple market risk factors (such as a convertible bond's exposure to interest rates, credit spreads, equities, and equity volatility), the sensitivity to each market risk factor is recognized. The sensitivity to each primary market risk factor will be aggregated across all positions to the portfolio level. This portfolio-level sensitivity to each stress test movement of each market risk factor is captured as a key risk fundamental of the portfolio. As standard scenarios are applied consistently across funds, the results can be compared and aggregated across funds. When a portfolio of funds is analyzed, the aggregate stress test behavior of each underlying fund will be utilized in the analysis.

Risk Fundamentals provides the fund manager with the detail sensitivities of each holding to a battery of standard stress tests. Risk Fundamentals summarizes

FIGURE 18.27 **Stress Test Analysis**

		RETURN	COMPOSITE AVG.	COMPOSITE % RANK	DIRECTIONAL AVG.	DIRECTIONAL % RANK	GLOBAL MACRO AVG.	GLOBAL MACRO % RANK
Portfolio	± 2 σ	–26%	–9%	11%	–15%	31%	–19%	37%
	± 4 σ	–64%	–16%	4%	–28%	22%	–48%	32%
Equity	+4 σ	21%	11%	79%	10%	83%	7%	97%
	+2 σ	9%	6%	67%	5%	62%	3%	87%
	–2 σ	–10%	–5%	45%	–7%	35%	–2%	15%
	–4 σ	–22%	–12%	34%	–10%	21%	–6%	9%
Rates	+4 σ	4%	3%	57%	4%	49%	6%	45%
	+2 σ	2%	1%	55%	3%	46%	4%	41%
	–2 σ	3%	–2%	76%	–1%	76%	–3%	67%
	–4 σ	–5%	–4%	45%	–5%	51%	–7%	62%
Credit	+4 σ	8%	6%	59%	5%	61%	4%	56%
	+2 σ	4%	3%	54%	2%	68%	1%	61%
	–2 σ	–4%	–1%	42%	–3%	42%	–2%	45%
	–4 σ	–8%	–4%	45%	–5%	38%	–5%	41%
Commodity	+4 σ	23%	2%	87%	2%	97%	10%	86%
	+2 σ	12%	1%	76%	0%	96%	3%	76%
	–2 σ	–8%	0%	27%	–1%	26%	–4%	42%
	–4 σ	–16%	–2%	21%	3%	12%	–7%	36%
Dollar	+4 σ	13%	5%	64%	5%	78%	6%	62%
	+2 σ	6%	3%	56%	2%	65%	3%	69%
	–2 σ	–6%	1%	34%	–1%	39%	–4%	46%
	–4 σ	–13%	–4%	22%	–4%	22%	–7%	42%

the position-level sensitivities to the portfolio level. In **Figure 18.27**, a global macro fund demonstrates relatively little sensitivity to a potential rise in interest rates (the duration of the portfolio is small). However, the sensitivity to an equity "event" is both significant and greater than that of comparable funds in the global macro peer universe. Relative to other global macro funds, the fund is in the 97th percentile of sensitivity to a potential four standard deviation move in the equity markets.

FIGURE 18.28 Convexity Analysis

		RETURN	MIN	AVERAGE	MAX
Equity	+4 σ	12%	5%	9%	15%
	+2 σ	–7%	–12%	–4%	4%
	–2 σ	–6%	–10%	–6%	–2%
	–4 σ	–17%	–17%	–13%	–9%
Rates	+4σ	–15%	–13%	6%	3%
	+2 σ	–8%	–9%	–5%	2%
	–2 σ	–8%	–11%	–6%	1%
	–4 σ	–4%	–8%	–2%	7%
Credit	+4 σ	–1%	–4%	1%	6%
	+2 σ	–3%	–5%	2%	7%
	–2 σ	–3%	–7%	–3%	3%
	–4 σ	–7%	–8%	–1%	1%
Commodity	+4 σ	17%	12%	19%	27%
	+2 σ	22%	10%	21%	32%
	–2 σ	20%	13%	23%	29%
	–4 σ	19%	11%	17%	27%
Dollar	+4 σ	0%	–3%	1%	5%
	+2 σ	–2%	–4%	2%	4%
	–2 σ	2%	–1%	1%	3%
	–4 σ	0%	–2%	0%	2%

Convexity

Risk Fundamentals analyzes the convexity of the portfolio based on the results of the standard stress tests. For each stress test scenario, in addition to the return calculation that incorporates the natural convexity of the instrument, another calculation applying the linear extrapolation of the risk-factor sensitivity is also performed. The difference between the result incorporating convexity and the result assuming a linear relationship isolates the impact of convexity.

Figure 18.28 displays the convexity analysis of the same global macro fund that was shown earlier. The convexity analysis shows the convexity of returns of the fund with respect to interest rates is significantly greater than in previous portfolio constructions.

FIGURE 18.29 **Risk-Return Analyses**

		MAR-04	MIN	AVERAGE	MAX
Returns	Compound Annual	9.5%			
Drawdowns	Largest	–13.1%	–5.3%	–8.4%	–12.1%
Worst Period	Month	–2.9%	–2.1%	–2.6%	–3.2%
	Calendar Year	–9.8%	–5.9%	–7.4%	–11.4%
	Rolling 12 Months	–11.9%	–7.5%	–9.7%	–12.4%
Best Period	Month	3.7%	2.2%	3.4%	4.9%
	Calendar Year	11.2%	4.3%	8.2%	12.4%
	Rolling 12 Months	14.3%	6.0%	12.1%	17.3%
Annualized Deviations	Standard	8.6%	3.6%	10.3%	15.9%
	Gain Standard	5.3%	2.2%	6.0%	8.7%
	Loss Standard	4.7%	2.3%	6.9%	11.7%
	Downside 0%	5.7%	2.4%	7.2%	11.7%
	Semi	8.3%	3.7%	11.0%	17.6%
	Tracking Error	18.7%	11.2%	16.8%	25.2%
Distribution	Skew	–0.3	–0.7	–0.2	0.5
	Kurtosis	1.1	–0.3	0.5	1.6
Correlation	S&P 500	0.61	–0.49	0.15	0.54
	MSCI World	0.52	–0.42	0.14	0.57
	HFR Composite	0.29	–0.37	0.16	0.39
VaR	95%	3.6%	1.7%	4.8%	7.2%
	99%	4.8%	2.3%	5.8%	8.9%
Relative VaR	95%	8.9%	5.0%	7.7%	12.6%
	99%	11.2%	6.8%	10.7%	16.2%
Absolute Ratios	Sharpe	0.7	0.5	0.8	1.1
	Sortino 0%	1.2	0.6	0.9	1.7
	Calmar	0.4	0.2	0.3	0.5
Relative Ratios	Information	–0.1	–0.4	–0.2	0.1
	Treynor	0.0	–0.4	–0.1	0.2

Risk-Return Analyses

Risk Fundamentals provides a wide range of return, risk, and risk-adjusted return statistics. These are based on the long-term historical simulation. The objective is to present risk in the language of hedge funds. For each measure, the comparable values for previous months' constructions (including the minimum, average, and maximum value) and averages and percentile ranking versus peer funds (funds with similar strategies and styles) and all hedge funds are provided.

Although the risk statistics are exclusively based on the historical simulation of the current construction, the risk-adjusted return statistics combine these with actual returns. This is logically consistent with the fact that risk tends to repeat whereas returns do not (discussed in Chapter 5). However, this raises the issue that the return histories of funds are of varying lengths, depending on when each fund launched. Risk Fundamentals solves this problem by presenting peer comparisons for these statistics utilizing the same period for the hedge fund, strategy, and style comparables.

Figure 18.29 shows the risk-return analyses for a European equity long/short fund. Risk Fundamentals projects the fund's drawdown potential (and underperformance for managers measured on relative performance). The largest drawdown of the simulated returns of the current construction of this fund (-13.1 percent) is greater than that of all previous constructions of the fund (ranging from –5.3 percent to –12.1 percent).

Risk Fundamentals similarly provides measures of volatility (and tracking error for managers measured on relative performance). Figure 18.29 shows that the standard deviation of the simulated returns of the current construction (8.6 percent) of this fund is relatively close to the average for all previous months' constructions for the fund (10.3 percent).

Risk Fundamentals provides information on the distribution of returns, also shown for the same European equity long/short fund in Figure 18.29. The fund displays relative high positive kurtosis and negative skew. Finally, Risk Fundamentals provides various measures of risk-adjusted return, including the Sharpe ratio for managers measured on absolute return and the information ratio for managers measured on relative return.

Constructing a Fund

A risk-factor framework provides a framework that can support the construction of a "risk-efficient" fund. It does this very differently from the way a portfolio is viewed by a portfolio manager. A portfolio manager generally thinks bottom up in terms of trades, such as a pair trade in equities or a hedge in fixed income. A statistically based construction does not explicitly recognize these relationships but instead recognizes the sources of risk and the resulting behavior of each individual position, and in doing so implicitly recognizes these relationships. For example, when a manager creates a covered call, he directly understands the relationship between the underlying position and the call. In contrast, a statistically driven construction maps both the long underlying position and the short call option (applying the delta sensitivity) to the same risk factors, and the exposures of these factors net out.

This is equally true when a portfolio manager hedges the interest rate exposure of a convertible bond with swaps. Although a statistical-based solution can in no way replace the thinking process of a portfolio manager, it can synergistically enhance it. A statistical approach is comprehensive, rigorous, and disciplined. As a complement to a strong portfolio manager, it can provide an independent, third-party perspective and control. It can also contribute insight to the portfolio management process.

Risk Fundamentals provides the following multiple views of the portfolio construction being analyzed:

- ***Units***—this view presents the portfolio in units:
  - —Shares for equities
  - —Face value for debt
  - —Contracts for exchange traded futures and options
  - —Notional amounts for OTC derivatives
- ***Invested capital***—This represents the amount of invested capital that is required to purchase or sell short cash instruments and the margin that is required to purchase or sell short notionally funded instruments:
  - —Market value for cash instruments (stocks and bonds) and other cash instruments
  - —Market value for options
  - —Initial margin for futures
  - —Market value for OTC derivatives
- ***Cash equivalents***—This represents the amount of cash that would be required to gain the equivalent exposure to cash instruments:
  - —Market value for stocks and bonds and other cash instruments
  - —Market value of the delta equivalent number of underlying securities of options
  - —Notional value for futures
  - —Notional value for OTC derivatives
- ***Risk equivalent***—This converts each position to its risk equivalent exposure. The user can select from alternative ways to view risk:

—Exposure to primary market risks (beta to S&P, duration)
—Marginal standard deviation (tracking error)
—Marginal drawdown (underperformance)
—Marginal Value at Risk (relative VaR)

Figure 18.30 is an example of the multiple views of a construction of an equity long/short fund. In this example, the ORCL 4/04 C12.5 options represent a relatively small percentage of invested capital (0.09 percent), a larger percentage of cash equivalent capital (0.31 percent), and a comparatively larger percentage of risk equivalents (1.06 percent of marginal standard deviation).

As discussed in Chapter 10, constructing a portfolio is generally an incremental process. Constructions typically evolve rather than being created de novo. This evolutionary process is generally guided by iteratively testing alternative solutions. Risk Fundamentals permits the user to create alternative what-if constructions and to analyze the behavior of these alternatives. Alternatives can be created by explicitly setting specific position sizes or by adjusting all positions to achieve specific aggregate targets of long or short exposure. In fact, the system

FIGURE 18.30 **Portfolio Analysis**

	INSTRUMENT	UNITS	INVESTED CAPITAL	NOTIONAL LEVERAGE
Portfolio	**50.1%**	**3.59%**	**53.66%**	**100.00%**
AA US	Cash	41,600	0.46%	0.00%
IBM 5/04 P80	Option	–85	–0.01%	0.16%
DELL US	Cash	–73,800	–2.46%	0.00%
EMC US	Cash	121,500	1.56%	0.00%
FISV US	Cash	–17,400	–0.67%	0.00%
IDTI US	Cash	102,400	1.73%	0.00%
ISIL US	Cash	145,100	3.48%	0.00%
ORCL 4/04 C12.5	Option	833	0.09%	0.22%
ORCL 4/04 C15	Option	3,665	0.20%	0.74%
SNPS US	Cash	56,300	1.88%	0.00%
TQNT US	Cash	–342,600	–2.46%	0.00%
WIND US	Cash	558,400	4.38%	0.00%

can simultaneously support both approaches (setting the sizes explicitly and adjusting all other positions to achieve an aggregate goal) as long as there is a feasible solution. (For example, one cannot have an aggregate target for long positions that is less than the sum of the sizes for long positions that have been explicitly set.) However, if the solution is not feasible, Risk Fundamentals will diagnose this and so indicate. The specific position size is expressed as the cash equivalent percent of equity capital.

As discussed in Chapter 5, historical risk (both volatilities and correlations) tends to repeat whereas historical returns do not. Consequently, Risk Fundamentals combines historical risk data with user-supplied prospective returns to drive the portfolio management process. The prospective return of a position is projected based on the sum of the product of the net exposure of that position to each risk factor times the prospective return of each risk factor (the return anticipated resulting from the construction's exposure to risk factors) plus the prospective alpha (the idiosyncratic return generated by selecting specific securities) of that position.

	RISK EQUIVALENTS				
CASH EQUIV CAPITAL	MARGINAL STD DEV	MARGINAL DRAWDOWN	MARGINAL VAR	CASH EQUIV/ CONTRACT	
100.00%	**100.00%**				
0.46%	0.50%	0.98%	0.12%		
0.16%	0.05%	–0.02%	0.09%	–5,032	**Underly Price: 79.25 Cntrct Size: 100 Delta: –0.635**
–2.46%	–0.94%	–5.10%	–2.74%		
1.56%	2.20%	4.65%	3.65%		
–0.67%	–0.23%	–0.59%	–0.86%		
1.73%	3.53%	2.87%	4.81%		
3.48%	5.68%	5.49%	7.98%		
0.31%	1.06%	1.18%	0.46%	957	**Underly Price: 13.91 Cntrct Size: 100 Delta: 0.688**
0.95%	3.26%	3.63%	1.41%	670	**Underly Price: 79.25 Cntrct Size: 100 Delta: –0.635**
1.88%	1.74%	3.92%	1.93%		
–2.46%	–0.97%	–3.22%	–4.25%		
4.38%	0.32%	0.35%	0.40%		

For example, let's assume a position has a beta to the S&P of 1.2 and a sensitivity to large cap of 0.5 (for simplicity we will assume only two risk factors). Furthermore, let's assume your prospective outlook for the next six months to one year was for the S&P to return 10 percent annually and for large cap (which has dramatically underperformed during the last several years) to outperform by 2 percent annually. The risk-factor–based prospective return would be 13 percent (a sensitivity of 1.2 times a prospective return of 10 percent for the S&P or 12 percent, plus a sensitivity of 0.5 times a prospective return of 2 percent for large cap, or 1 percent). Furthermore, if you projected a prospective alpha (the position-specific return above and beyond that of market and secondary risks) of 2 percent, the expected annual return for the position would be 15 percent (the combination of the 13 percent risk-factor–based prospective return and the 2 percent prospective alpha).

By using a standard set of prospective risk-factor returns across all positions in a portfolio, the returns that are explained by these factors are consistently handled. The selection of a specific holding will be driven by the prospective outlook for that position.

Risk Fundamentals provides measures of marginal risk and risk-adjusted return to guide the portfolio management process. The measures of marginal risk provide a perspective of how sensitive the risk of the overall portfolio is to changes in the weights of specific positions. Remember that one cannot measure the risk of a position in isolation but that it must be measured in the context of the overall portfolio. This approach accomplishes that.

However, remember that the objective is not to avoid risk but to target the risk that is most attractively compensated. Therefore, even more valuable than the marginal risk measures are the marginal risk-adjusted return measures that Risk Fundamentals provides. The marginal risk-adjusted return measures are calculated by combining the marginal risk measures with the prospective returns. As discussed in Chapter 10, a portfolio is "risk efficient" when all of the marginal risk-adjusted return measures are equal. When these measures are not equal, increasing the exposure to positions with favorable marginal risk-adjusted-return characteristics and reducing the exposure to those with unfavorable marginal risk-adjusted-return characteristics can improve the efficiency of a construction.

Risk Fundamentals ranks the marginal risk-adjusted-return measure of each position and shades the top 20 percent in green (shown in gray) and the bottom 20 percent in red (shown in black). Increasing the weight of those positions in green and reducing the weight of those in red will increase the "theo-

FIGURE 18.31 **Alternative Risk-Adjusted Optimizer Objectives**

	ABSOLUTE MEASURES	RELATIVE MEASURES
Volatility	Sharpe ratio based on standard deviation	Information ratio based on tracking error
Declines	Sharpe ratio based on largest drawdown	Information ratio based on largest underperformance
VaR	Sharpe ratio based on VaR	Information ratio based on relative VaR

FIGURE 18.32 **Alternative Optimizer Risk Limits**

	ABSOLUTE MEASURES	RELATIVE MEASURES
Volatility	Standard deviation	Tracking error
Declines	Largest drawdown	Largest underperformance
VaR	VaR	Relative VaR

retical" attractiveness of the portfolio. I say "theoretical" because, although I fully believe that this is a powerful framework to analyze the construction of a portfolio, I want to strongly warn against mechanically responding to the analysis without repeatedly reviewing and questioning the assumptions that are driving it.

As discussed in Chapter 14, an optimizer is not as practical an approach to constructing a portfolio as it might appear. However, it can be an insightful tool for providing an objective perspective and can promote "outside-the-box" thinking. The optimizer utilizes the risk (volatilities and correlations) of the historical simulation in combination with the prospective returns to optimize the construction of the portfolio.

Risk Fundamentals provides a sophisticated optimizer. The user can select from a variety of alternative risk-adjusted objective functions to guide the development of a risk-efficient portfolio, as shown in **Figure 18.31**. Additionally, Risk Fundamentals can incorporate transaction costs for buying or selling the securities. Furthermore, the user can also establish a variety of constraints:

- Risk limits, as shown in **Figure 18.32**
- Maximum scenario analyses

- Maximum stress test loss
- Minimum position size (largest short position)
- Maximum position size

Constructing a Portfolio of Funds

As previously discussed, the construction of a portfolio of funds by Risk Fundamentals is exactly the same as the construction of a fund. As Risk Fundamentals does not differentiate between a fund (of securities) and a portfolio of funds, and because the risk profile of both a fund (of securities) and a portfolio of funds is exactly the same, the risks of a portfolio of funds can be aggregated into a portfolio of funds that invests in the other portfolios of funds (such as a large institutional investor investing in a fund of funds). Therefore, the Risk Fundamentals framework permits an unlimited number of levels in aggregating funds.

Consequently, all of the capabilities discussed in the previous section apply to the construction of a portfolio of funds. However, in the case of the portfolio of funds, the underlying positions are individual funds rather than securities. In fact, funds and securities can be intermingled in a portfolio construction. This capability supports the analysis of potential hedging strategies (such as buying or selling SPDRs or S&P futures to hedge the equity market exposure of a portfolio of funds).

The ability to construct a portfolio of funds is enabled by the fact that the summary risk profile created by Risk Fundamentals can be reloaded as a fund. I will use a sample portfolio of funds with five underlying U.S. equity long/short funds (called Fund A, Fund B, Fund C, Fund D, and Fund E) to demonstrate how this works. The various components of the risk profile of each of the underlying funds get aggregated as follows:

Concentration data. The detail position data of each underlying fund get aggregated to a summary level that captures the primary market exposures while masking the specific positions. Risk Fundamentals automatically reloads these concentration summaries by fund into the position detail worksheet of the portfolio of funds construction, as shown in **Figure 18.33**.

The summary exposures by fund are aggregated to provide concentration data on the portfolio of funds level. Because the long and short exposures are separately captured at the fund summary level, the portfolio of funds concentration separately aggregates the longs and the shorts of the underlying funds. Across the five underlying funds in the portfolio of funds, the concentrations by

FIGURE 18.33 **Concentration by Position Type of a Portfolio of Funds**

	LONG	SHORT	GROSS	NET	MIN	AVG	MAX
Total	**1137.3%**	**–1055.9%**	**2193.2%**	**81.4%**	**65.4%**	**76.4%**	**85.4%**
Equity	**24.3%**	**–16.7%**	**41.0%**	**7.6%**	**2.1%**	**6.2%**	**11.4%**
Equity	24.3%	–12.5%	36.8%	11.8%	6.4%	11.5%	17.2%
ETF		–4.2%	4.2%	–4.2%	–6.3%	–4.2%	–2.1%
Debt	**639.1%**	**–605.1%**	**1244.2%**	**34.0%**	**29.5%**	**33.4%**	**37.2%**
Sovereign	625.0%	–607.4%	1232.4%	17.6%	15.3%	18.4%	21.4%
Corporate	5.2%	2.3%	2.9%	7.5%	6.1%	7.5%	8.9%
Convertible	8.4%		8.4%	8.4%	6.4%	7.3%	8.7%
ABS	0.5%		0.5%	0.5%	0.3%	0.5%	0.7%
Muni							
Currency	**0.5%**		**0.5%**	**0.5%**	**–2.0%**	**–0.1%**	**1.2%**
Futures	**468.3%**	**–429.7%**	**898.0%**	**38.6%**	**23.9%**	**28.4%**	**37.2%**
Equity Fut	7.6%	–5.2%	12.8%	2.4%	0.5%	2.1%	4.5%
Finan Fut	459.3%	–423.4%	882.7%	35.9%	23.4%	29.3%	34.5%
Cmdty Fut	0.5%	–0.4%	0.9%	0.1%	–0.3%	0.1%	0.4%
Crncy Fut	0.9%	–0.7%	1.6%	0.2%	0.1%	0.2%	0.3%
Options	**2.7%**	**0.0%**	**2.7%**	**2.7%**	**1.1%**	**2.2%**	**3.4%**
Equity Opt	0.3%	–0.1%	0.4%	0.2%	–0.1%	0.2%	0.5%
Finan Opt	0.8%	–0.3%	1.1%	0.5%	0.1%	0.5%	0.9%
Cmdty Opt	0.4%	0.0%	0.4%	0.4%	0.2%	0.5%	0.7%
Crncy Opt	1.2%	0.4%	0.8%	1.6%	–0.5%	0.4%	1.8%
OTC Derivatives	**2.4%**	**–4.4%**	**6.8%**	**–2.0%**	**–3.2%**	**–1.3%**	**–0.1%**
IRS	2.3%	–4.2%	6.5%	–1.9%	–3.3%	–1.3%	–0.1%
CDS	0.1%	–0.2%	0.3%	–0.1%	–0.2%	–0.1%	0.0%
FI Options							
Real Estate							
Funds							
Hedge Funds							
Mutual Funds							

industry are as shown in Figure 18.33. In this example, the portfolio of funds has greater exposure to financial futures (35.9 percent) than at any prior time (ranging from 23.4 percent to 34.5 percent).

FIGURE 18.34 **Risk-Factor Detail of a Portfolio of Funds**

	MARKET	RISK FACTOR CATEGORY	RISK FACTOR	POSITION SIZE	SENSITIVITY	NET EXPOSURE	MARGINAL STD DEV
Fund A	US	Idiosyncratic	Correlated	16.45%	0.206	0.034	4.52%
Fund A	US	Idiosyncratic	Independent	16.45%	0.997	0.164	1.85%
Fund A	US	Market	Beta	16.45%	0.590	0.097	6.92%
Fund A	US	Style	LargeCap	16.45%	–0.830	–0.137	2.52%
Fund A	US	Style	Value	16.45%	–0.142	–0.023	0.32%
Fund A	US	Style	Volitility	16.45%	0.275	0.045	1.95%
Fund A	US	Style	EPSGrowth	16.45%	0.126	0.021	0.25%
Fund A	US	Style	EPSVariability	16.45%	0.159	0.026	0.10%
Fund A	US	Style	Illiquidity	16.45%	–0.121	-0.020	0.12%
Fund A	US	Style	Leverage	16.45%	0.073	0.012	0.00%
Fund A	US	Industry	Energy	16.45%	0.029	0.005	0.19%
Fund A	US	Industry	Materials	16.45%	–0.003	0.000	0.00%
Fund E							
SPY US	US	Market	Beta	–10.00%	1.000	–0.100	–7.14%

Risk-factor data. Risk factors have been explicitly developed to be additive. In **Figure 18.34**, Risk Fundamentals loads the portfolio aggregate risk-factor sensitivities of each underlying fund as the risk-factor sensitivities of that fund in the construction of a portfolio of funds. Note that in Figure 18.34 the risk-factor sensitivities for Fund A are exactly those presented earlier in the risk factor summary for that fund (Figure 18.24).

The detail risk-factor exposures (by underlying fund) are aggregated by risk factor to the portfolio of funds level (parallel to what was previously shown for the aggregation of risk-factor sensitivities of instruments to the fund level). The same risk-factor decomposition analysis that was previously shown for the fund can be performed at the portfolio of funds level. **Figure 18.35** shows that approximately 38.2 percent of the risk of the current construction of the portfolio of funds results from the exposure to the equity risk factors. Furthermore, the risk attributable to exposure to physical commodities (9.4 percent) is significantly greater than the 3.9 percent average of that statistic for diversified fund of funds, resulting in the portfolio being ranked

FIGURE 18.35 **Risk-Factor Decomposition of a Portfolio of Funds**

			MAR-04	COMPOSITE AVG.	COMPOSITE % RANK	FUND OF FUNDS AVG.	FUND OF FUNDS % RANK	DIVERSIFIED FOF AVG.	DIVERSIFIED FOF % RANK
Equity			**38.2%**	**42.3%**	**47%**	**44.0%**	**44%**	**43.5%**	**46%**
Market		Beta	27.3%	31.2%	45%	34.1%	41%	33.2%	45%
Secondary		**Total**	10.9%	11.1%	40%	9.9%	57%	10.3%	52%
	Style	LargeCap	2.4%	1.2%	53%	2.2%	61%	2.4%	50%
		Value	3.1%	2.1%	56%	1.5%	67%	2.4%	63%
		Other Style	2.4%	3.9%	42%	3.2%	39%	3.1%	45%
	Industry		1.5%	3.4%	36%	2.4%	37%	2.1%	41%
	Volatility	Equity Vol	1.5%	0.5%	59%	0.6%	57%	0.3%	62%
Interest Rates			**8.8%**	**12.2%**	**32%**	**11.7%**	**41%**	**12.3%**	**34%**
Market		Curve Shift	4.3%	7.2%	37%	6.9%	35%	7.5%	36%
Secondary		**Total**	4.5%	5.0%	39%	4.8%	41%	4.8%	42%
	Curve	Curve Twist	2.4%	2.6%	45%	2.2%	55%	2.4%	50%
		Curve Butterfly	1.4%	1.6%	41%	1.4%	49%	1.7%	44%
	Volatility	Rate Vol	0.7%	0.8%	46%	1.2%	42%	0.7%	51%
Credit			**10.2%**	**11.6%**	**46%**	**8.3%**	**61%**	**11.9%**	**43%**
Market		Spread Shift	6.5%	5.6%	59%	4.4%	59%	7.3%	39%
Secondary		**Total**	3.7%	6.0%	37%	3.9%	45%	4.6%	32%
	Spread	Spread Twist	0.5%	1.2%	29%	0.9%	37%	0.7%	34%
		Spread Butterfly	0.9%	1.5%	34%	0.4%	74%	0.9%	49%
	Quality	High-Grade Spread	0.6%	0.9%	36%	0.7%	43%	0.5%	57%
		Junk Spread	1.6%	2.1%	37%	1.5%	59%	2.3%	41%
	Volatility	Credit Vol	0.1%	0.3%	29%	0.4%	37%	0.2%	45%
Commodity			**9.4%**	**4.3%**	**85%**	**4.7%**	**79%**	**3.9%**	**96%**
Market			1.2%	0.5%	91%	0.7%	87%	0.6%	92%
Secondary		**Total**	8.2%	3.8%	77%	4.0%	75%	3.3%	87%
	Group	Cmdty Group	3.2%	1.5%	79%	2.1%	81%	1.7%	81%
		Commodity	4.9%	2.3%	83%	1.9%	88%	1.6%	77%
	Volatility	Cmdty Vol	0.1%	0.0%	67%	0.0%	72%	0.0%	79%
Currency			**6.4%**	**7.8%**	**41%**	**7.7%**	**45%**	**6.8%**	**42%**
Market		Dollar Index	0.7%	1.2%	32%	1.1%	34%	0.9%	39%
Secondary		**Total**	5.7%	6.6%	43%	6.6%	42%	5.9%	43%
	Currency		5.4%	6.3%	45%	6.5%	41%	5.9%	41%
	Volatility	Currency Vol	0.3%	0.3%	51%	0.1%	61%	0.0%	61%
Idiosyncratic			**27.0%**	**21.8%**	**59%**	**23.6%**	**56%**	**21.6%**	**59%**
Independent			11.8%	8.3%	62%	8.7%	59%	8.4%	56%
Correlated			15.2%	13.5%	56%	14.9%	53%	13.2%	61%

FIGURE 18.36 **Underlying Fund Detail**

DATE OF LAST CONSTRUCTION		PORTFOLIO 8-MAR	FUND A 28-FEB	FUND B 15-FEB	FUND C 28-FEB	FUND D 31-JAN	FUND E 5-MAR
Drawdown	Last Construction	–6.5%	–13.1%	–2.3%	–12.3%	–15.2%	–7.5%
	Avg. Last 12 Months	–8.2%	–13.2%	–2.9%	–13.5%	–18.2%	–5.6%
Std Dev	Last Construction	5.6%	8.6%	3.1%	6.4%	12.2%	5.2%
	Avg. Last 12 Months	6.3%	9.1%	3.4%	6.2%	11.2%	6.4%
Semi Dev	Last Construction	7.2%	8.3%	5.1%	5.9%	13.4%	7.2%
	Avg. Last 12 Months	6.9%	9.5%	6.2%	5.4%	13.2%	6.9%
Skew	Last Construction	0.32	–0.30	1.21	–0.25	0.03	0.69
	Avg. Last 12 Months	0.39	0.15	1.15	–0.34	0.45	0.52
Kurtosis	Last Construction	0.14	1.10	0.53	–0.15	0.09	0.18
	Avg. Last 12 Months	0.11	–0.01	0.39	–0.21	0.19	0.19
VaR 95%	Last Construction	4.6%	3.6%	2.0%	4.2%	8.0%	3.4%
	Avg. Last 12 Months	4.9%	4.5%	2.2%	4.1%	7.3%	4.2%
Correlation S&P	Last Construction	0.18	0.61	0.05	0.35	0.57	–0.03
	Avg. Last 12 Months	0.21	0.01	0.19	0.42	0.53	0.02
Sharpe Ratio	Last Construction	1.0	0.7	1.9	0.9	0.7	1.5
	Avg. Last 12 Months	0.9	0.8	1.8	1.0	0.8	1.3

in the 96th percentile based on exposure to physical commodities.

Idiosyncratic returns data. Risk Fundamentals captures the portfolio-level weekly idiosyncratic returns of each underlying fund and reloads them as the idiosyncratic return of that fund in the construction of a portfolio of funds. To be able to isolate the correlated idiosyncratic returns from the independent idiosyncratic returns across underlying funds (see "***Idiosyncratic***" in Figure 18.35), the weekly returns must be appropriately aligned. As Risk Fundamentals distributed methodology cannot guarantee that the risk profile of all of the underlying funds are snapshots from the same date (in fact, it is highly unlikely that they will be), synchronizing the data permits a rigorous analysis of idiosyncratic returns across funds despite their inconsistency in reporting dates. The summary idiosyncratic returns of each portfolio are loaded as the position-level data for that fund in the portfolio of funds.

Liquidity data. We have already demonstrated how Risk Fundamentals captures the portfolio-level aggregation of the liquidity information (the percent of the construction that could be liquidated within varying periods of time). This includes the percentage of both assets and risk that could be liquidated, separately for long and short positions. When analyzing a portfolio of hedge funds, Risk Fundamentals reloads the summary liquidity data of each of the underlying funds at the position level for each fund in the portfolio.

Risk-return statistics. Risk Fundamentals calculates a historical simulation for the portfolio of funds. Based on this historical simulation Risk Fundamentals calculates all of the same risk-return statistics for the portfolio of funds that have already been presented for each of the underlying funds.

Figure 18.36 shows how Risk Fundamentals presents comparable risk-return statistics across all underlying funds so that they can be compared and analyzed (note that the statistics presented for Fund A are exactly those presented earlier in Figure 18.29). This example highlights that, based on the most current constructions of each fund, Fund D has the greatest drawdown exposure of all underlying funds (–15.2 percent for the last construction and –18.2 percent as the average of the constructions of the prior 12 months).

Portfolio analysis. Risk Fundamentals' portfolio management capabilities can be applied to the portfolio of funds. In **Figure 18.37**, S&P SPDRs have been added to the five underlying funds, permitting the Risk Fundamentals management logic to support the analysis of shorting equity market exposure to beta hedge the portfolio of funds. The portfolio analysis function permits the user to create "what-if" portfolio constructions. In Figure 18.37 the user has specified the weights of two positions: the weight of Fund E should be 20 percent of equity capital, the weight of the S&P SPDRs should be –10 percent of equity capital. Furthermore, the user has specified that the long holdings of the portfolio of funds (there are no short holdings besides the S&P SPDR hedge) should be levered to 115 percent of equity capital. Risk Fundamentals has automatically adjusted the weights of all the positions for which no specific weights were established to achieve the portfolio level leverage targets.

This analysis in Figure 18.37 shows that based on marginal risk Fund E is the most attractive fund to increase (adding a small increment of the fund increases the risk of the portfolio less than adding an equal amount of any other fund) but that based on marginal risk-adjusted returns Fund B is the most attractive fund to increase (adding a small increment of the fund increases the risk-adjusted return of the portfolio more than adding an equal amount of any other fund).

I stated in the previous section that an optimizer is generally not a useful tool in constructing a fund, but it can be significantly more valuable in constructing a portfolio of funds. There are two reasons for this:

FIGURE 18.37 **Portfolio Analysis of a Portfolio of Funds**

	ALTERNATIVE 1			ALTERNATIVE 2		
		LONG	SHORT		LONG	SHORT
	TARGET	115.00%		**TARGET**		
Portfolio	**105.00%**	**115.00%**	**–10.00%**	**80.00%**	**110.00%**	**–30.00%**
Fund A		36.73%		25.00%	25.00%	
Fund B		13.22%		25.00%	25.00%	
Fund C		7.01%		25.00%	20.00%	
Fund D		38.04%		20.00%	20.00%	
Fund E	20.00%	20.00%		20.00%	20.00%	
SPY US	–10.00%		–10.00%	–30.00%		–30.00%

- Portfolios of funds are long only. This avoids the tendency of optimizations with both long and short positions to select positions that are highly correlated but with different returns. In such cases, optimizers tend to go long the correlated position that has the higher return and short the correlated position with the lower return, capturing the difference in return while hedging out the risk. This is an excellent decision if the risks and returns are going to repeat, but often these relations are anomalous and the resulting construction flawed.
- A portfolio of funds typically includes a relatively small number of holdings (often fewer than thirty) and the results of applying an optimizer to a portfolio of this size is significantly more insightful than applying it to a broadly diversified portfolio.

Performance Attribution

Risk Fundamentals retains all the constructions and utilizes them to undertake and deliver a performance attribution. Hedge funds have coined the term alpha. Alpha is the incremental return that hedge funds generate above that which would be generated by simply being long or short market or secondary risks. Alpha can be generated through selecting the right idiosyncratic risk or by the successful active management of market or secondary risk exposures. When long and short positions are independent selections, rather than components of relative value or arbitrage strategies, it is useful to separately attribute returns to long and short positions, which Risk Fundamentals

	MARGINAL RISK						MARGINAL RISK ADJUSTED RETURN	
	STANDARD DEVIATION		DRAWDOWN		VAR		SHARPE RATIO	
	Marginal	Rank	Marginal	Rank	Marginal	Rank	Marginal	Rank
	109.7%	80%	103.2%	60%	143.2%	100%	–0.01	60%
	31.5%	20%	46.7%	20%	42.3%	20%	0.13	100%
	185.1%	100%	156.0%	100%	121.7%	80%	–0.02	40%
	96.8%	60%	124.3%	80%	103.4%	60%	0.04	80%
	22.7%	0%	22.7%	0%	39.7%	0%	–0.18	0%
	81.1%	40%	65.2%	40%	81.1%	40%	–0.05	20%

does. The performance attribution decomposes returns into the following root sources:

Market bias. This is the return generated by consistently being either long- or short-biased market risk factors. The market bias contribution is calculated by isolating the return of the average market exposure of a portfolio (the product of the net exposure to each market risk factor times the performance of that market risk factor during the period).

Market alpha. This is the return generated by actively managing the portfolio's exposure to market risk factors. The active market alpha is determined by calculating the contribution of the actual market exposure for a portfolio minus the market bias contribution.

Secondary bias. This is the return generated by consistently being either long- or short-biased secondary risk factors. The factor bias contribution is calculated by isolating the return of the average secondary risk factor's exposures of a portfolio (the product of the net exposure to each secondary risk factor times the performance of that secondary risk factor during the period).

Secondary alpha. This is the return generated by actively managing the portfolio's exposure to secondary risk factors. The active factor alpha is determined by calculating the contribution of the actual secondary risk factor's exposures of a portfolio minus the factor bias contribution.

Asymmetric trading. This is the return generated by applying an asymmetric strategy in managing specific holdings. If the fund is biased in the decision to

FIGURE 18.38 **Performance Attribution**

	TOTAL	2004	2003	2002
BEGIN	FEB-02	JAN-04	JAN-03	FEB-02
END	FEB-04	FEB-04	DEC-03	DEC-02
MONTHS	25	2	12	11
Market Risk	**9.0%**	**1.7%**	**5.2%**	**2.0%**
Market Bias	3.2%	0.9%	3.5%	–1.2%
Market Alpha	5.7%	0.8%	1.6%	3.2%
Secondary Risks	**12.5%**	**2.0%**	**1.3%**	**8.9%**
Secondary Risks Bias	1.7%	1.5%	–3.9%	4.2%
Large Cap	1.4%	0.7%	–1.2%	1.9%
Value	0.0%	0.9%	–3.2%	2.4%
Other Style	-0.1%	–0.2%	0.5%	–0.4%
Industry	0.4%	0.1%	0.0%	0.3%
Secondary Risks Alpha	10.6%	0.5%	5.4%	4.4%
Large Cap	5.1%	–0.5%	2.4%	3.2%
Value	5.0%	1.2%	2.5%	1.2%
Other Style	0.2%	0.3%	0.1%	–0.2%
Industry	0.0%	–0.5%	0.3%	0.2%
Idiosyncratic Alpha	**9.1%**	**1.2%**	**3.5%**	**4.2%**
Asymmetric Trading	**0.2%**	**0.1%**	**0.2%**	**-0.1%**
Trading Returns	**34.1%**	**5.1%**	**10.5%**	**15.5%**
Net Interest	0.6%	0.2%	0.2%	0.2%
Gross Returns	**34.9%**	**5.3%**	**10.7%**	**15.7%**
Fees	9.9%	1.3%	3.6%	4.6%
Net Returns	**23.6%**	**4.0%**	**7.0%**	**11.1%**

hold winning and losing positions, the fund will demonstrate option-like (generally long-volatility) behavior when market volatility increases or decreases. This isolates this behavior phenomenon. All of the other sources of performance are a function of the "snapshot" of each construction. This source recognizes the dynamic trading strategy across snapshots.

Net interest. Net interest income or expense is calculated based on the net cash position.

Fees and expenses. The fees and expenses paid to the manager include the management fee, performance fee, and expenses.

Idiosyncratic alpha. This is the return generated through idiosyncratic risk taking. The idiosyncratic alpha is calculated as the residual between the actual net return of the fund and all of the other components of return that have been isolated. The other components of return that have been isolated include market bias and alpha, factor bias and alpha, asymmetric trading, and net interest minus fees and expenses.

Investors in hedge funds should seek risk exposures that they cannot access through their traditional investments. The most attractive exposure is to idiosyncratic risk, especially independent idiosyncratic risk. Market and factor alpha is attractive because although traditional investments can provide exposure to both market and secondary risks they do not permit active management of these exposures. Therefore hedge funds represent a unique opportunity not available through traditional investments. Investors can gain exposure to secondary risks through traditional investments, so returns generated through a factor bias are less attractive. Finally, most investors already have significant exposure to market risks through their traditional investments. Furthermore, such exposures can be achieved with significantly lower fees through ETFs (SPDRs). Consequently, hedge funds that have material long-biased exposure to primary market risks do not provide diversification and charge comparatively high fees.

Figure 18.38 is an example of the portfolio attribution for an equity long/short fund beginning in February 2001 through February 2004. The fund generated a 23.6 percent net return during this 25-month period. The fund generated trading returns of 34.1 percent that has been relatively evenly split among return from market risk exposure (9.0 percent), secondary risk exposure (12.5 percent), and idiosyncratic alpha (9.1 percent). The biggest single contributor is market alpha (5.7 percent), the ability of the fund to actively manage the funds' exposure to market risk.

Note the difference between *risk decomposition* (discussed earlier in the "Risk Factors" subsection of this chapter) and *performance attribution*. Risk decomposition is a view of the risk inherent in the current portfolio. The performance attribution is undertaken across all of the constructions of a specific portfolio or fund (over time) to identify the sources of return (rather than risk). Although conceptually different, consideration of risk factors provides a valuable framework for both analyses.

Notes

[1]The Global Classification Standard (GICS)[SM] was developed by and is the exclusive property and a service mark of Standard & Poor's and MSCI. Neither Standard & Poor's nor MSCI is affiliated with or endorse Risk Fundamentals.

[2]Risk Fundamentals maps more than 200,000 equities and significantly more corporate debt issues globally to the four-level GICS classification hierarchy.

CHAPTER 19

$\sum_{i=1}^{18} \text{Chapter}_i$

I lied! In the Introduction, I promised that I would not use any Greek symbols. In this chapter, I do. To translate the above, the Greek letter sigma (Σ) is used by mathematicians to express the summation of a series. The series I am summing is Chapters 1 through 18 of this book.

The basics of risk management are actually quite simple. The objective is to understand the potential behavior of your investments. The key components of risk are:

- Volatility
- Diversification
- Leverage
- Liquidity

A basic knowledge of these fundamentals permits an investor (whether you are a fund manager managing a fund composed of securities or you are an investor managing a portfolio of funds) to perform the three critical processes in managing an investment portfolio:

1 Understand the risks being taken and ensure they are consistent with the objectives of the portfolio (the risk cop).
2 Apply this fundamental understanding to the construction of a risk-efficient portfolio (the risk strategist).
3 Ex post, analyze the sources of the actual performance of the portfolio (the risk pathologist).

Risk management is something that every investor does. The issue is how well. Understanding and proactively managing your risk will reward you with better (or superior or improved) returns. Especially in the hedge fund world, where risk management and transparency practices are in a period of rapid evolution, neophytes have the opportunity to quickly catch up, and experienced investors (or practitioners) have the opportunity to become leaders.

Government and industry committees have repeatedly called for hedge funds to provide standardized summary risk and return reporting, while rejecting position disclosure. Despite this consistent conclusion, in the more than half-decade that has passed since the crises of the fall of 1998 (Long-Term Capital Management), no concrete industry solution has emerged. Although some funds have individually implemented their own unique reporting, the lack of consistency precludes comparing and aggregating this information across funds, so it has limited value. It can be argued that an "industry utility" solution, equivalent to that provided by the credit rating services, is required.

Kenmar believes the value of such an industrywide standard solution is so great that the firm plans to provide a basic service as an "industry utility." This basic service includes

- The NAV/return reporting provided by Bloomberg as part of the Bloomberg Professional service,
- A complete risk transparency report presenting all of the standard fundamental risk measures for the fund, and
- Access to the fundamental risk statistics (both for specific funds and aggregations).

As described in detail in Chapter 18, the full offering includes the following three components:

1 ***NAV/Return Reporting.*** Net asset values (NAVs) and returns are reported on a real-time basis. Other hedge fund return reporting services currently do so on a monthly basis, significantly after returns have been e-mailed, faxed, or telephoned to investors. The real-time reporting eliminates the need for such nonroutine, nonstandardized reporting and can form the standard approach to distributing return data on a timely basis. Furthermore, investors are able to receive real-time returns of all of the underlying funds in their portfolio. Despite the argument presented in Chapter 5 that risk measures based on monthly actual return histories are not the best approach to measuring risk, Risk Fundamentals uses the historical simulation to provide a complete set of these risk measures, in the unique language of hedge funds.

2 ***Risk Management/Transparency System.*** The Risk Fundamentals risk management/transparency system was designed by Kenmar to be distributable to hedge funds so that funds can apply a standardized framework while maintaining complete control of their position data. The system is a sophisticated risk management application that uses a standard template to create a comprehensive risk profile of the fund without disclosing any position data. The system automatically tracks the fundamental risk measures over time and compares each measure to those of the fund's peer group and the universe of hedge funds. The risk profile includes measures of:

- Returns
- Liquidity
- Leverage
- Risk-factor sensitivity
- Volatility
- Diversification
- Risk-adjusted return
- Value at Risk
- Stress tests
- Performance attribution

The system can automatically distribute these risk profiles electronically. These risk profiles can be compared and aggregated across funds to analyze the risks of a portfolio of funds.

3 ***Risk Fundamentals.*** Comparable to financial fundamentals representing the key measures of corporate performance and equity returns, what in this book are termed *risk fundamentals* represent the key measures of hedge fund performance and returns. Although the Risk Fundamentals system provides a comprehensive set of tools to analyze risk, a significant part of the value delivered by the application derives from the use of a standard template for measuring and reporting risk across funds. The risk fundamentals calculated by the application are the essential "industry standard" measures of risk and return.

These measures are aggregated to indices, and individual funds are ranked (by percentile) based on each of these measures within the universe of all hedge funds, by strategy and by style. This standardization permits investors to evaluate individual funds against norms and understand how a specific measure of a fund compares to that of its various peer groups.

Appendix

Integrating Market Correlation into Risk-Adjusted Return

APPENDIX

Integrating Market Correlation into Risk-Adjusted Return

Institutional and high net worth investors are increasingly looking at hedge funds, as their expectations for returns from their equity investments range anywhere from low to bleak. Essentially, they are looking for investments that are not correlated with the equity market and that can perform well in any environment—particularly when their long-only equity investments are not. As the world has become more global, and international markets more correlated, diversification has become more difficult to achieve and therefore more valuable.

If you are an investor with a significant exposure to the S&P 500 through traditional investments, which of the following hedge funds would be the most attractive to you (assuming that the S&P earns a 12 percent return, the risk-free rate is 5 percent, and the standard deviation of each of the hedge funds and the S&P is 18 percent)?

HEDGE FUND A: Generates an annualized return of +12 percent and is perfectly correlated with the S&P 500.

HEDGE FUND B: Generates an annualized return of +8 percent and is uncorrelated with (100 percent independent of) the S&P 500.

HEDGE FUND C: Generates an annualized return of –2 percent and is perfectly negatively correlated with the S&P 500.

The correct answer is *all of the above.* An investor with significant exposure to the equity market should find these alternative investments equally attractive.[1]

My Kenmar colleagues and I published our research on hedge fund diversification in an article titled "Squeezing the Best from Hedge Fund Diversification" in the March 2002 issue of *Risk,* in which we made two key observations with respect to the correlation of hedge funds to the equity market:

- Although hedge funds can provide valuable diversification from the equity market, the performance of most hedge funds is, in fact, highly correlated with the equity market.

- Traditional measures of risk and return (such as the Sharpe ratio) do not differentiate between risk that is correlated with the equity market—to which most investors have significant exposure, through traditional investments—and risks that are not correlated with the market.

This research sent us in search of a measure of risk-adjusted return that, in addition to adjusting returns for volatility, as the Sharpe ratio does, also adjusts returns for correlation to the market (beta). This quest led to the development of the BAVAR (***b***eta ***a***nd ***v***olatility ***a***djusted ***r***eturn) ratio. The BAVAR ratio adjusts the beta of various investments to be equivalent, so that a fund that has a lower return but is uncorrelated to the market can be *appropriately* compared to a fund that achieves a higher return but is highly correlated to the market. (This appendix assumes the "market" to be the S&P 500; however, the methodology works equally well for any other market.)

We based the formulation on the Sharpe ratio:

$$\frac{\text{[Return of Fund]} - \text{[Risk-Free Rate]}}{\sigma\,\text{[Return of Fund]}}$$

Because volatility and correlation are nonadditive, we cannot compare two funds with different correlations to the S&P (beta) simply by subtracting the exposure of each to the S&P. However, we do know how return, volatility, and correlation combine. Using this knowledge, our methodology brings parity, and therefore comparability, to hedge funds with different levels of correlation with the S&P by normalizing the beta of each investment to 1. We do this by combining each hedge fund with the appropriate level of long/short exposure to the S&P, in order to bring the hedge fund's total S&P exposure to a beta of 1. We then recalculate the new return and new volatility of the beta-adjusted hedge fund. The results are then plugged into the Sharpe ratio to create the BAVAR ratio:

$$\frac{(\text{[Return of Fund]} - \text{[Risk-Free Rate]}) + (1-\beta) * (\text{[Return of S\&P]} - \text{[Risk-Free Rate]})}{\sqrt{(1-R^2) * \sigma^2\text{[Return of Fund]} + \sigma^2\text{[Return of S\&P]}}}$$

σ^2[Return of Fund] is the variance of the return of the fund

σ^2[Return of S&P] is the variance of the return of the S&P

R^2 is the coefficient of determination of the regression of the [Return of Fund] with the [Return of S&P]

β is the coefficient of the [return of the S&P] in that regression

The amount of additional S&P exposure required to bring the hedge fund to a beta of 1 would be $(1-\beta)$, where β is the coefficient of the regression of the returns of the fund as the dependant variable and that of the S&P as the independent variable. The Capital Asset Pricing Model (CAPM) tells us that the expected return generated from this amount of additional S&P exposure would be $(1-\beta)$ multiplied by the equity risk premium, the difference between the return of the S&P and the risk-free rate. Consequently, the return of the beta-adjusted hypothetical hedge fund would be the combined return of the hedge fund and this additional exposure to the S&P, as shown in the numerator above.

The returns of a hedge fund combined with $(1-\beta)$ exposure to the S&P are equal to the residuals of the regression that calculated the beta above combined with the S&P. We use this fact to facilitate the calculation of the volatility of the beta-adjusted hedge fund. However, the residuals of the regression are independent of the S&P, and therefore the variance of the beta-adjusted hedge fund is equal to the sum of the variance of the residuals and that of the S&P. By definition, the coefficient of determination (R^2) of the regression is $1 - \sigma^2$ {Residuals}/σ^2{Return of Fund}. Consequently, the variance of the residuals, σ^2{Residuals}, is equal to $(1-R^2)*\sigma^2${Return of Fund}. The standard deviation of the beta-adjusted hedge fund is the square root of the sum of the variance of residuals and the variance of the S&P. The denominator of the BAVAR ratio is determined by plugging the standard deviation of the beta-adjusted hedge fund into the Sharpe ratio formulation, as shown above.

We vetted the BAVAR ratio by testing that it worked for the following key conditions:

- ***Perfect positive correlation to the S&P 500 (Hedge Fund A, above).*** In this case, $R^2 = \beta = 1$ and the BAVAR ratio simplifies to the Sharpe ratio. Hedge Fund A thus has a BAVAR ratio of:

$$\frac{(12\%-5)}{18\%} = \frac{7\%}{18\%} = 0.39$$

- ***Perfect negative correlation to the S&P 500 (Hedge Fund C, above).*** In this case, $R^2 = 1$ and $\beta = -1$, and the BAVAR ratio again simplifies to the Sharpe ratio. Hedge Fund C thus has a BAVAR ratio of:

$$\frac{(-2\%-5\%) + [(1+1) * (12\%-5\%)]}{18\%} = \frac{7\%}{18\%} = 0.39$$

- ***Uncorrelated (statistically independent) to the S&P 500 (Hedge Fund B, above).*** In this case, $R^2 = \beta = 0$. In addition to the return generated by the hedge fund, the beta-adjusted hedge fund earns the equity risk premium from the additional exposure to the S&P. Because the returns of the hedge fund and the returns of the S&P are independent, the standard deviation of the beta-adjusted hedge fund is equal to the sum of the variances of the two. Assuming that the volatility of the hedge fund equals that of the S&P, the standard deviation of the beta-adjusted fund will equal the square root of two times the volatility of the S&P. HEDGE FUND B thus has a BAVAR ratio of:

$$\frac{(8\%-5\%) + (1-0) * (12\%-5\%)}{\sqrt{(1-0) * 18\%^2 + 18\%^2}} = \frac{10\%}{25\%} = 0.39$$

When using monthly returns to calculate the BAVAR ratio, it will be subject to the same, and no greater, data problems as is the Sharpe ratio, such as: limited data, the length of actual records varying across funds, changes in the underlying portfolios, and the hedge fund managers' ability to "manage" monthly valuations. BAVAR's value may be maximized when the underlying investments in hedge funds are processed through a risk management system that maps positions to risk factors. The factor and idiosyncratic risk can then be appropriately isolated from the beta risk (see the aforementioned *Risk* article; "Squeezing the Best from Hedge Fund Diversification," March 2002), permitting a more rigorous quantification of the BAVAR ratio.

Use of the BAVAR ratio can significantly enhance an investor's ability to construct risk-efficient portfolios by providing a methodology of appropriately comparing the risk-adjusted returns of funds that have varying correlations to the S&P (varying betas). Investing in hedge funds that are not market neutral and have a positive beta can make sense, as long as the higher correlation to the equity market is appropriately compensated by higher returns. If the risk-reward is justified, the investor can simply hedge out the market exposure, resulting in an investment with attractive alpha, known as "alpha transport." BAVAR provides a holistic framework to support this decision.

Notes

[1]It is not intuitive that one should find equal appeal in:

HEDGE FUND A: an investment that is perfectly positively correlated with the S&P (beta of 1) and earns 12 percent with a volatility of 18 percent, and

HEDGE FUND C: an investment that is perfectly negatively correlated with the S&P (beta of –1) and earns –2 percent with a volatility of 18 percent.

The reason is that combining a long-only equity portfolio with Hedge Fund A results in the identical risk-adjusted return as the combination of the long-only equity portfolio with Hedge Fund B. The former would, of course, have a higher return and a higher risk than the latter, but on a risk-adjusted basis, the returns would be identical.

One could also equalize the return and risk of the combined portfolios by equalizing the return and risk of Hedge Fund C to Hedge Fund A; this is accomplished by increasing the S&P exposure (representing a beta of 2) in Hedge Fund C. The added S&P exposure would earn 14 percent (two times the equity risk premium of 7 percent); when added to the original return of Hedge Fund C of –2 percent, it now returns 12 percent—equal to that of Hedge Fund A.

Glossary

active. The exposure to a risk factor is actively managed if it is continuously adjusted on an ongoing basis.

allocation. Allocation is a top-down process by which equity capital is assigned to various strategies/investments.

alpha. The return generated by a fund that cannot be attributed to market performance. The value added of the fund or manager.

arbitrage. A simultaneous sale of a security or commodity in different markets to profit from unequal prices.

asymmetric trading. Trading strategies that employ asymmetric rules and, consequently, result in option-like behavior.

asymmetry. The degree to which a distribution is not symmetrical around the mean, but rather is skewed to one side or the other.

attribution. The classification of actual results to explain the root source of the performance.

BAVAR ratio. An extension of the Sharpe ratio which additionally adjusts for correlation to the market (see the Appendix).

beta. Measures percentage change in the price of the dependent variable (stock) given a 1 percent change in the independent variable (equity market).

bias. A consistent tendency to have either a long or short exposure to a risk factor. Portfolios are either market neutral, actively long or short, or biased in their exposure to particular risks.

borrowing leverage. The leverage created by borrowing funds (generally at a risk-free rate plus some relatively small premium) and investing the borrowed funds. The borrowing leverage is calculated as the ratio of the gross invested capital and the equity capital.

Capital Asset Pricing Model. A theory which concludes that the only risk that is compensated is market risk because all other risks can be shed through diversification, and therefore a rational market will not compensate for them.

CAPM. See ***Capital Asset Pricing Model***

cash equivalent. The value of a cash security that has equivalent behavior as a notionally funded instrument.

cash securities. Securities that are purchased by investing cash, in contrast to securities that are notionally funded such as futures or OTC derivative.

commingled fund. An investment vehicle in which the assets of multiple investors are combined.

commodity. Physical commodities including energies, precious metals, basic metals, agricultural products, and livestock. Exposure to these markets is gained through futures.

concentrations. Concentration is the exposure of a portfolio construction to a specific instrument or to a group of instruments.

construction. The constituency of a portfolio at a point of time. The combination of positions that a portfolio comprises.

construction leverage. Construction leverage is the percentage of the instrument risk that is retained in the construction of the portfolio. It is calculated as the ratio of the net cash equivalent to the cash equivalent.

convexity. Convexity is the nonlinear behavior of financial instruments. This can result from both optionality and other nonlinear relationships (e.g., the duration of a bond changes as interest rates move).

correlation. A measure of the relationship between two series. A correlation of 1 implies that the two series move 100 percent synchronously. A correlation of –1 implies that the two series move 100 percent inversely. A correlation of 0 implies that the two series are independent of each other.

counterparty risk. The risk that a counterparty will not satisfy its obligations in an over-the-counter (OTC) transaction.

credit default swap. OTC instruments in which a counterparty seeking credit protection agrees to pay a premium to the protection seller for the right to be compensated in the case of a default of the reference issuer.

credit rating. The rating designated by a rating service (S&P, Moody) that indicates an individual's or company's ability to repay obligations or its likelihood of not defaulting.

credit risk. The risk in a fixed-income security that the interest and principle will not be paid in full (the default risk). This risk is compensated through credit spreads.

CTA (commodity trading advisers). Advisers specifically licensed to trade futures.

decomposition. The process of isolating the causal components of a measure. Risk decomposition explains the component sources of risk.

diversification. The benefit of investing in uncorrelated holdings. Investors should be willing to accept lower returns from diversifying investments.

drawdown. The maximum cumulative decline in value from a peak to the subsequent trough before the fund achieves a new peak.

due diligence. The process of reviewing and assessing candidate hedge fund managers. Although the most intensive effort is made before investing with a manager, this should be an ongoing process.

duration. The sensitivity of the price of a fixed-income instrument to a parallel shift of the yield curve.

dynamic trading. See ***asymmetric trading***

embedded options. Cash instruments that are bundled with related options.

equity capital. The capital that shareholders of a fund have contributed to that fund.

event driven. Strategies that bet on the outcome of a specific event or series of events. The outcomes are generally characterized by very large moves around specific events. Such strategies include merger arbitrage (the event is the completion of an acquisition) or distressed debt (the event is that of reorganization/liquidation).

exchange. A marketplace where securities and the like are traded, in contrast to instruments that are brokered in the over-the-counter (OTC) markets.

fat tails. See ***kurtosis***

financing leverage. Financing leverage is the total leverage created from financing. It is the combination of the borrowing leverage and the notional leverage. It is calculated as the ratio of the gross invested capital to the equity capital.

fund. Used generically to represent managed money including hedge funds, mutual funds, and separate accounts (although separate accounts are technically not funds).

fund of funds. A hedge fund that invests in multiple underlying hedge funds.

futures. A security in which one agrees to buy or sell a specified amount of a commodity on a specified future date at a specified price.

futures leverage. Futures leverage is the leverage resulting from the notional financing of futures and forwards. It is calculated as the difference between the futures notional value minus the margin requirement.

GICS. See ***Global Industry Classification Standard***

Global Industry Classification Standard. A four-level hierarchical grouping of industries jointly established by Standard and Poor's (S&P) and Morgan Stanley Capital International (MSCI).

hedge fund. A privately offered, pooled investment vehicle that is not widely available to the public, the assets of which are managed by a professional investment management firm. A fund may employ a variety of techniques to enhance returns, such as both buying and shorting stocks according to a valuation model.

hedging. The process of eliminating a risk exposure by taking an exposure in the opposite direction. Because hedges are in instruments that have correlated behavior but are typically not exactly the same, hedges generally result in basis risk, the risk that the hedging instrument will behave differently than the primary instrument.

historical simulation. A method of calculating risk and/or VaR by simulating how the current portfolio construction would have performed based on historical market performance.

idiosyncratic risk. The residual risk after removing all of the market and secondary risks (the risk explained by the risk factors). Also called *security-specific risk.*

illiquidity. The lack of "liquidity."

implied volatility. The volatility implied by the current pricing of an option. This is different from the historical volatility, which is the actual volatility of the price of the underlying instrument in the recent past.

instrument risk. Instrument risk is the internal leverage inherent in a specific security. It is calculated as the ratio of the risk of the instrument to the net cash equivalent value of the instrument.

interest rate swap. An over-the-counter transaction issued by a broker/dealer that approximates the risks and returns of a repoed Treasury bond.

invested capital. The gross capital invested, which is the sum of the value of the long positions and the absolute value of the short positions.

kurtosis. The degree to which a distribution is flatter or more peaked than a normal (or "bell-shaped") distribution. Also called a *fat tail.*

leverage. The amount of risk per dollar of equity capital. The property of instruments rising or falling at a proportionally greater amount than the comparable [or underlying] investments.

levered risk. The total leverage of a portfolio. It is the risk expressed as a percentage of equity capital. It is calculated as the product of the financing leverage and the unlevered risk.

liquidity. The speed at which an investor can monetize an investment without adversely impacting the market valuations of the underlying security.

marginal sensitivity. The sensitivity of a measure to a very small change in value of a factor on which the measure is dependent. For relationships that behave linearly, the marginal sensitivity remains constant. For relationships with convexity, the marginal sensitivity changes as the underlying exposure changes.

market capitalization. The market value of the shares outstanding of all the equities related to a company.

market risk. The risk related to directional market movements. This is the risk that cannot be diversified away in a long-only portfolio. The six primary market risks are equity, interest, credit, commodity, currency, and real estate.

maturity. The period until fixed-income instruments come due or is payable. For a bond, the date on which the principal is required to be repaid. In an interest rate swap, the date that the swap stops accruing interest.

Monte Carlo simulation. A method of simulation that generally synthesizes history into a variance and covariance matrix. This matrix is used to iteratively create hypothetical scenarios by using a random number generator to transform the variance/covariance into stochastic series. These scenarios are used to calculate risk and VaR.

NAV. See ***net asset value***

net asset value. A measure of the value of a fund per share. The percent change for the NAV is the return during a period.

non-market risk. See ***operational risk*** and ***counterparty risk***

notional capital. The component of cash equivalents that are not funded by equity capital or borrowing. This derives from instruments such as futures, options, and OTC derivatives that represent risk exposures significantly greater than their cash value.

notional leverage. The component of financing leverage that is created through notional funding of options, futures, and swaps. It is the sum of the option leverage, futures leverage, and the swap leverage. It is calculated as the ratio of the cash equivalent of these instruments divided by the invested capital.

operational risk. Risk other than market risk or credit risk that results from potential problems in the operations. This can include procedural or system errors, fraud, misvaluations, business interruptions, and the like.

optimizer. A mathematical algorithm that can maximize (or minimize) an objective function within an established set of constraints. This can be used to construct a portfolio.

option leverage. The leverage an investor creates by paying or receiving a small premium to respectively buy or sell an option that could ultimately represent a very large exposure dependent on the outcome on the performance of the underlying security. It is calculated as the difference between the delta equivalent cash value of the underlying minus the market value of the option (the premium).

optionality. Optionality is created when the return of an instrument is dependent in a nonlinear relationship with some other instrument. Optionality can result from directly investing in an option, investing in instruments that have embedded options (e.g., convertible bonds), or through dynamic trading strategies that result in synthetic options.

orthogonal. The quality or state of being independent; orthogonal risk factors are independent of each other (no correlation). Orthogonalization is the process of adjusting risk factors so that they are orthogonal.

OTC. See ***over the counter***

OTC derivative. An over-the-counter instrument (generally fixed income) including swaps, swaptions, caps, and floors.

over the counter. Instruments that are not traded on an exchange.

parametric model. A closed form solution using the variance and covariance to calculate risk and/or VaR.

pari passu. A construction in which the relative size of each position is the same as that of another construction.

passive. The exposure to a risk factor is passively managed if it is not actively managed, i.e., not continuously adjusted on an ongoing basis.

peer universe. A universe of funds that are considered peers. Risk Fundamentals® applies a three-level structure consisting of all hedge funds, hedge funds with the same strategy, and hedge funds with the same style.

percentile rank. The ranking of a universe of funds by percentile based on a specified criteria. The rankings will range from 0 percent to 100 percent.

probabilistic. A process in which the result cannot be determined based on a known relationship. Also called *random.*

prospective returns. Forward-looking expectations of returns for each risk factor and for each position. The position-specific return, or alpha, is the compensation for the idiosyncratic risk of that position.

rating. See ***credit rating***

relative value strategies. Strategies that target the relative performance of specific securities (called "pairs" trading) or groupings of positions.

return. The percent change in the value of a holding or portfolio. The ratio of the profit and loss to the net asset value.

risk. Risk results from the uncertainty of returns. The two key components of risk are volatility and correlation/diversification.

risk-adjusted return. A measure that appropriately adjusts returns for the fact that one should expect a higher level of return with greater risk (either greater volatility or greater correlation).

risk budgeting. A comprehensive approach to planning, executing, and monitoring the full investment process.

risk culture. The orientation of an organization to risk taking. Having a fundamental understanding of risk integrated into the investment process.

risk equivalent. A measure of risk that converts all types of risk to a common basis.

risk factors. Indices of market data that explain the behavior of specific holdings.

risk-free rate. The return an investor should anticipate as a risk-free return on capital employed.

risk visualization. Reporting risk in a visual or graphic presentation to facilitate communicating something that is inherently difficult to describe.

secondary risk. Correlated risks other than market risks. These include style and industry risks in equities; and yield curve, credit ratings, and basis risks in fixed income.

security-specific risk. See ***idiosyncratic risk***

sensitivity. The sensitivity to a risk factor is the percent change a particular instrument will experience in response to a 1 percent change in the risk factor. For example, the beta is the percent change in the value of an equity resulting from a 1 percent change in the underlying equity market.

separate account. An investment vehicle that contains the assets of single investor (versus commingled fund).

Sharpe ratio. A ratio that adjusts return premium (the difference between the return and the risk-free return) for volatility.

short positions. A strategy in which the holder effectively sells a position she does not hold. It is accomplished by borrowing the security and then selling the security in the open market.

skew. See ***asymmetry***

standard deviation. A measure of volatility. Calculated as the expected squared deviation of each value from the mean.

stochastic. See ***probabilistic***

strategy. The general or specific approach to investing that an individual, institution, or fund manager employs. Specific to hedge funds, a high level of grouping hedge funds that characterizes both the asset class exposure (equity, fixed income, future, multi-asset) and the risk characteristics (directional, market neutral, event).

stress test. An analysis of the potential impact of "crises" on the returns (profit and loss) of a portfolio construction by applying crisis scenarios. On the sell-side, this is an adjunct to VaR, which is typically used to measure risk in "normal" markets.

style. A more granular level of grouping hedge funds, subordinate to strategy.

style drift. The process by which hedge funds migrate between styles; the negative aspect of "flexibility." Judging with hindsight, a nimble fund has moved in and out of positions and enhanced returns; a fund with style drift has not hewn to the strategy and returns have suffer as a result. As an investor is seeking nimbleness in hedge funds, there is an unclear line between style drift and nimbleness.

swap. An over-the-counter instrument including interest rate swaps and credit default swaps. An arrangement in which two entities lend to each other on different terms, e.g., in different currencies, and/or at different interest rates, fixed or floating.

swap leverage. Swap leverage is the leverage resulting from the notional financing of swaps. It is calculated as the difference between the swap equivalent value minus the market value of the swap.

swaptions. Options on interest rate swaps. The buyer of a swaption has the right to enter into an interest rate swap agreement by some specified date in the future. The swaption agreement will specify whether the buyer of the swaption will be a fixed-rate receiver or a fixed-rate payer. The writer of the swaption becomes the counterparty to the swap if the buyer exercises.

transparency. The process of providing risk information to an investor. One extreme solution is providing position disclosure.

unlevered risk. The unlevered risk is the component of risk leverage that results from the selection of specific instruments and the combination of these securities in a specific construction. It is the product of the instrument risk and the construction leverage. It is calculated as the ratio of the total risk to the cash equivalent.

value at risk (VaR). A measure of risk that represents the largest loss that should probabilistically be anticipated at some specified level of confidence. The sell-side has adopted this as a standard measure of risk (although the confidence level, historic period, period over which the return is calculated, method of calculation, etc. vary significantly).

volatility. A measure of the variability of returns. The most common measure of volatility is annualized standard deviation of returns.

Index

ILLUSTRATION CREDITS

The author and publisher gratefully acknowledge permission to reprint the following:

Page 1, left	Antique microscope. © Tony Cordoza/Stone/Getty Images.
Page 1, right	Antique telescope. © Jody Dole/The Image Bank/Getty Images.
Page 15	Nicolas Copernicus, Heliocentric system of the universe from his treatise *De Revolutionibus Orbium Coelstium libri six,* Nuremberg, 1543. Image Select/Art Resource, NY.
Page 37	Engraving of Archimedes from *Mechanics Magazine,* London, 1824. Courtesy of Chris Rorres.
Page 47	Mona Caron, *The Titanic Sinking.* Watercolor/digital. © 2004, used with permission of the artist.
Page 88	*The Rosetta Stone.* © Copyright The British Museum, reprinted with permission.
Page 91	British constable. © Topical Press Agency/Hulton Archive/Getty Images.
Page 123	Report card. Courtesy of Judy Scholin.
Page 151, left	Leonardo da Vinci, *The Vitruvian Man.* Pen and ink drawing, Accademia, Venice, Italy. Scala/Art Resource, NY.
Page 151, right	Leonardo da Vinci, *The Mona Lisa.* Oil on wood, 77 x 53 cm, Louvre, Paris. Réunion des Musées Nationaux/Art Resource, NY.
Page 159	Sherlock Holmes. © Archive Holdings Inc./The Image Bank/Getty Images.
Page 167	Mercury and the Three Graces—a detail from Sandro Botticelli's *La Primavera.* Tempera on wood, 203 x 314 cm, Uffizi, Florence. Scala/Art Resource, NY.
Page 179	Pieter Bruegel the Elder, *The Tower of Babel.* Wood, 114 x 155 cm. Reprinted with permission of Kunsthistoriches Museum, Vienna.

Good faith efforts have been made to contact the copyright holders of the art in this book, but in a few instances the publisher has been unable to locate them. Such copyright holders should contact Permissions Department, Bloomberg Press, 731 Lexington Avenue, New York, NY 10022.

About the Author

Amy Genkins

Richard Horwitz is managing director of manager assessment and risk management of Merrill Lynch's Hedge Fund Development and Management Group (HFDMG). He has implemented Risk Fundamentals, a proprietary risk transparency and management system. The system is risk factor based, permitting underlying funds to provide structural risk transparency without requiring position disclosure and for this transparency to be used to provide a fundamental understanding of each underlying fund and to construct risk-efficient portfolios of funds. Previously, Horwitz was senior vice president and director of risk management and investment analytics at Kenmar Global Investment Management Inc., a $2 billion fund of funds. He gained his fundamental knowledge of hedge funds as a principal at Capital Market Risk Advisors, Inc., the boutique risk management consulting firm. Horwitz had previously been a buy-side senior equity analyst at Sanford C. Bernstein & Co. and a consultant in financial services at Booz Allen Hamilton Inc. He earned an MS in management (Sloan School) and a BS in electrical engineering from the Massachusetts Institute of Technology. Horwitz has also written numerous articles on hedge funds.